Civil Servants and Their Constitutions

John A. Rohr

 University Press of Kansas

Published by the University Press of Kansas (Lawrence, Kansas 66049), which was organized by the Kansas Board of Regents and is operated and funded by Emporia State University, Fort Hays State University, Kansas State University, Pittsburg State University, the
University of Kansas, and Wichita State University

Library of Congress Cataloging-in-Publication Data

Rohr, John A. (John Anthony), 1934–
    Civil servants and their constitutions / John A. Rohr.
       p. cm. — (Studies in government and public policy)
    Includes index.
    ISBN 0-7006-1162-2 (cloth : alk. paper) — ISBN 0-7006-1163-0 (pbk. : alk. paper)
    1. Civil service—History. 2. Administrative law—History. 3.
Constitutional history. I. Title. II. Series.
    K3440.R64 2002
    342'.068—dc21
                        2001006343

British Library Cataloguing in Publication Data is available.

Printed in the United States of America

10 9 8 7 6 5 4 3 2

The paper used in this publication meets the minimum requirements of the American
National Standard for Permanence of Paper for Printed Library Materials Z39.48-1984.

Civil Servants and
Their Constitutions

STUDIES IN GOVERNMENT AND PUBLIC POLICY

To the Constitution of the United States

By the same author:

Prophets Without Honor: Public Policy and the Selective
    Conscientious Objector (1971)
Ethics for Bureaucrats: An Essay on Law and Values (1978, 1989)
To Run a Constitution: The Legitimacy of the Administrative State (1986)
The President and the Public Administration (1989)
Founding Republics in France and America: A Study
    in Constitutional Governance (1995)
Public Service, Ethics, and Constitutional Practice (1998)

Contents

Preface

My purpose in this book is to present a gentle corrective to certain excesses and deficiencies in the New Public Management (NPM) movement. A corrective is in order because "the New Public Management has obfuscated any discussion of political power and left us with only a managerial leitmotif that has made the notion of 'political' seem almost problematic."[1] The corrective, however, must be gentle because, properly understood, "the economic ideas invoked by the New Public Management" need not collapse into "a sterile technocratic view of governance."[2]

In mentioning the New Public Management movement, I wish I could give the reader a crisp definition of just what I have in mind. This I cannot do because, as anyone familiar with the NPM realizes. it is a moving target. I include, of course, David Osborne and Ted Gaebler's *Reinventing Government* and the National Performance Review developed under the guidance of Vice-President Al Gore at the beginning of the Clinton administration.[3] I also round up the usual suspects one finds featured in the articles and symposia on the NPM that have enriched (and, alas, at times burdened) the major business and public administration journals for the past decade or so.

If a definition of the NPM is hard to come by, there is no dearth of vivid descriptions. Phillip Cooper gets to the heart of the matter when he describes its "common element" as including "downsizing . . . deregulation, decentralization, delayering, right-sizing, reinventing and reengineering."[4] Anne Khademian sees its salient characteristics as including efforts to let performance "replace process as the focus for accountability" and letting "performance-driven, short-term contracting . . . take precedence over vertical integration in defining responsibilities." while "devolution and flexibility—not rule books and centralized and executive oversight—should shape the job of the manager."[5] More succinctly, Andrew Dunsire captures the new mood as one in which traditional "administrative, hierarchical and professional cultures" yield to a "private, commercial market culture."[6]

I have noted my intent to direct my gentle corrective to deficiencies and excesses in the NPM literature. To grasp my meaning, consider the writings of two of the most highly regarded scholars in the NPM movement, Barry Bozeman and Robert Behn.

Bozeman's introduction to an edited volume on public management provides a good example of a deficiency in the NPM literature. His essay, "Two Concepts of Public Management," skillfully develops the differences between the public management that originates in the business schools on the one hand and in the public policy schools on the other—the "B-Approach" and the "P-Approach," as he calls them.[7] The former is less inclined to fret over the distinction between public and private; the latter emphasizes substantive policy and political questions as opposed to the process questions favored by the B-Approach.

Adherents to the P-Approach can be found at the meetings of the Association for Public Policy Analysis and Management, and their publications appear in the pages of the *Journal of Policy Analysis and Management.* Their B-Approach colleagues participate in the public-sector division of the Academy of Management and favor the *Academy of Management Review* for their publications. Bozeman develops an impressive list of contrasts between the two approaches before addressing the problem of how a synthesis might be effected that would enhance the distinctive strengths of each approach. The paths to synthesis are many and varied, but conspicuous by its absence is any reference to the Constitution of the United States, which provides the overarching framework within which American public managers of both the policy and business persuasions must do their managing. Managers ignore the distinctively American challenges arising from the constitutional principle of separation of powers only at their peril. Bozeman's failure to see the managerial relevance of the Constitution stands in stark contrast to James Q. Wilson's reminder to readers of his classic study, *Bureaucracy,* that the failure of some of the best ideas on management has "nothing to do with the limitations or inadequacies of individual bureaucrats and everything to do with the constitutional regime of which they are a part."[8] Indeed, he urges readers eager to get to the "bottom line" to "spare themselves the hundreds of pages that follow and turn immediately to Federalist Paper number 51 written two centuries ago by James Madison."[9]

Robert Behn provides a telling example of an excess in the NPM literature when he draws an analogy between public management and engineering.[10] His article testifies to the accuracy of the observation by David Rosenbloom and Rosemary O'Leary that "the consequences of defining public administration as management cannot be overstated."[11] The problem with Behn's article becomes clear when one locates it within the broader framework of the NPM. Taken by itself, the article is clever and enlightening; but when seen as part of a larger whole—that is, the NPM movement—the bloom is off the rose. The analogy between management and engineering has the unwholesome effect of taking management one further step away from governance. Engineering, like science, music, and theology, knows no national boundaries, and this is why scientists, artists, and theologians—often to their credit—make statesmen uneasy. Such men and women operate from a different normative base from those who govern. Despite the salience of the NAFTAs, the WTOs, and the EUs of this world, governing remains overwhelmingly the business of nation-states. Behn's analogy is excessive because it takes public management too far afield from its natural home—the nation-state established within a constitutional order.

Many avenues are available for those who want to see constitutional principles assume their rightful place in administration. An obvious starting point is the remarkable emphasis on administration in *The Federalist Papers,* where the word *administration* and its cognates appear more frequently than the words *Congress, president,* or *Supreme Court.* Indeed, *administration* is one of the few words Publius, the pseudonymous author of *The Federalist,* bothers to define—along with such constitutional stalwarts as *republic, tyranny,* and *faction.* In fact, he defines it twice. "In its largest sense," administration "comprehends all the operations of the body politic, whether legislative, executive or judiciary, but in its most usual and perhaps in its most precise signification, it is limited to executive details, and falls peculiarly within the province of the executive department."[12] Even this "most precise signification" is breathtakingly broad, for among the "executive details" we find nothing less than "the actual conduct of foreign negotiations, the preparatory plans of finance, the application and disbursement of the public monies, in conformity to the general appropriations of the legislature, the arrangement of the army and navy, the direction of the operations of war."[13]

Publius's grand vision of administration contrasts sharply with Woodrow Wilson's famous 1887 essay on administration, which offers a more measured view of it as simply the "detailed and systematic execution of public law."[14] Even Wilson, for all his efforts to confine administration to quarters subordinate to politics, cannot avoid using the word *Constitution* and its cognates over forty times in a short essay ostensibly on administration.

More directly related to the NPM is the impressive current literature criticizing it for its sometimes cavalier treatment of the rule of law, especially its free and easy slogans about eliminating red tape and letting managers manage.[15] Particularly helpful along these lines is an article by Laurence Lynn, a sympathetic critic of the NPM, who argues that what its partisans "pejoratively deride as bureaucracy run amok is in fact the institutional manifestation of the continuous effort to create responsive, accountable government, to prevent abuse of discretion."[16] He reminds those too quick to condemn a government that fails to serve its customers that that very failure may be due to that same government's "attempt to insure that discretion is not abused, that due process is the rule rather than the exception and that undue risks are not taken in the people's name."[17]

In this book I build on the rule-of-law critique of the NPM but do so by calling for the *integration* of the rule of law into the movement rather than its simple *addition*. I do this by building a case for the intimate connection between administration and constitutionalism. Nothing is more fundamental to governance than a constitution, and therefore to stress the constitutional character of administration is to establish the proper role of administration as governance that includes management but transcends it as well. I hope to bring constitutional standards to support George Frederickson's wise observation "that public administration is repositioning itself to deal with the problems of the disarticulated state."[18]

In building my case for the intimate connection between constitutionalism and administration, I begin by looking at constitutions abroad. Here I follow de Tocqueville's sound advice that one can best learn about one's own country by studying the ways of other countries—or, as Kipling puts it, "What knows he of England who only England knows?" In Part I, "Constitutions Abroad," I examine the close connection between administration and constitutions in France, the United Kingdom, and Canada—countries I have selected because they are sufficiently similar to the United States to make comparisons meaningful and sufficiently different to make them interesting. In the title of this book, *constitutions* is in the plural because four are examined in these pages.

In Part II, "The Constitution of the United States," I examine the American constitutional-administration nexus under the aspects of separation of powers, individual rights, and federalism. Throughout these three chapters, I focus on American civil servants in the hope of instilling in them a sense of the crucial role they play in managing the Constitution they are sworn to uphold, hence, the appearance of *civil servants* in the book's title.

Readers familiar with my earlier writings will be aware that, on balance, I am rather favorably disposed toward civil servants. I continue to hold this position with no apologies. Nevertheless, in rehearsing constitutional-administrative relations in this book, I present many examples of administrative behavior that was less than edifying and a few examples of scandal, corruption, and bureaucratic disaster. I do so because my purpose is not to celebrate the glories of administration but to document its presence. When it comes to great constitutional crises, for better or for worse, administration is always there.

Throughout the book, I make extensive use of historical materials as well as more recent events. The examples extend from the French Revolution through the founding of the Canadian Confederation in the 1860s to such contemporary issues as the influence of administrative directives from Brussels on the British courts and recent American developments in separation-of-powers principles. In casting my net so broadly, I hope to establish the point that the constitutional-administrative nexus is no short-lived conceit. It cuts across space (four countries) and time (three centuries). It is stable, pervasive, and enduring. If the NPM is to be more than a passing fad, it must integrate constitutional principles.

In writing this book over the past four years, I have called upon many friends, colleagues, and institutions to help me. At the top of the list is my profound gratitude to the Woodrow Wilson International Center in Washington, D.C., and to Michael J. Lacey, the director of its Division of United States Studies. I spent the academic year 1998–1999 as a fellow at the Wilson Center, where most of the research for this book was completed. During this fellowship year I had the good fortune to work with Michael Lacey, whose insights and encouragement were invaluable. I am also indebted to the men and women who shared the fellowship year with me. They are too many to name, but I would be remiss if I failed to mention Donald Wolfensberger and Richard John.

I am also most grateful to the Earhart Foundation for financial assistance that helped defray some of the formidable expenses of living in Washington, and to Virginia Tech for the sabbatical year that enabled me to accept the Woodrow Wilson Fellowship.

My colleagues and students at Virginia Tech's Center for Public Administration and Policy have, as always, provided the supportive academic atmosphere so conducive to research and writing. I am especially grateful to Joseph Rees, the Center's director, for his academic leadership and to doctoral students Brandy Faulkner, Chad Miller, Tammy Trimble, and Susan Willis-Walton for their insightful comments on this book when it was in manuscript form.

In completing the comparative chapters of this book, I received considerable assistance from personnel at the French, British, and Canadian embassies. In particular, I am grateful to Gary M. Dwor-Frécaut and Bernard Rabitel of the French embassy, David Arkley of the British embassy, and Daniel Abele of the Canadian embassy. My thanks also to librarians Brien St. Jacques and Barbara Donahue at the Canadian embassy for their gracious assistance.

The nature of this book required a good number of interviews with experts in the fields I was examining. I am especially obliged to Professor Thomas Sargentich of the Washington School of Law at the American University for the brilliant insights into administrative law he shared with me. I am also grateful to Judge Welton Curtis Sewell for educating me on the role of federal magistrates; to Judge John Vittone of the Department of Labor for explaining his central role in the PATCO case discussed in chapter 4; and to Henry Wray of the House Committee on Government Reform, Virginia Thomas of the Heritage Foundation, and Chris Wye of the National Academy of Public Administration for initiating me into the mysteries of the Government Performance and Results Act.

The University Press of Kansas provided its customary care and dedication in preparing my manuscript for publication. My thanks to the anonymous and insightful referee whom Fred Woodward, director of the University Press of Kansas, selected to read the initial draft I submitted. The comments and criticisms of this unknown benefactor have strengthened my work considerably.

Authors usually dedicate their books to family members or to close professional associates. I have dedicated earlier books to my wife, Kathy, my sons, Paul and Mark, my students, my colleagues at Virginia Tech, the Jesuits who educated me, and to American civil servants. This book is dedicated to the text whose themes unify all my previous work, the Constitution of the United States.

Several sections of this book rely in part on writings of mine that have been published elsewhere. I am grateful for the permissions I have received to make use of "Ethics, Governance, and Constitutions: The Case of Baron Haussmann," in *Ethics in Public Service for the New Millennium,* ed. Richard A. Chapman (Aldershot, U.K.: Ashgate Press, 2000), 203–216; "Constitutionalism and Administrative Ethics," in *Handbook of Administrative Ethics,* ed. Terry L. Cooper, 2d ed. (New York: Marcel Dekker, 2001), 673–678; "Public Administration and Comparative Constitutionalism: The Case of Canadian Federalism," *Public Administration Review* 57 (July/August 1997): 339–346; "Current Canadian Constitutionalism and the 1865 Confederation Debates," *American Review of Canadian Studies* (winter 1998): 413–444; and "Delegation," in *The President and the Public Administration* (Washington, D.C.: American Historical Association, 1989), 55–59.

PART I
Constitutions Abroad

1

France

When Americans think of their Constitution, they usually think of their courts as well because of their remarkable power to declare acts of Congress and state legislatures unconstitutional. When the Supreme Court of the United States exercises this power, it does so definitively, save the cumbersome process of amending the Constitution. Americans unhappy with their courts voice their displeasure by scoring the antidemocratic character of nonelected, federal judges, contrasting them unfavorably with their democratically elected congressmen or state legislators.

The French republican tradition grants a sympathetic ear to Americans who complain of judicial excesses, calling their own version of this problem *le gouvernement des juges,* a term of opprobrium dating back to the Revolution of 1789. Indeed, so worried have the French been about judges trumping their democratically elected National Assembly that they waited until the establishment of the Fifth Republic in 1958 to create an institution empowered to strike down an unconstitutional statute. That institution is the Constitutional Council *(Conseil Constitutionnel),* which, as its name suggests, is not really a court with litigants before it but a council whose jurisdiction can be invoked only by certain constitutionally designated officers to examine the constitutionality of a statute before it goes into effect. Although today the Constitutional Council enjoys great prestige in France, it was eyed suspiciously in 1958 as a highly problematic innovation. Not surprisingly, it was criticized on the conventional grounds of democratic legitimacy—how can nonelected councillors serving a nine-year term void a statute voted by an elected parliament? More important for the purpose of this book, however, was a distinctively French argument one would never hear in the United States, an argument that affords a good insight into the relationship between constitutionalism and administration in France.

The argument in question arose in the context of a discussion as to whether ordinary citizens should be permitted to challenge the constitutionality of a statute after it has gone into effect, as is the practice in the United States, or whether the challenge should be limited to certain officials who would voice their objection after the law had been voted but before it was promulgated by the president of the Republic—the position that eventually prevailed. Raymond Janot, who represented General Charles de Gaulle's government before an advisory group of parliamentarians during the process of drafting the Constitution of 1958, argued against permitting ordinary citizens to challenge a law after it had been promulgated. His reason is quite instructive for those who study and practice the art of administration.

Janot maintained that many laws will require elaborate administrative regulations before they can be implemented effectively and therefore the government would often be unable to act until the constitutionality of a statute had been judicially confirmed in litigation initiated by a disgruntled citizen. This could cause "some serious delays in governmental activity and that in turn could have an adverse effect on the institutions of the State as a whole."[1] This is a telling comment that illuminates a dark corner of French public administration. For Janot, a distinguished French jurist, a statute is the foundation of an impressive administrative superstructure that is crucial for governance in France. To permit a court to nullify a statute would not only embarrass parliament, but it would also unconscionably delay the government's power to govern by regulation. Janot does not even consider the possibility that the government might enact regulations pursuant to a statute before it undergoes a constitutional challenge, because if the challenge were successful, it would bring down not only the statute itself but the elegant regulatory scheme based upon it. This would destroy a network of rights and duties based on administrative regulations grounded in the doomed statute.[2]

Americans who criticize the excesses of judicial power would never do so because of the bad effect of such excesses on administrative regulations. Americans simply do not think this way, but French jurists do because they take the constitutional aspects of the administrative state far more seriously than Americans. I shall pursue this idea of the importance of administration in French constitutional history by examining three themes from the past three centuries: de Tocqueville on the salience of administration during the French Revolution at the end of the eighteenth century, the constitutional background for the stunning administrative achievements of Baron Haussmann in the nineteenth century, and the central role assigned to administration in the Constitution of the Fifth Republic in the twentieth century.

DE TOCQUEVILLE ON ADMINISTRATION
AND THE REVOLUTION OF 1789

Alexis de Tocqueville's great classic, *The Old Regime and the French Revolution,* is best known for illustrating the paradox that has come to be associated with his name: the more things change, the more they remain the same. He begins his book by stating the profound changes the revolutionaries of 1789 had in mind, changes that included but went far beyond introducing a new constitutional order. Their goal was nothing less than to effect the total transformation of society, "to break with the past, to make, as it were, a scission in their life line and to create an unbridgeable gap between all they had hitherto been and all they now aspired to be."[3] Indeed, "they spared no pains in their endeavor to obliterate their former selves."[4] Despite their apocalyptic goals, de Tocqueville says of the revolutionaries of 1789 "that, in fact, though nothing was further from their intentions, they used the debris of the old order for building up the new."[5]

Thus, the opening paragraphs of de Tocqueville's *The Old Regime* clearly intone the theme of continuity amid change, a theme that nicely captures his great literary endeavor. To establish the continuity between pre- and postrevolutionary France, de Tocqueville turns to the administrative records of the old order, an obvious place to look in "a country whose strong central administration has gained control of all the national activities."[6] His research revealed that despite the profound constitutional and societal changes initiated by the revolution, "many of the laws and administrative methods which were suppressed in 1789 reappeared just a few years later, much as some rivers after going underground re-emerge at another point, in new surroundings."[7]

Chief among the practices surviving the Revolution was the administrative principle of centralization. Here de Tocqueville calls his readers' attention to the widely held but erroneous belief that the highly centralized administrative system of nineteenth-century France was the product of the Revolution of 1789. Quite the contrary, centralization "was a legacy from the old regime and, I may add, the only part of the political constitution of that regime which survived the Revolution for the good reason that it alone could be adapted to the new social system sponsored by the Revolution."[8] Thus, de Tocqueville identifies the administrative principle of centralization as the sole survivor of what he calls the "political constitution" of the old order. That is, the Revolution destroyed such venerable institutions as the king, the nobility, the established Church, the traditional courts, and so forth, but it preserved administrative centralization. The revolutionaries needed centralized administration to spread their principles from Paris to the rest of France. Centralization was nothing less than "the Revolution's starting-off point and one of its guiding principles."[9] One can hardly imagine a stronger affirmation of an intimate connection between public administration and constitutional upheaval.

Writing in 1856, de Tocqueville details many instruments of administrative centralization from the old regime that his contemporaries would recognize at once as roughly similar to the Council of State, the prefects, and the jurisdictions outside the ordinary courts as these were known in mid-nineteenth-century France. The Council of State was created by the Constitution of 1800 (year VIII of the Revolution) under the watchful eye of Napoleon to serve as both the highest administrative court in France and as the political and legal adviser to the emperor. By 1856, it was well on its way to developing the excellent reputation it enjoys today as one of France's most prestigious institutions. De Tocqueville describes the crucial functions of the Royal Council *(le conseil du roi)* of the old regime, which served as the precursor of the Council of State. It centralized power in its own hands, because, though subject to the pleasure of the king, it exercised broad legislative, executive, and judicial powers. As de Tocqueville puts it: "All the affairs of the realm came before it in the last instance and it gave directives in every field of the administration."[10]

The office of prefect was another Napoleonic innovation that survives to the present day. Although it has undergone many changes during its long history, the prefect's office still serves the centralizing role of representing the national government in each of the ninety-six departments of metropolitan France. The prefect's role was anticipated in the old regime by the office of the intendants, junior members of the Royal Council dispatched throughout the kingdom to represent the Royal Council and the king. The intendant was usually "a young man of humble extraction, who . . . was never a native of the province to which he was posted."[11] Since he served at the pleasure of the king, he was in every sense the king's man and performed a crucial centralizing role by leaning against the powerful centrifugal forces of the offices created over the centuries in haphazard fashion by local princes, barons, bishops, and town councils, which, taken together, created "a bewildering confusion of powers."[12] The intendants, enjoying the support of the king and the Royal Council, gradually established their control over the collection of taxes, militia service, road building, police work, relief for the poor, agriculture, and all sorts of public works.

A third centralizing instrument was the king's policy of creating "exceptional" jurisdictions to avoid subjecting royal interests to the independent decisions of the judges of the ordinary courts. De Tocqueville states the problem with characteristic clarity: "In no other European country were the judges so independent of the government as in France, but in no other country was so much use made of 'exceptional' courts of justice."[13] It was precisely because the judges of the ordinary courts had achieved such independence from the king that he yielded to the temptation to remove politically sensitive cases from the ordinary courts and place them before specially created jurisdictions favorably disposed toward royal interests. At first, only cases directly involving royal authority were removed from the ordinary courts, but gradually this practice was extended to suits against civil servants and eventually to all litigation involving "traffic regulations, public conveyances, the upkeep of the highways, inland navigation, and the like."[14] This practice became routinized with the appearance in nearly every administrative regulation of the clause, "Furthermore, his Majesty orders that all disputes arising from the execution of this decree and its appurtenances shall be heard by the Intendant, who will pass final judgment on them, subject to a right of appeal to the [Royal] Council."[15]

Thus, before the Revolution of 1789 France had established the harbinger of what we know as French administrative law today—a special jurisdiction staffed by administrators rather than by ordinary judges empowered to adjudicate controversies of public interest with no appeal to the ordinary courts. The creation of this exceptional jurisdiction played a major role in centralizing French administrative justice both before and after the Revolution.

Many indeed were the causes for the extreme centralization of French administration, but none was more important than the perennial financial needs of the king to bankroll foreign wars and other dynastic ambitions. Traditionally, French kings had raised revenue with the cooperation of the Estates General, a body composed of the three great "estates" or orders in France—the nobility, the high clergy, and the ordinary people. To summon this body, however, was always risky for the king because the nobility would invariably demand concessions before approving any financial support. The fact that no French king had summoned the Estates General from 1615 to 1789 was a good indication of just how risky this strategy was.

Among the revenue-raising methods adopted by the French kings during this period of 174 years was the singularly ill-advised policy of selling all kinds of public offices. In the short term, this practice flattered what de Tocqueville called "the keen desire for office" he had observed among his countrymen. He opines that there are "few, if any, parallels for this intense desire of middle class Frenchmen to cut an official figure." Indeed, he maintains that no sooner did a middle-class Frenchman "find himself in possession of a small capital sum than he expended it on buying an official post instead of investing it in a business."[16] Many offices also brought with them exemption from burdensome taxes that fell on ordinary citizens unwilling or unable to buy an office.

The problem with this system of raising revenue was that public office became a form of private property. In an appendix to his book, de Tocqueville recounts a tale that underscores this development. The lieutenant-general of police in Mans brought suit against the financial department of that city to vindicate his right to pave the streets and to collect fees from those who used them. The paving of streets, he argued, was a police function that had fallen to him when he bought his office. The financial department denied the police officer's claim, arguing that it had the responsibility to pave the streets. Interestingly, de Tocqueville notes that "this time it is not the King's council which decides between them." The case went to an ordinary court, where it was treated as a civil suit because the key legal issue was "the interest of the capital invested by the lieutenant in the purchase of his office."[17]

For the king, the most fundamental problem with the system of selling offices was that he lost control over the ones he had sold, as each officer, with impeccable logic, treated his public office as a matter of private interest—as in the case of the lieutenant-general of police from Mans. Since the officer owned the office, the king could not replace him with a more congenial subordinate. Under these circumstances, the king could not impose his will upon those who were nominally his subordinates. De Tocqueville neatly summarizes the dilemma facing the royal power: "Its greed frustrated its ambition."[18]

Hence, the attraction of the streamlined, rationalized, and centralized system that linked the king to his council and the council to the intendants. Significantly, the office of intendant was never for sale. The centralized system, "at once simpler and easier to manipulate," was established alongside the inefficient system of purchased offices, which "had to be left running idle." In practice, the centralized system "carried out the function nominally performed by the hordes of office holders who had bought their way into the bureaucracy."[19]

Looking back from his 1856 vantage point, Alexis de Tocqueville explained why the Revolution of 1789 had brought lasting changes to France whereas the results of the revolutions in the first half of the nineteenth century were ephemeral by comparison. The reason for the different results, he maintained, is that in the years immediately preceding 1789, the king had finally been compelled to introduce a series of important administrative reforms in such matters as public finance, taxation, and the structure of governance. These changes in what de Tocqueville calls "secondary laws" had led to "much confusion and ill-feeling." Indeed, this "abrupt, wholesale remodeling of the entire administration which preceded the political revolution" had brought about "one of the greatest upheavals that have ever taken place in the life of a great nation." The importance of far-reaching administrative change lies in its immediate impact on the everyday lives of ordinary people. Through administration, a government "keeps every citizen constantly aware of its existence and affects his daily life." The dramatic changes in what de Tocqueville calls the "subordinate" aspects of government just before the Revolution had unsettled the citizens' acquiescence in the established order and predisposed them to accept and even to embrace changes at the highest level of the state that would eventually topple the king himself. In the nineteenth-century revolutions, on the other hand, "the administration was, so to speak, decapitated," but "its body survived intact and active." Consequently, the citizens saw that "the same duties were performed by the same civil servants whose practical experience kept the nation on an even keel through the worst political storms."[20]

This is a remarkably strong statement on the constitutional significance of administration by one of history's most astute political observers. The great Revolution of 1789 produced lasting results because it had been preceded by the "abrupt, wholesale remodeling of the entire administration." Such administrative changes did not precede the revolutions of the nineteenth century and, therefore, their results were far less enduring.

BARON HAUSSMANN AND THE SECOND EMPIRE

The life and times of Baron Haussmann reveal the intimate connection between the career of one of the world's most brilliant administrators and the constitutional regime he served. My focus is not on specific constitutional texts but on the spirit of the Second Empire, a spirit Haussmann grasped and embodied. The narrative here is intended to show the extent to which Haussmann's spectacular administrative career depended on the authoritarian standards of the Second Empire.

My argument follows Aristotle's observation that polities have a way of shaping the character of their citizens so that there are discernible differences between Athenians, Spartans, Thebans, and others.[21] Aristotle's famous discussion of whether a good citizen is necessarily a good person appeared in this context. This can be a question of great moral significance, as it surely was in Hitler's Germany, where to be a good Nazi was, by definition, to be a bad person. Nazi Germany, however, is fortunately the extreme case. Most regimes define their citizens' characters more gently and subtly, without abandoning the field of political morality altogether, e.g., individual rights in the United States, compassion and community in Canada, a certain residual class-consciousness in the United Kingdom, and grandeur (both illusions of and the real thing) in France. To succeed in these countries, it helps to be at ease in conforming to these loose and amorphous standards rather than to kick against them. Because of the moral overtones implicit in the question of the relationship between constitutions and character, I have organized our examination of Baron Haussmann's career by looking first at his virtues and then at his vices.

Georges-Eugène Haussmann was born in Paris in 1809. He attended the prestigious Lycée Henri IV, then as now a wise choice for parents with grand ambitions for their children. After studying law at the Sorbonne, he entered the prefectoral corps in 1831 and filled a wide variety of administrative posts during the Orleanist regime of Louis Philippe, the citizen king. He was serving as prefect of the Gironde when, in 1853, Emperor Napoleon III appointed him prefect of the Seine, "the most important administrative appointment in the administrative state,"[22] a position he held until a financial scandal led to his dismissal in 1870. He served briefly, but without distinction, in the Chamber of Deputies of the Third Republic. Haussmann died in 1891.

He is best known for bringing about nothing less than the transformation of Paris, with the grand boulevards and elegant parks that grace that city today. No less important were his stunning improvements in sanitation, lighting, and transportation. Neither Haussmann's friends nor his foes nor Haussmann himself would dispute the judgment of Napoleon III that he was, quite simply, a "great administrator."[23] He was a man who "craved order in his life, his work and his world," a man who "found poetry in a budget."[24] Haussmann's spectacular successes were due primarily to his effective and at times ruthless use of power, which in turn rested on his informal status as a favorite of Emperor Napoleon III and his formal status as prefect of the Seine, a position that made him the de facto mayor of Paris.

Since I am focusing on the relationship between constitutions and administration, a brief chronology of the constitutional changes during Haussmann's lifetime is in order. He was born under the Empire of Napoleon I, which was replaced by the Bourbon Restoration of 1815 and which in turn yielded to the Orleanist regime, also known as the July Monarchy, in the revolution of 1830. In 1848, another revolution brought the Second Republic to power, whose president, Louis Napoleon, a nephew of the first Napoleon, was elected by popular vote. In 1851, Louis Napoleon led a coup d'état against the republic he headed, an action legitimated (at least to Napoleon's satisfaction) by the overwhelming support he received in a plebiscite. The next year saw the establishment of the Second Empire with Napoleon III at its head and a new, authoritarian constitution to replace its short-lived republican predecessor. In 1870, France suffered a crushing defeat in the Franco-Prussian War, which ended the Second Empire. After the bloody suppression of the Paris Commune in 1871, the first steps were taken toward what eventually emerged as the Third Republic, with a series of constitutional laws voted in 1875.

Haussmann's vices are more interesting for our purposes than his virtues because they are more directly related to the constitutional standards of the regime in which he flourished. To do justice to his memory, however, we should not ignore the brighter side of his character.

Virtues

Let me begin by correcting the common misapprehension that the splendid, wide boulevards Haussmann designed for Paris were really military highways intended to move troops more quickly against oppressed and unruly Parisians. Although military considerations were not entirely irrelevant, far more important were the aesthetic values of open spaces, such practical matters as the public health benefits of clearing out dismal slums, and the commercial advantages of expediting the flow of traffic. Military plans, such as they were, had been laid long before Haussmann's arrival. The *rue de Rivoli,* for example, had been begun by the first Napoleon as a convenient path to dispatch soldiers to the troublesome neighborhoods on the east side of Paris as well as for the aesthetic purpose of leading into an open urban space around the Hôtel de Ville. To the extent that military purposes played any part in Haussmann's plans, one can only savor the irony in the fact that the most important military use of his boulevards came in 1871 when the supporters of the Paris Commune (not exactly Haussmann's kind of folks) used them to descend on the center of Paris.

Many of Haussmann's virtues would be welcome in civil servants of any regime, e.g., his indomitable energy and his unflagging loyalty to his political master. Although questionable practices in matters of public finance eventually led to his downfall, there is no evidence that these practices redounded to his personal financial advantage.[25] For our purposes, however, his most interesting virtue was surely his clearheaded view of the public interest as he understood it. I mention this virtue last not because it is least, but because its problematic character tends to spill over into the category of vice, thereby serving as a bridge between his virtues and vices. In his *Mémoires,* written after his fall from power, Haussmann asserts that "the only practical form of Democracy is the Empire" and that "I was an imperialist by birth and conviction."[26] He explains the link between imperialism and democracy: "It [imperialism] is a democracy whose authoritarian form assures stability, whose chief receives from the People an indispensable title that allows him to treat on equal footing with the most powerful sovereigns, but whose strong constitution does not permit him to compromise the imprescriptible and inalienable rights of the Nation."[27]

Haussmann's commitment to the empire was rivaled only by his devotion to Paris as its center. In the first sentence of his *Mémoires,* he introduces himself to the reader as "quite simply a parvenu Parisian, determined to make a name for himself, even a controversial name, in his beloved natal city." No small part of the controversial name he won for himself was due to his incessant conflicts with fellow Parisians who saw little advantage for themselves in Haussmann's spectacular public works. His reply was characteristically direct: "Paris belongs to France and not to Parisians by birth or by choice. . . . The central power, which represents the nation, ought to be armed at Paris with the necessary authority to make the general interest prevail over all the others." David Jordan summarizes nicely Haussmann's view of the public interest: "Grandeur, rational order, purposeful and incessant movement, progress, cleanliness, an urban life lived in public are the qualities he forcefully imposed on Paris."[28]

There is something admirable about a man with a firm sense of who he is and what he must do but something unsettling as well. Jordan has it right in referring to the qualities of life Haussmann *"imposed* on Paris." Haussmann was a single-minded man. He describes himself as one who always "followed a direct route, without letting myself to be diverted." This, he believed, gave him a certain advantage over adversaries more devious than himself: "Clever men, little accustomed to the straight and narrow, did not lie in wait for me along this road." Those who dared to cross the self-righteous Haussmann paid dearly for their transgressions: "I strike back with usury."[29]

Vices

Baron Haussmann was not a pleasant man. To find flaws in his character is not difficult. Indeed, such an endeavor is soon overwhelmed with an embarrassment of riches. To keep the discussion of Haussmann's vices within manageable bounds, I shall concentrate on only three of them: arrogance, financial irregularities, and political meddling.

Arrogance. An arrogant public official is unwelcome in any regime, but the offense is less serious in an authoritarian one. Haussmann was insufferably arrogant by any standard, but the long success he enjoyed under the Second Empire suggests that the authoritarian milieu of the regime spared him the early dismissal he almost certainly would have merited had he served during a republican era.

Examples of Haussmann's arrogance abound. Consider his title of baron, which he claimed through his maternal grandfather, Georges-Frédéric Dentzel, a brigadier-general under Napoleon I upon whom the latter conferred the title of baron of the empire. Haussmann's critics pointed out that he had no legitimate claim to the title since such honors could not be handed on through the maternal line, but Haussmann felt no embarrassment because "many of his contemporaries used titles just as questionable."[30]

His arrogance did not escape his superiors. One of the letters in his personnel file from his early days in the provinces notes that in fulfilling his assignments, "he is inclined to substitute his own personal policy and ideas for those of his superiors, by reason of the excellent opinion he has of his personal merit."[31] In the same vein, the duc de Persigny, who served as minister of the interior in the early years of the Second Empire, recounts in his *Mémoires* the interview in 1853 that prompted him to select Haussmann for what he knew would be the extremely difficult post of prefect of the Seine. Acknowledging that, paradoxically, he was more impressed by Haussmann's "character faults" than by "his remarkable intelligence," he observed that the prospective prefect delighted in explaining the great events of his administrative career and that he "could have gone on for six hours without stopping provided the conversation stayed on his favorite topic, himself." Well aware of the toughness the new prefect would need to implement the ambitious urban renewal projects of Napoleon III, Persigny took considerable pleasure in knowing he had the right man. Somewhat ominously, he added, "while this fascinating personality revealed itself to me with a certain brutal cynicism, I could barely contain my utter satisfaction."[32]

For a good example of Haussmann's high opinion of himself, consider his instructions to the painter charged with decorating the Municipal Council chamber at the Hôtel de Ville in 1865. Four murals were called for. The first three depicted Clovis choosing Paris as his capital, Philippe-Auguste embarking on a crusade to regain the Holy Land, and Francis I establishing the Hôtel de Ville. The fourth mural presented none other than Haussmann himself receiving from Napoleon III the decree annexing several communes adjacent to Paris.[33]

He enlisted his arrogance in advancing his own career on one of the many occasions when he found himself at odds with the Council of State and Napoleon's ministers. As prefect of the Seine, Haussmann was technically subordinate to the minister of the interior. Ordinarily, this hierarchical disadvantage had little practical significance because Haussmann could usually finesse ministerial opposition by his ready access to the emperor. In November 1860, Haussmann found several of his projects languishing in the Council of State and various ministerial bureaus. Weary of these delays, he decided to draft a decree for the emperor's signature creating a new Ministry of Paris with himself as minister. The emperor found this too bold an innovation but offered him instead an invitation to attend cabinet meetings and an appointment as an extraordinary member of the Council of State. The draft decree Haussmann prepared for the emperor's signature was accompanied by a letter reminding his majesty that there was to be a banquet the very next day at which Haussmann was to "propose the Emperor's health." To coax the emperor to sign the decree, he bluntly assured him that "I should be happy to have a new cause for gratitude for the generosity which your Majesty has already shown me."[34]

Haussmann's arrogance assumed international implications at a banquet sponsored by the municipality of Paris to honor the king and queen of Belgium. Having "by now become very blasé about crowned heads," Haussmann created quite a stir when he took the queen by the arm and "snapped at the King: 'Come along, then, King of the Belgians, take Mme. Haussmann's arm. . . .' And he led the way to dinner."[35]

Haussmann's arrogance did not desert him as his career came to an unhappy end. At the first hint in December 1867 of the revelations of the financial legerdemain that eventually brought him down, he stonewalled in the grand style worthy of an imperial favorite: "Everyone has seen that threats have no effect on an administration convinced of its duty. . . . A great administration knows neither anger nor resentment. It remains calm and firm in the struggles which it has increasingly to wage against ill-founded pretensions."[36]

The press was not amused. The rumors of scandal continued apace with a string of political misfortunes for the emperor, which forced him to make significant changes in his cabinet at the end of 1869. The new members of the government were of a more liberal persuasion than their predecessors. Part of the liberal agenda was to demand Haussmann's resignation, a measure in which the emperor reluctantly acquiesced. Imagine the emperor's astonishment when his personal letter advising Haussmann that he would have to resign received the following reply: "*I refuse to resign.* I do not wish to appear to evade the difficulties of the final hour. I wish to render my accounts, to pay off the debt of the City, and go out by the main doorway, handing over my administration to my successor in good order." For good measure he added, "A man like me does not resign, neither does he cling to power. Either you sack him or keep him."[37] The emperor sacked him.

As a final example of Haussmann's arrogance, consider his way of referring to the poor of Paris as "nomads." There was a cruel irony in this particular appellation, for these nomads were, as David Jordan aptly notes, "a tribe of his creation, some of them displaced by the demolitions, many newly arrived to enlist in his construction and demolition armies."[38] Contempt for such people was a necessary concomitant of Haussmann's administrative triumphs. His interest lay with boulevards, sewers, parks, and lighting—areas of state responsibility that benefited rich and poor alike. His favorite metaphor for the city as a body with lungs, bowels, and arteries "considered neither the soul nor the repose of the body itself, neither the citizens nor their daily private lives."[39] Had he cared about people as people, he would not have succeeded in his great life work. His arrogance led him to believe his own high-minded rhetoric on public spiritedness, which caught so well the spirit of the regime he served so faithfully.

Financial Irregularities. A recurring theme throughout Haussmann's long tenure as prefect of the Seine was the resentment of elected officials toward him. He solved part of this problem in 1855 when he persuaded the emperor to call for legislation changing the municipal council of Paris from an elected to an appointed body whose members were de facto chosen by Haussmann himself and then officially appointed by his nominal superior, the minister of the interior.[40] Parliament, however, presented a more difficult problem. When Haussmann became prefect of the Seine in 1853, he was pleased to discover that his predecessors had left a modest surplus in the municipal treasury. Although the prevailing orthodoxy of the day, championed by elected officials, held that "every surplus belongs to the public," Haussmann saw the surplus as the fiscal foundation for an extensive and largely clandestine plan of borrowing the capital needed for the emperor's ambitious urban renewal projects. Thus, Haussmann embarked on a creative financial adventure that eventually led to his downfall but not before he had accomplished far more than either he or the emperor dreamed possible at the outset. As a public financier, Haussmann was far ahead of his time. He grasped intuitively the remarkable potential for growth in what came to be known as deficit spending, but what he called "productive spending."

At first he relied on shrewd schemes of shuttling funds back and forth between the city's ordinary and extraordinary budgets in such a way as to mask the true extent of the city's debt. The key to his system, however, was the establishment of the Public Works Fund for Paris *(Caisse des Travaux de Paris)* in 1858. Not coincidentally, this fund was established at the same time that he annexed the suburbs surrounding Paris. Informed opinion estimated that it would take ten years to provide adequate sewers, lighting, and water in the annexed zone if ordinary revenues alone were used. This was far too long for the impatient prefect. Hence, he prevailed upon the emperor to issue a decree creating the Public Works Fund. Because this fund was established by imperial decree as opposed to parliamentary statute, Napoleon's Constitution enabled Haussmann to escape the burden of close legislative scrutiny. The fund was his *caisse noire.*

The Cour des Comptes, then as now the official auditing office of the French state, occasionally questioned some of Haussmann's uses of the fund, but its writ ran no further than to call the alleged irregularity to the attention of a parliament whose reduced role in the imperial regime enabled it to do little more than issue feckless after-the-fact warnings that Haussmann ignored. For all practical purposes the emperor's favorite was untouchable.

When Napoleon's health and political power began to wane in the late 1860s, Haussmann became an attractive target for those whose real aim was to topple the imperial regime itself. A constitutional change in 1867 brought ministers into a closer working relationship with parliament. This institutional change, combined with a rejuvenated and increasingly hostile press, gradually subjected Haussmann's financial practices to a closer scrutiny than they could bear.

The indomitable Jules Ferry led the attack, charging that Haussmann "lacks all sense of legality" and that "he breaks the law with abandon."[41] Haussmann conceded his methods were unorthodox but insisted they were legal as well as effective. It is beyond the scope of this chapter to try to settle the legality of Haussmann's creative public finances. For our purposes, the interesting point is the argument he made to support the legality of his actions. Acknowledging that there was no statute to support his Public Works Fund, he argued that there was ample precedent for his reliance upon an imperial decree as the legitimating source of his revenue-raising policies. He noted that under the Second Republic, a decree, not a statute, had enabled the state to purchase the toll concessions on bridges over the Seine, and the city of Paris had issued bonds to finance the purchase. There was no challenge to this arrangement at that time, despite the absence of any national law to support it. If a republic can regulate its finances by decree, surely an empire can do the same.[42]

Political Meddling. Throughout his long career, Haussmann was always involved in politics. One can hardly imagine a clearer illustration of the inherently political character of administration than the brilliant career of Georges Haussmann. As a young man of twenty-one, he played a minor role as a messenger in the revolution of 1830 that ushered in the reign of Louis Philippe. Fortunately (and characteristically), Haussmann backed the winning side. He showed considerable bravery during the three days of fighting in the streets of Paris and received a minor wound, which became "the stroke of good fortune he exploited to launch his career."[43] Having received legal training at the Sorbonne, he decided to apply for a post in the prefectoral corps shortly after the revolution of July 1830. He probably selected this corps because it was part of the Ministry of the Interior, where his father had some influence. When he submitted his application, he mentioned the wound he had received in helping to bring the Orleans regime to power as well as his distinguished lineage as grandson of a general of Napoleon on his mother's side and of a member of the Legislative Assembly of 1791 on his father's side. Prudently, however, he passed over in silence his paternal grandfather's expulsion from France as a regicide at the time of the Bourbon Restoration in 1815. Grandfather Haussmann had failed to oppose the sentence of death visited upon Louis XVI in 1793.

In the early years of his career, he often invoked his friendship with the duc d'Orléans, a classmate from his days at Lycée Henri IV and a son of King Louis Philippe. The young duke was Haussmann's patron until his premature death in 1842, a serious blow to his ambitious client. Through the long years from 1831 to 1853 when Haussmann was working his way up the ladder of the prefects' corps, he carefully cultivated the goodwill of the rich and powerful, without, however, shrinking from controversy with them when professional duty required it.

The republican revolution of 1848 presented an acute problem for Haussmann as a loyal supporter of the fallen Orleans monarchy. His *Mémoires* reveal his careful political calculations as he navigated the swirls and eddies of that tumultuous year. At the time, Haussmann was serving as subprefect in the Department of the Gironde. Upon the abdication of Louis Philippe at the end of February, the Second Republic was proclaimed at first in Paris and then gradually throughout all of France. When the representatives of the newly proclaimed republic offered Haussmann the opportunity to retain his office of subprefect, he declined, stating that "I could absolutely not, without dishonor, become the representative of the policies of the republic after having served the recently overthrown July Monarchy for seventeen years."[44] He was then offered the position of president of the *Conseil de Préfecture* of the Gironde, which his tender conscience permitted him to accept because he found it "pure administration"—a rather ironic comment in view of the politically charged character of Haussmann's administrative career.

By summer 1848, the revolution had turned exceedingly violent, and Haussmann watched in dismay as four different prefects arrived in rapid succession to represent the fledgling republic in the Gironde. Amid this instability, Haussmann was offered a promotion, which he shrewdly declined, saying he was reluctant "to reenter the administration before the Constitution was voted and a definitive government installed."[45] Writing of these events some forty years later, he candidly acknowledged that he did not want to be too closely identified with the shaky republic, especially as he sensed a growing sentiment for more firm government under Louis Napoleon. Thus Haussmann found himself well positioned in December 1848, when Louis Napoleon was elected president of the Second Republic, from which office he led a coup d'état three years later that resulted in the Second Empire and the long reign of the erstwhile republican president as Emperor Napoleon III.

Haussmann's appointment as prefect of the Seine in 1853 was the crucial event in his career. He was selected with Napoleon's ambitious urban projects in mind. Although Haussmann was neither an architect nor an engineer, the emperor and his able interior minister, the duc de Persigny, saw other attractive qualities in him. We have already observed the delight Persigny took in Haussmann's "brutal cynicism." No less important, however, were his demonstrated skills in the overtly political arena of electoral campaigns. Napoleon's coup d'état of 2 December 1851 had to be legitimated by a plebiscite. Having been promoted to the office of prefect of the Gironde, an area that included the great city of Bordeaux, Haussmann was expected to deliver a strong majority in support of the coup. (At that time, it was not unusual for prefects to use their influence in elections to support the government of the day in Paris, whose representatives they were.) Haussmann did not disappoint his political masters, even though the Gironde had never been known for its support of Napoleon I. The plebiscite, held on 21 December 1851, found the Gironde giving Louis

Napoleon overwhelming support—a larger majority than he had won as candidate for president of the Republic in 1848.

To consolidate the powers he had assumed in the coup d'état, Napoleon needed strong support in the Legislative Corps *(Corps legislatif),* an innovative parliamentary body created by the new, authoritarian Constitution of 14 January 1852, which established institutions more congenial to the new regime than those of the fallen Second Republic of 1848. Once again, Napoleon turned to the prefects to deliver the vote, this time in the legislative elections of March 1852. Haussmann rallied his subprefects and the mayors in his department to the task at hand, even allowing himself the indulgence of sharing his thoughts on constitutional theory. Since the plebiscite of 21 December had given popular support to Louis Napoleon's retaining the powers of president of the Republic, Haussmann saw the task of the Legislative Corps as one of reinforcing these powers. Therefore, he told his electioneering subordinates, it is imperative to elect men who will support Louis Napoleon so that there will be "harmony as complete as possible" between the two institutions—the presidency and the Legislative Corps—selected independently of one another.[46] Utterly innocent of any notion of separation of powers, Haussmann's view on the distribution of constitutional power agrees perfectly with his administrative worldview that values unity, order, and harmony above all else. Apparently, Haussmann's fellow citizens agreed, for all but a handful of the victorious legislators supported Napoleon.

Although the coup d'état of 2 December 1851 set in motion the events that would lead to the establishment of the Second Empire, exactly one year passed before the formal change came into effect. In the meantime, Louis Napoleon retained the title of president of the Republic, although rumors swirled around Paris that the Second Empire would soon be established. To prepare the people for this event, Napoleon traveled extensively throughout France in 1852, explaining his vision of the country's future. One of the most notable of these trips brought him to Bordeaux, where Haussmann organized a splendid reception worthy of an emperor in waiting. His efforts were rewarded with a speech by Napoleon that must have delighted Haussmann. Addressing the Bordeaux Chamber of Commerce on 9 October 1852, Napoleon allayed fears that a new empire would mean ceaseless wars, as the old one had. He assured his listeners that should an empire be established, it would be a peaceful one: "We have huge uncultivated areas to develop, roads to build, ports to construct, rivers to make navigable, our whole networks of railways to complete. . . . This is what I understand by the Empire if the Empire is to be re-established. These are the conquests I envisage, and all you around me who want, like me, the good of our country, you are my soldiers."[47] One can only imagine Haussmann's profound satisfaction with the grand vision of nothing less than an administrative empire.

Six weeks later the French people approved by plebiscite this text: "The imperial dignity is re-established. Louis Napoleon Bonaparte is Emperor of the French with the name Napoleon III."[48] The Second Empire was formally proclaimed on 2 December 1852; and on 22 June 1853, Haussmann, whose imperial credentials were impeccable, was appointed to the high office of prefect of the Seine.

Since Paris had no mayor at that time, the prefect of the Seine exercised many of the functions normally associated with the office of mayor. Although constitutional theory made the prefect of the Seine the subordinate of the minister of the interior and prevented him from dealing directly with the emperor, Haussmann skillfully circumvented these legal niceties and managed to interact with Napoleon on virtually a daily basis. This personal contact with the emperor was key to Haussmann's power and served him well until the power of the emperor faltered and with it the power of his loyal servant. Thus, Haussmann, like so many of his tribe, eventually met the unhappy fate of those who put their trust in princes.

THE CONSTITUTION OF THE FIFTH REPUBLIC

The Text

If one reads the text of the Constitution of the Fifth Republic of 1958 with an eye on its administrative institutions, the most striking impression is the matter-of-fact way in which they are treated.[49] The Constitution of the United States treats administrative institutions in a brief but highly formal manner, providing only that executive departments and any other offices will be created "by law," that is, by Congress, without naming these offices or hinting at the role they will play. The administrative life of the new American Republic lay in the future and would be determined by Congress. Not so the French Constitution of 1958. Important administrative organizations that predated the new Constitution are simply *there,* with no discussion of their legal foundations or their specific functions. Thus Article 13 describes certain powers of the president of the Republic in relation to such familiar administrative institutions as the Council of Ministers, the Audit Office *(La Cour des Comptes),* the Council of State, and so forth. Several articles refer to the prefects without any further explanation. The text says nothing about these offices and organizations because they needed no introduction to French citizens of 1958, for whom they were familiar household words with well-known historic tasks. In a word, the text presupposes an elaborate administrative structure already established to welcome the new constitution as soon as it shall have won the support of the people. In France, constitutions come and go but administrative institutions remain.

The immediate cause for a new constitution in 1958 was the disastrous colonial war in Algeria. A cabal of army officers, disgusted by what they considered halfhearted support for the war from the government in Paris, created a "revolutionary committee," which seized power from the legitimate colonial authorities in Algiers with no opposition from the army. Shortly thereafter, they seized control of Corsica, and politicians in Paris had to face the serious possibility of a military coup d'état. There was even talk of civil war. In this charged atmosphere, René Coty, the president of the Republic, asked General de Gaulle to come out of retirement and to form a government to deal with the crisis.

De Gaulle had left political life in 1946 when the French people approved the Constitution of the Fourth Republic, a text that the general found utterly unacceptable. Because of his heroic role in heading the Resistance during World War II, de Gaulle had become the leading French statesman during the unstable period from the liberation of Paris in 1944 until the establishment of the Fourth Republic in 1946. His principal objection to the 1946 Constitution was its support for the principle of parliamentary sovereignty. De Gaulle had always maintained that France's humiliating defeat at the hands of the Germans in 1940 was due primarily not to a failure of French arms but to the failure of political leadership in the closing days of the Third Republic (1870–1940) and that the primary cause of this failure was the unhappy principle of parliamentary sovereignty.

De Gaulle and his followers realized that parliamentary sovereignty worked well in the United Kingdom but was unsuitable for France because of its exceedingly diverse political culture. French republicanism tended to divide the people into a multiparty system in which governments could be formed only by unstable alliances of parties temporarily united only by a common interest in holding power. When difficult decisions had to be made, these governments could not develop coherent strategies and often succumbed to motions of censure that drove them from power. According to the Gaullists, this governmental instability deprived France of the firm executive leadership it needed to face the German military threat at the outset of World War II. Consequently, General de Gaulle, as the leading statesman of the immediate postwar period, tried in 1946 to persuade his countrymen of the need for a strong executive and to dissuade them from adopting a new constitution grounded in what he saw as the fatal error of the past, the principle of parliamentary sovereignty.

The reasons the French rejected de Gaulle's advice were many and varied, but prominent among them was the profound value of parliamentary sovereignty in the French republican tradition. During World War II, the only part of France that was not under direct rule of the German army was governed by Maréchal Philippe Pétain's authoritarian regime at Vichy, which was explicitly antirepublican. Indeed, the device affixed to the coins issued during the Vichy years substituted the telling expression *l'Etat français* for *la République française*. By 1946, the French people were eager to return to their republican ways, which were inextricably linked to the principle of parliamentary sovereignty. When the people rejected his advice and approved the 1946 Constitution of the Fourth Republic, General de Gaulle withdrew from public office and, to a certain extent, from public life itself.

When the Algerian crisis brought him back to public office as president of the Council, the title used in the Fourth Republic for the prime minister, de

Gaulle was determined to use his office not only to put down the rebellion in the army but also to try once again to give the French a constitution with stronger executive powers than the principle of parliamentary sovereignty had allowed in the past. To do this, however, he and his followers had to convince the French people that they still had a republican regime. This was no easy task since parliamentary sovereignty was considered a condition sine qua non of French republicanism. The Gaullists' problem was not unlike that of the framers of the American Constitution in 1787, who had to convince skeptical Anti-Federalists that the new government they proposed was still a republic even though its vast size was at odds with the traditional understanding that republican government could be exercised only over small territories.

To meet this challenge, de Gaulle called upon his minister of justice, Michel Debré, who brought together a working group *(groupe de travail)* to draft a new constitutional text. Significantly for our purposes, all the members of this working group, including Debré himself, were members of the Council of State and therefore career civil servants. They were often helped by constitutional experts, nearly all of whom were professors at the leading faculties of law and therefore, as such, civil servants of the French State. So important a role did civil servants—councillors of state and professors—play in drafting the constitution that its critics soon came to refer to the Fifth Republic as the regime of the bureaucrats *(le régime des fonctionnaires).*

A striking innovation in the Constitution of the Fifth Republic is the enumeration of specific powers in its Article 34. Just as the Constitution of the United States enumerates the powers of Congress in such areas as taxation, commerce among the states, naturalization, rules to govern the armed forces, and so forth, so also the French Constitution gives parliament the power to legislate in matters concerning nationality, marriage, inheritance, education, taxation, crimes and their corresponding punishments, national defense, and so forth. Both constitutional texts carry the clear implication that the enumeration of certain powers excludes all other powers not so enumerated. The Tenth Amendment to the U.S. Constitution renders this implication explicit when it provides that "the powers not delegated to the United States by the Constitution, nor prohibited by it to the States, are reserved to the States respectively, or to the people." Thus, in American constitutional theory the residual powers of the State remain with the several states or the people, but the national powers are exceptional—that is, they exist only because the Constitution says they exist. Like the Americans, the French were unwilling to leave as a mere implication the denial of plenary powers to parliament. Thus, Article 37 states that "matters other than those that fall within the domain of law shall be of a regulatory character." The regulatory power is vested in the prime minister and the government he or she heads. Therefore, whatever areas of French life escape the reach of parliament's legislative powers necessarily fall squarely under the regulatory powers of the prime minister and the government.

The consequence of this division of powers is that the parliament of the Fifth Republic is no longer sovereign. Its powers are extensive, but precisely because they are enumerated, with all nonenumerated powers reserved to the government's regulatory domain, it cannot be sovereign. Neither is the government sovereign because its powers are limited by those granted to parliament, and the concept of limited powers is at war with the meaning of sovereignty. To reinforce this limitation on parliament's powers, the Gaullists established an institution without precedent in French legal history, the Constitutional Council (*Conseil Constitutionnel*).

This council has become one of the most important institutions in French governance today, but in 1958 its primary task was to police the border between parliament and the government to be sure that ambitious legislators did not take actions beyond their appointed limits. To this end, the Constitutional Council was given the power to declare acts of parliament unconstitutional. This was a remarkable departure from French republican tradition because the bedrock principle of parliamentary sovereignty had hitherto meant that no institution of the State could void an act of parliament. Not infrequently, French parliaments under the Third and Fourth Republics passed laws that seemed to be clearly unconstitutional and did so with impunity. The justification for such actions lay, not surprisingly, in appeals to parliamentary sovereignty. Parliament was sovereign because it *re-presented* the people; that is, it presented the people a second time in microcosm, as it were. Since parliament spoke for the people, what political institution could prevail against it? Surely not a constitution that derived its binding authority from the people, the same source that legitimated the power of parliament. Constitutions state the will of the people yesterday, but the allegedly unconstitutional statute represents the will of the people today, and who is to say that the people cannot change their mind? Unlike Americans, French constitutional theorists were not always convinced of the value of looking upon a constitution as a form of higher law, higher even than laws expressing the will of the people at a particular point in time.

The relationship between Articles 34 and 37, combined with the creation of the Constitutional Council, turned a new page in French constitutional history, and it did so to empower the government to govern by "autonomous rules" (*réglements autonomes*), that is, rules promulgated "spontaneously" by the government without necessarily having the support of an underlying statute. If we look back over the forty-three-year history of the Fifth Republic, the wisdom of hindsight shows that the practical effects of this change in republican doctrine have not been as important as their theoretical underpinnings might suggest. There have been relatively few serious conflicts between governments and the parliamentary majorities that supported them. This happy outcome was hidden from the eyes of the men who drafted the Constitution of 1958. They knew they were introducing bold constitutional innovations. As one astute observer put it, "The Constitution makes the Government the legislator of common law and the

Parliament the legislator by exception."[50] This was nothing less than a Copernican revolution in the constitutional theory of French republics. In Haussmann's time, parliament was weak both in theory and practice, but that was quite fitting for the authoritarian regime he served. Republican regimes had been traditionally grounded in parliamentary sovereignty, which meant that at least in theory every administrative regulation was supposed to be grounded in some way in an act of parliament. As of 1958, this was no longer the case. Just as the American Congress possesses the exceptional, as opposed to the residual, powers of the State, the parliament of the Fifth Republic is now "the legislator by exception." All this was done to emancipate the autonomous rule-making power of the government from parliamentary control so that future French governments, unlike those at the beginning of World War II and during the Algerian crisis, would be able to act on their own if parliament was unwilling or unable to do so. This is a profound example of the administrative imperative for action transforming constitutional principles.

The departure from parliamentary sovereignty, reinforced by the creation of the Constitutional Council, is the most important textual consideration for our purposes, but it is not the only one. Other provisions impose severe limits on the powers of parliamentary committees to amend bills submitted by the government, and still others limit the number of permanent committees in each chamber to six while permitting the government to call for the creation of special committees to examine specific bills when the government finds it expedient to do so. Other texts permit the government to exercise considerable influence on parliament's agenda. All these provisions have the common goal of empowering the government to act expeditiously when legislation is called for. That is, the text of the Constitution grants the government significant inroads into the legislative process itself even though this is parliament's proper domain.

The most extreme example of governmental control of the legislative process, however, appears in the third paragraph of Article 49, commonly referred to simply as "49,3." Here the prime minister is empowered to link his support for a proposed legislative text to a pledge of his government's responsibility before the National Assembly, the lower and far more powerful chamber of parliament whose members are chosen by direct universal suffrage. If he should do this, 49,3 provides "the text shall be considered as adopted, unless a motion of censure, filed in the succeeding twenty-four hours, is voted under conditions laid down in the previous paragraph." The "previous paragraph" (49,2) details the procedure by which parliament can censure a government and thereby bring about its demise. What 49,3 means in practice is that a bill can be considered as adopted by parliament—i.e., it can become a law—*without a vote*. To avoid this, the National Assembly could censure the government and thereby bring it down, but this would risk the likelihood of new parliamentary elections, a prospect obviously distasteful to the majority coalition. Prudence dictates that an unhappy parliamentary majority swallow its pride and let the government have its way.

This has sometimes been called "rationalized parliamentarianism," a splendid euphemism for governmental control of the legislative process in an advanced administrative state.

Institutions

Having touched upon the Constitutional Council as an institutional innovation in the Constitution of the Fifth Republic, I shall now examine it more closely, especially its relationship to the well-established Council of State. The present inquiry, then, might be considered "a tale of two councils."

One of the most interesting aspects of the creation of the Fifth Republic is the central role played by the Council of State in fashioning the precise language that describes the Constitutional Council and its tasks. Although the broad outlines of the Constitution of the Fifth Republic came from General de Gaulle himself, the exacting task of finding the appropriate language to express his ideas fell largely to the councillors of state who formed the working group assembled by de Gaulle's Minister of Justice, Michel Debré. Before submitting their text to the people, the members of the working group sought the approval of their parent body, the Council of State itself. Both the Constitutional Committee of the Council of State and its General Assembly gave careful consideration to the proposed text and introduced important changes.

There was nothing surprising about the Council of State playing an important role in preparing the constitutional text. Traditionally, it has had the twofold responsibility of giving legal advice to the government of the day and serving as the highest administrative court in France. What is surprising, however, are the generous powers the councillors of state conferred upon the Constitutional Council, which they correctly surmised would soon become an institutional competitor. Of particular interest is the second paragraph of Article 62, which provides that the decisions of the Constitutional Council "must be recognized by the governmental authorities and by all administrative and judicial authorities." This language came directly from the Constitutional Committee of the Council of State and was formally approved in plenary session of its General Assembly. Quite clearly, the Council of State subordinated itself to the new institution it was creating in the sense that "all administrative authorities," including the Council of State itself, were to recognize the constitutional decisions handed down by the Constitutional Council. This self-denying action challenges the received wisdom on the self-interested nature of organizational behavior and reveals a striking example of high-minded administrative statesmanship.

The early years of the Constitutional Council were relatively uneventful. Although it had the power to declare acts of parliament unconstitutional, it was not a court of law. No litigants appeared before it. Prior to 1974, its jurisdiction could be invoked only by four officers designated in the Constitution to do so: the president of the Republic, the prime minister, the president of the National Assembly, and the president of the Senate. During the first ten years of its existence, it made only seven decisions, all of them favorable to the government at the expense of parliament. Its early history confirmed François Luchaire's telling metaphor that the Constitutional Council was simply "a cannon aimed at Parliament."[51]

All this changed, however, on 16 July 1971 when the Constitutional Council rendered a decision that Didier Maus has aptly characterized as a "fundamental psychological turning point" that transformed the council from "an executive auxiliary" to the "guardian of liberty."[52] The origin of this decision can be traced to a challenge brought by Alain Poher, the president of the Senate, to an act of parliament amending a well-known law dating back to 1901 protecting the freedom of association for nonprofit organizations, including political parties. The text in question would have permitted state officers to impose certain burdens on associations suspected of pursuing illegal purposes. The Senate rejected the proposed legislation on the grounds that it violated a specific constitutional provision protecting political parties, but the National Assembly was able to vote the text into law by using a special constitutional provision enabling it to bypass a reluctant Senate under certain circumstances—a procedure not unlike the manner in which the British House of Commons can pass laws without the approval of the House of Lords.

Poher did not challenge the National Assembly's authority to circumvent the Senate, but he did challenge the statute on its merits, specifically, the threat he thought it posed to the constitutional protection of political parties. Poher's appeal to the Constitutional Council was extraordinary because it had nothing to do with parliament encroaching on the regulatory powers of the government, which theretofore had been the sole basis for the council to strike down acts of parliament. Indeed, the government supported the law in question. Poher's appeal invited the council to void an act of parliament on the straightforward grounds that it violated fundamental civil liberties specifically protected by the Constitution. Remarkably, the council upheld Poher's challenge, but in doing so, it reached far beyond the specific constitutional text cited by Poher and rested its decision on extremely broad language from the preamble to the Constitution.

This decision clearly signaled the Constitutional Council's willingness to confer upon itself a wide range of powers that included traditional civil liberties of speech, press, and religion as well as a host of unspecified powers lurking in "the fundamental principles recognized by the laws of the Republic."[53] It has been aptly called the French version of *Marbury v. Madison,* the famous decision of 1803 in which the U.S. Supreme Court conferred upon itself the power to declare acts of Congress unconstitutional, despite the absence of any textual language giving the federal courts this extraordinary power. Regardless of the technical merits of the Constitutional Council's decision of 16 July 1971, it launched the council on an illustrious career that has made its power to strike down statutes proposed by the government and voted by parliament a prominent feature of contemporary French governance.[54]

I have mentioned that prior to 1974, the jurisdiction of the council could be invoked only by officers authorized by the Constitution to do so. In 1974, an important constitutional amendment permitted sixty members of the National Assembly or sixty senators to convene the council for the purpose of examining the constitutionality of a statute before it goes into effect. This power has been used extensively by political parties of both the Right and the Left when in opposition to the parties that support the government. There is always the chance that the opposition, having lost in the legislative arena, will prevail on constitutional grounds before the council. Consequently, the Constitutional Council is a far busier jurisdiction today than it had been in its first ten years when its writ ran no further than the border dividing parliamentary powers from those of the government. Indeed, some critics complain that it has become a third legislative chamber. Be that as it may, no one denies the importance of the Constitutional Council today.

As the power and influence of the Constitutional Council grew, inevitable tensions arose between it and the Council of State, most notably over the controversial nationalization policies of the Socialist government that came to power in 1981. By that time, many jurists seemed to agree that although the Council of State had to recognize the authority of decisions made by the Constitutional Council, it did not have to follow its reasoning. That is, the Council of State was bound to follow res judicata but not the jurisprudence of the Constitutional Council. In an illuminating study published in 1987, Louis Favoreu revealed that the distinction between res judicata and jurisprudence is not as clear as some scholars would have it.[55] He presented impressive evidence to show that as a matter of fact the Council of State often does follow the jurisprudence of the Constitutional Council, even though it is not technically obliged to do so. This tendency contributes significantly to the goal of developing a consistent body of constitutional and administrative law in France.

For our purposes, however, it is important to note that the path of influence between the two councils is not a one-way street. As the Constitutional Council has expanded its jurisdiction to include questions of civil liberties, it has often relied on administrative law principles developed by the Council of State long before the Constitutional Council had been created. Thus, the Constitutional Council can be said to be in tutelage to the Council of State. In applying the jurisprudence of an administrative court to further the constitutional rights of the individual, the Constitutional Council challenges the stereotype of administrative institutions as the sworn enemy of human freedom.

In this chapter I have examined the intimate connection between public administration and constitutions in three centuries of French history in support of the broad theme of this book. To take the argument beyond the confines of one country, I now turn to the United Kingdom for further evidence of the constitutional-administrative nexus.

2

The United Kingdom

The election of Tony Blair as prime minister of the United Kingdom in 1997 signaled the dawn of what promised to be an era of far-reaching constitutional change in his country. No incoming American president would ever dream of proposing the sweeping constitutional reforms envisaged and, for the most part, delivered by the first Blair government. By century's end, his government had already brought about the expulsion of the vast majority of hereditary peers from the House of Lords and the devolution of significant constitutional powers to newly established parliaments in Scotland and Wales. It had also taken all the necessary steps preparatory to incorporating the European Convention on Human Rights. Serious attention was being given to changing Britain's electoral system of first past the post in favor of a modified proportional representation system that would work to the advantage of minority parties, most notably the Liberal Democrats. These changes took place in a climate that entertained further speculation on such drastic constitutional changes as a formal Bill of Rights, a written constitution, and even the abolition of the monarchy. The constitutional dimensions of public administration cannot compete with the attention given to such spectacular changes as the reformed House of Lords or the new parliament in Edinburgh, but thoughtful observers of British government have noted the probable long-term effects on the British Constitution of the striking administrative innovations introduced by the governments of Prime Minister Margaret Thatcher during her long tenure from 1979 to 1990.

Before examining the details of administrative reform, a few preliminary comments on broader questions of administration and the British Constitution are in order. Let us consider briefly the extent to which the British Constitution is unwritten, constitutional conventions, and the prerogative power.

The relationship between administration and constitutionalism in the United Kingdom differs markedly from the same relationship in France, Canada, and the

United States. This is hardly surprising since the Constitution of the United Kingdom is so different from those of the other three countries. The most obvious difference is that the other three constitutions are written, but the British is not, an obvious difference, to be sure, but one that is perhaps overstated. To characterize the British Constitution as unwritten *tout court* is not entirely correct. Indeed, one knowledgeable commentator dismisses the idea as "absurd."[1]

The British Constitution is unwritten only in the sense that there is no single document to which one can point as the Constitution. There are many important documents that, along with long-standing unwritten conventions, together form the British Constitution. Chief among these documents are famous statutes addressing such bedrock issues as how one defines the precise nature of the United Kingdom itself, the status of the established church, the role of the judiciary, certain fundamental rights of Englishmen, the United Kingdom's relationship to the European Union, and, quite recently, the composition of the House of Lords and the powers devolved upon Scotland and Wales.[2]

Common law principles expressed in important judicial decisions provide another written source of the British Constitution. Particularly significant for our purposes is the inclusion among constitutional sources of administrative regulations taken pursuant to statute or "subordinate legislation made under the authority of the parent act," as Philip Norton puts it.[3] Still another source of the British Constitution is major scholarly treatises, which, though not legally binding, enjoy a certain persuasive authority, not unlike that of *The Federalist Papers* in American constitutional jurisprudence. The works of John Austin and Albert V. Dicey come readily to mind as nineteenth-century authorities, and the twentieth century produced the writings of such prominent scholars as Ivor Jennings, O. Hood Phillips, E. C. S. Wade, and Kenneth Wheare. One of the most important functions of these treatises is to explain and interpret the unwritten conventions that are themselves part of the British Constitution as a whole.

Because of the blend of written and unwritten elements in the British Constitution, we would do well to accept Philip Norton's pithy description of it as "part written but uncodified."[4] Precisely because it is uncodified, it is difficult to know just what one means when one invokes "the Constitution" in British discourse on public administration—other than that the point at issue is of some importance to the speaker. Indeed, one of the most striking aspects of constitutionalism in British public administration is its amazing breadth. Consider the vast range between the following two narratives. First, Henry Parris tells the story of the constitutional relationship between the civil service and the Crown as it developed from 1780 to 1830. "As the monarchy rose above party," he says, "so the civil service settled below party. Constitutional bureaucracy was the counterpart of constitutional monarchy."[5] Next, consider Peter Hennessey's account of what he considers "quite a significant constitutional change," which involved changes in the public spending system introduced by Sir Leo Pliatzky in 1975 and 1976. No longer could the chancellor be overruled on a spending matter in a cabinet committee; only the full cabinet could do this. "And 'shifting the onus of appeal on to the spending minister would make a great deal of psychological difference' as in [Prime Minister] Wilson's words, it would give the Treasury 51 percent of the votes."[6] Thus constitutional issues in British public administration seem to run the gamut from matters of such stunning importance as the flowering of constitutional monarchy to an interesting but surely less-than-monumental change in financial management.

The place of conventions in the British Constitution presents a problem for Americans and other persons from countries whose legal and political orders are grounded in a written constitution. It would be a serious error to underestimate the importance of conventions in the British constitutional tradition. For example, the absolutely fundamental principle of "ministerial responsibility," whereby ministers are responsible to Parliament for their actions, is a convention of the British Constitution. In a technical, formal sense, ministers are responsible to the Queen, as the common expression "her majesty's government" suggests. The evolving democratic character of British society, however, required that those who actually governed would be accountable to a parliament elected by the people, and the convention of ministerial responsibility to this body met this need. Before legislative measures approved by Parliament become law, another convention requires that the Queen give her royal assent. So powerful is this convention that no monarch has withheld assent since 1707.

Because of the importance of constitutional conventions in our study of the United Kingdom, let us consider Philip Norton's definition of conventions as "rules of behavior that are considered binding by and upon those responsible for making the Constitution work, but rules that are not enforced by the courts or by the presiding officers in either house of Parliament."[7] If this definition does not entirely clarify the British notion of convention for American readers, they might consider some important aspects of their own government that find no textual support in the U.S. Constitution. Congressional committees and political parties are indispensable elements of American governance, but the Constitution says nothing about them. Eight of our presidents have died in office, and in each case, the vice-president who replaced him was considered to be the president of the United States. This was due more to constitutional convention (American style) than to the constitutional text. Article 2, section 1, provides: "In Case of the Removal of the President from Office, or of his Death, Resignation, or Inability to discharge the Powers and Duties of the said Office, the Same shall devolve on the Vice President." The first vice-president to whom this text applied was John Tyler, after the death of William Henry Harrison in 1841. Although the Constitution says that the powers and duties of the president's office "shall devolve on the Vice-President," Tyler insisted that he was nothing less than president of the United States, and his viewpoint prevailed, thereby creating an American version of a constitutional convention for each of his seven successors. Perhaps because

Americans are not quite as comfortable with conventions as their British cousins, the Constitution was amended in 1967 to provide quite simply that on the death of the president, "the Vice-President shall become President." Nevertheless, for 126 years most Americans, despite occasional grumbling in some quarters, were content to let convention alone settle the question of whether a vice-president succeeding a deceased president was himself president or merely one upon whom the powers and duties of the presidency had devolved.

Like the British monarchy, the office of president of the United States lends itself to powerful conventions. Perhaps the best known is the two-term tradition, which is traced to President Washington's refusal to serve a third term. When Franklin Roosevelt successfully broke this tradition in 1940, his action led to the Twenty-second Amendment, which explicitly forbids any president from serving more than two terms. The president's annual State of the Union address provides such compelling political theater that breathless television commentators can be forgiven for speaking of the president's "obligation" to address the Congress on this great topic of state. The text of the Constitution merely requires that "from time to time" the president must "give to Congress Information of the State of the Union, and recommend to their Consideration such measures as he shall judge necessary and expedient." Clearly, this duty can be discharged in writing and was so discharged during the century that elapsed between the presidencies of Thomas Jefferson and Woodrow Wilson. Finally, the constitutional text that empowers the president to make treaties and appointments to certain high offices only with "the Advice and Consent of the Senate" has meant in practice that the Senate's power is only one of consenting or withholding consent. This practice dates from President Washington's displeasure with the Senate's reluctance to advise him on an Indian Treaty in 1789. Feeling snubbed by the Senate, Washington never again formally sought its advice on a treaty, and his successors have followed suit. Treaties are made by the executive alone and submitted to the Senate for its consent. In effect, convention has deleted the word *advice* from the constitutional text. Although these American examples lack the binding force of British constitutional conventions, they do serve to illustrate that well-established practices can assume a certain normative value alongside a written constitutional text.

My third point concerns the prerogative powers—"the powers and privileges recognized by common law as belonging to the Crown."[8] These powers are particularly important in matters of public administration because they govern the legal status of the civil service. The United Kingdom has never had a comprehensive civil service statute, although as far back as 1855 the famous civil service reformers Sir Stafford Northcote and Sir Charles Trevelyan tried in vain to get one. They had to settle for an administrative decree known then and now as an Order-in-Council.[9] There was a certain logic to the government's reliance on its prerogative powers to regulate the civil service because civil servants have always been considered servants of the Crown.

Americans will recognize a certain similarity between the prerogative powers of the Crown and the authority of the president of the United States to issue "executive orders," but the similarity is quite superficial. Presidential executive orders always begin by invoking the powers vested in the president "by the Constitution and laws of the United States" or with some other, similar formula. Although presidents frequently fail to specify the precise constitutional text or statutes on which they rely, the crucial point is that they must acknowledge in principle that whatever powers they might have must have come from some other legal source. Citizens who find no connection between the presidential power exercised in the executive order and the constitutional or statutory authority the president invokes can challenge the legality of the executive order in court. If the connection is found to be nonexistent or extremely tenuous, the executive order could be annulled. All this is quite compatible with the norms and standards of a constitutional republic.

The prerogative powers of the Crown are quite different in principle because they are grounded in a royal power exercised today by ministers in accordance with the imperatives of a constitutional monarchy. In practice, many of the powers traditionally associated with the Crown have been superseded by statute, but enough remain, especially in foreign and military affairs as well as in the governance of the civil service, to provide contemporary British governments with a flexibility their American counterparts can only envy from afar. Take, for example, the provision in Article 2, section 2 of the U.S. Constitution that offices must be established "by law," that is, by Congress. In the presidential campaign of 1980, Republican candidate Ronald Reagan pledged that, if elected, he would abolish the Departments of Energy and Education. He was unable to deliver on his promise because the Democrats controlled the House of Representatives and would not agree to pass a law abolishing the targeted departments. Conversely, Congress denied President Jimmy Carter's request for a Department of Trade, thereby depriving him of an administrative instrument he wanted, just as it later insisted that President Reagan retain administrative instruments he did not want. This explicitly constitutional power of Congress seriously limits the president's power as chief executive officer of the Republic.

British governments have far more flexibility in such matters. Peter Hennessy relates an instructive tale from the 1970s wherein Prime Minister Edward Heath created a "mega-ministry, the Department of Trade and Industry which had absorbed the Ministry of Technology which, in turn, had swallowed up the old Ministry of Fuel and Power."[10] In January 1974, reacting to the pressures of the oil crisis, Heath broke up the megaministry and created a new Department of Energy to deal with the crisis. When Harold Wilson succeeded Heath in March 1974, he split the Department of Trade and Industry even further, "mainly to meet his need to find sufficient Cabinet portfolios." Thus, Tony Benn headed a new Department of Industry and Peter Shore took over the Department of Trade.[11] At the same time, a new Department of Prices and Consumer Protection was created and headed by a Wilson loyalist. All this took place without benefit of statutes passed by Parliament because the government's prerogative powers include the authority to create and abolish offices.

A more recent example of the government's free hand in these matters comes from Tony Blair's early days as prime minister when he created a new ministry, "Environment, Transportation and the Regions." Previously, Environment and Transportation had been separate departments. In combining them, Blair added "the Regions" because of the widespread impact of environmental and transportation matters throughout the United Kingdom. No statute was required to effect these changes. Nor was a statute required to undo them when, immediately after his reelection in June 2001, the prime minister dispatched Environment to the Ministry of Agriculture, leaving Transportation and the Regions on their own.

With the background of the uncodified Constitution, conventions, and prerogative powers in mind, let us now look at three specific issues that develop the theme of the intimate connection between administration and constitutionalism: the Clive Ponting affair, a case study of this intimate connection in practice; ministerial responsibility and civil service anonymity, two of the salient principles in the Ponting affair; and the influence of the great constitutional scholar Albert V. Dicey on British administrative law.

THE PONTING AFFAIR

An important corollary of the principle of ministerial responsibility to Parliament is the principle of civil service anonymity. If the minister is responsible for what takes place in his ministry, he may not dodge the bullet by blaming his wayward subordinates when things go wrong. Before examining these principles closely, I offer a concrete example of how they played out in practice in the Ponting Affair, a dramatic constitutional-administrative crisis in the aftermath of the Falklands War.

Clive Ponting was a senior civil servant in the Ministry of Defence during the Falklands War of 1982. On 2 May of that year, the HMS *Conqueror,* a nuclear-powered submarine of the Royal Navy, sank the Argentine cruiser *General Belgrano,* an action that resulted in the deaths of 368 Argentineans. The action came at a time when Peru and the United States were still trying to find a peaceful solution to the Falklands crisis, but the sinking of the *Belgrano* contributed substantially to the inevitability of war as the only solution to the conflict—and a marvelously successful war it was for the United Kingdom, the Royal Navy, and the Thatcher government.

Shortly after the *Belgrano* had been sunk, however, opposition members of Parliament questioned the government closely on the precise circumstances that surrounded the event. Specifically, the opposition queried ministers as to whether the attack was consistent with the Royal Navy's rules of engagement then in effect. The official replies were uncertain, confused, and inconsistent. Once the war was over, the opposition pressed the Ministry of Defence more closely on these matters, as government critics became increasingly convinced that the *Belgrano* had never been within the "total exclusion zone" declared by the Royal Navy's rules of engagement. As one wag queried later, the Falklands War proved that Britannia ruled the waves, but did she also waive the rules?[12]

Further, there was growing evidence to challenge the government's claim that the *Belgrano* was on its way to rendezvous with an Argentinean aircraft carrier in order to attack ships of the Royal Navy. Indeed, much of the evidence suggested that the *Belgrano* was on its way home to Argentina when it met its unhappy fate.

As these troubling questions dragged on throughout 1983 and early 1984, the Ministry of Defence became increasingly uneasy, and for good reason, because its original version of the events had been deliberately misleading. Ponting, who had no part in the original deception, was asked in March 1984 to prepare a chronology of the events that would satisfy the government's critics. He urged a policy of openness that would put an end to the cover-up and thought that the Secretary of State for Defence, Michael Heseltine, had agreed. By the end of April, he realized that Heseltine had decided deliberately to mislead members of Parliament who were inquiring about just when and where the *Belgrano* had originally been sighted by the Royal Navy. As Ponting tells it: "I had never come across anything so blatant in my fifteen years in the Civil Service. It was a deliberate attempt to conceal information which would reveal that Ministers had gravely misled Parliament for the previous two years."[13]

On 24 April, he took the decisive action of anonymously leaking information to Tam Dalyell, a Labour MP, who had been particularly aggressive in challenging the official version of the *Belgrano* affair. The information was unclassified but of such a nature as to alert Dalyell to the fact that his questions were right on target. Meanwhile, the cover-up continued apace as the ministry escalated the deception to include not only individual members of Parliament but the Select Committee on Foreign Affairs as well. Ponting agonized over whether he should leak additional documents to Parliament that would surely expose the government's deception. Baring his soul, he asks:

> Could I really bring myself to send the documents to Parliament? All my instincts after fifteen years in the Civil Service told me that my loyalty was to Ministers and the department. But then I realised that Ministers had broken their side of the bargain in attempting to evade their responsibilities to Parliament. If they could just simply shrug off their duties, refuse to answer questions, give misleading answers or refuse to correct false statements to Parliament how could there be any effective control over what the Government did? In the end Ministers had to be responsible to Parliament or the whole British constitutional system would break down.[14]

In a word, Ponting seemed to think that it was his duty to alert Parliament to the fact that ministers were not fulfilling their constitutional duty of responsibility to that body.

Having mulled this over, he once again anonymously leaked unclassified but seriously compromising documents to Dalyell. This time, however, he was identified as the source of the leak, arrested, and subjected to criminal prosecution under the Official Secrets Act of 1911.[15] His trial began on 28 January 1985. As the Official Secrets Act was worded at that time, the only defense available to Ponting was that he had communicated the offending information "to a person to whom it is in the interests of the State his [the defendant's] duty to communicate it." The language is tortured, but the legal point is clear enough. In order to be found not guilty of violating the sweeping prohibitions of the Official Secrets Act as it was worded in 1985, Ponting had to show that he had a duty "in the interests of the State" to send the documents to Dalyell, an opposition member of Parliament. Clearly, the nub of the matter was the meaning of "the interests of the State." This of course is a point of law and, as such, it fell to the trial judge, Justice McCowan, to instruct the jury as to its meaning: "What, then, of the words 'In the interest of the State'? Members of the Jury, I direct you that those words mean the policies of the State as they were in July of 1984 when Mr. Ponting communicated the information to Mr. Dalyell and not the policies of the State as Mr. Ponting, Mr. Dalyell, you or I might think they ought to have been. The policies of the State mean the policies laid down for it by its recognized organs of government and authority."[16]

In framing the issue in this way, Justice McCowan virtually directed the jury to convict Ponting. If the interests of the State are the interests of the government of the day, Ponting could not credibly claim to have acted in the interests of the State. Remarkably, however, after a brief deliberation, the jury found Ponting not guilty.

As might be expected, this decision sent shock waves through Whitehall. Within a fortnight, Sir Robert Armstrong, head of the Home Civil Service, had issued a statement repeating the traditional doctrine that only ministers, not civil servants, are responsible to Parliament, a statement that echoed Justice McCowan's instruction to the jury. The fact that the jury clearly disregarded McCowan's instruction may have been a meaningful indication of the state of public opinion on the implications of ministerial responsibility and its corollary principle, civil service anonymity.

The specific facts of the *Belgrano* incident put Ponting's violation of these principles in a rather favorable light. From a straightforward ethical viewpoint, it is hard to position Ponting anywhere but on the side of the angels. Nevertheless, his argument is somewhat unsettling when seen in a different light. Consider Defence Minister Heseltine's perspective on the Ponting affair as he stated it on the floor of the House of Commons shortly after Ponting's acquittal. In its enthusiasm for Ponting, the opposition, according to Heseltine, was asking the

House to support the proposition "that the most trusted civil servants, in the most secure parts of our defence establishments, should be free anonymously to draft questions for Opposition back benchers to submit to Ministers on which the self-same leaking civil servants may then brief Ministers on the answers which they consider appropriate."[17] As one of the Defence Minister's critics candidly concedes, "Mr. Heseltine's rhetorical onslaught does contain an element of uncomfortable truth."[18]

MINISTERIAL RESPONSIBILITY AND CIVIL SERVICE ANONYMITY

Clive Ponting voiced the traditional spirit of the British civil service when he said, "All my instincts after fifteen years in the Civil Service told me my loyalty was to Ministers and the department." He felt this way because he had been schooled in the doctrine of ministerial responsibility, a principle knowledgeable experts call "part of the morality of the constitution."[19] Ministerial responsibility flows from the British constitutional principle that sovereignty belongs to Parliament or, more precisely, to the Queen-in-Parliament. Ministers, in both their collective and individual capacities, must answer to Parliament for their actions. Civil service anonymity is the constitutional corollary of ministerial responsibility. If the minister is responsible for what takes place in his ministry, he must not expose civil servants who may have given him bad advice. Thus the principle of anonymity protects civil servants from political reprisals for advice they may have given to ministers. Conversely, it also silences them, and that is why Sir Robert Armstrong stated in the aftermath of Ponting's acquittal that civil servants had no responsibility to Parliament. His language was most emphatic: "Civil servants are servants of the Crown. . . . In general, the executive powers of the Crown are exercised by and on the advice of Her Majesty's Ministers, who are in turn answerable to Parliament. The civil service as such has no constitutional personality or responsibility separate from the duly elected Government of the day."[20]

Sir Robert, like Justice McCowan, believed that Ponting, whatever his motives might have been, had violated the principle of civil service anonymity when he leaked sensitive information to a member of the parliamentary opposition. We do not know what Ponting's jurors thought of this principle—or even if they thought about it at all—but clearly their sense of fair play convinced them that Ponting should not be punished for his deeds.

A good example of how seriously the principle of civil service anonymity is taken comes from the immediate aftermath of World War II, when Sir Edward Bridges (later Lord Bridges), the cabinet secretary in Winston Churchill's wartime government, supported the idea of commissioning a team of scholars to prepare a multivolume history of the war. When it came to naming names of civil servants associated with specific wartime decisions, however, the historians were admonished: "We all remain bound in our historical writing by the constitutional convention of ministerial responsibility. Nor must we allow ourselves to give good or bad marks to officials who are debarred from explaining or defending their action. . . . Our concern is with the problems, the differing attitudes and policies put forward for tackling them, the methods followed and the results achieved. The biographical method is *taboo* for us."[21]

Since civil servants, or "officials" as they are often called in Britain, have no public forum in which to defend themselves against charges of foolish advice or decisions, they must not be singled out by name. Neither, however, are they to be commended by name for their wise advice or decisions. Praise and blame go to ministers, who alone answer to Parliament. Officials must preserve their anonymity because, as Sir Robert explained the constitutional-administrative orthodoxy, they are "servants of the Crown" and, as such, have "no constitutional personality or responsibility separate from the duly elected Government of the day."

One of the earliest examples of a formal consideration in Parliament of the principle of civil service anonymity focused on what has come to be known as the Scudamore affair of 1873. Frank Scudamore was a midlevel official in the British Post Office who was placed in charge of integrating telegraph systems purchased by the state in 1868 into a national system. He approached his task with "desperate, unflagging zeal," but unfortunately, his entrepreneurial spirit led him to play fast and loose with the rules of financial management in force at that time. Although no one accused Scudamore of diverting public funds to his personal advantage, he had clearly acted illegally when he "devised an ingenious system for turning aside Post Office revenues from their established route to the Exchequer into the telegraph purchase account."[22]

The ruse went undetected for several years, but when the scandal broke, Scudamore confessed that he alone was responsible for the whole scheme, which involved some £800,000 in misallocated public funds. When the issue was debated in Parliament, R. Bernard Osborne maintained that it was "all nonsense, and worse than nonsense . . . to put the onus on a Second Clerk in the Post Office." Anticipating the convention of civil service anonymity, Osborne argued that "this House [of Commons] has nothing to do with Mr. Scudamore. He is not responsible to us. We ought to look to the heads of departments." He added that "to shuffle off those questions" by letting the blame rest on the shoulders of a postal clerk would put "an end to parliamentary government." Historian Henry Parris notes significantly that no one rose to contradict Osborne's analysis, which would eventually lead to the full flowering of the principle of ministerial responsibility, whereby ministers would be held accountable for the errors, misdeeds, and poor judgment of their subordinates. In extreme cases, this could even mean that, at least in theory, the minister might be compelled to resign while the erring official remained in office.[23]

Parris presents an insightful analysis of these events by suggesting a certain symmetry between the relationship of a civil servant to his minister and the minister to the Crown. Both the minister and the civil servant give advice on how power should be exercised. When the minister advises the Crown, the adviser holds office for a relatively short time, but the advisee, the Crown, is permanent. This pattern is reversed, however, when the official advises the minister. Now the adviser is permanent and the advisee transitory. What the official and the Crown have in common is permanence in office, the precise quality that is lacking for the minister, who is responsible both for the advice he gives to the Crown and the advice he accepts from his subordinate official. The great constitutional scholar F. W. Maitland told only half the story when he said that "royal immunity is coupled with ministerial responsibility"; the rest is on the flip side of the coin of ministerial responsibility: "The permanent official, like the King, can do no wrong."[24] This clever insight provides a suitable context for Parris's comment: "As the monarchy rose above party, so the civil service settled below party. Constitutional bureaucracy was the counterpart of constitutional monarchy." The British notion of civil servants as servants of the Crown is meaningful.

No one would deny that there is a certain logic, clarity, and even elegance in the complementary constitutional conventions of ministerial responsibility and civil service anonymity. In practice, however, the obviously important role of civil servants in day-to-day British governance puts considerable pressure on those who defend the traditional orthodoxy. The great success of the delightful television satire *Yes Minister!* shows how readily British viewers recognize the powerful political role of high-ranking civil servants. The history of the British civil service reinforces this point, a history so rich and complex that one is hard-pressed to know where to begin. A historian of the Treasury Department is credited with finding the "first properly identifiable civil servant" in the entourage of William the Conqueror in the eleventh century. For our purposes, however, it will suffice to go back no further than the famous Northcote-Trevelyan Report of 1854, which is often credited with initiating the modern British civil service. There we find the authors calling for *ambitious* men to enter the reformed public service, a call that put the world on notice that feckless pawns need not apply.[25] Indeed, Sir Henry Taylor's splendid essay of 1878, *The Statesman,* looks forward to the day when ministers will be advised by permanent officials who are nothing less than "efficient closet statesmen."[26] Writing in the early twentieth century, Graham Wallas saw in the civil service a constitutional check against abuse of power by a sovereign parliament. For him, "The real 'Second Chamber,' the real 'constitutional check' in England is provided, not by the House of Lords and the Monarchy, but by the existence of a permanent Civil Service appointed on a system independent of the opinion or desires of any politician and holding office during good behaviour."[27]

Closer to our own time, Richard Crossman describes his feelings as a new minister vis-à-vis the career civil service:

> At first I felt like someone in a padded cell, but I must now modify this. In fact I feel like somebody floating on the most comfortable support. The

whole Department is there to support the Minister. Into his in-tray come hour by hour notes with suggestions as to what he should do. Everything is done to sustain him in the line which officials think he should take. But if one is very careful and conscious one is aware that this supporting soft framework of recommendations is the result of a great deal of secret discussion between the civil servants below. There is a constant debate as to how the Minister should be advised or, shall we say, directed and pushed and cajoled into the line required by the Ministry. There is a tremendous *esprit de corps* in the Ministry and the whole hierarchy is determined to preserve its own policy. Each Ministry has its own departmental policy, and this policy goes on while Ministers come and go. And in this world, though the civil servants have a respect for the Minister, they have a much stronger loyalty to the Ministry. Were the Minister to challenge and direct the Ministry policy there would be no formal tension at first, only quiet resistance—but a great deal of it. I am therefore always on the look-out to see how far my own ideas are getting across, how far they are merely tolerated by the Ministry, and how far Ministry policies are being imposed on my own mind.[28]

Crossman is describing what Sir Edward Bridges had in mind when he spoke of a "departmental point of view," meaning a department's "store of knowledge and experience in the subjects handled," which through "the slow accretion and accumulation of experience over the years" eventually becomes a "practical philosophy" or "departmental point of view."[29] Bridges wrote these words when he headed the postwar British civil service. In this position, he relied on his considerable expertise in constitutional matters to explain the important role the civil service played "in the balance of power networks within the British Constitution."[30] Not only did Bridges comment on the Constitution, but he also influenced its development by seeing to it that "his own expert understanding and interpretation of the political activities of civil servants was reinforced through significant constitutional documents."[31]

To catch the spirit of the constitutional-administrative interface in the United Kingdom, it is helpful to note that a constitutional expert, like Bridges, was appointed head of the civil service. (One cannot imagine an American with a similar expertise heading the Office of Personnel Management.) Even more significant is the fact that Bridges's academic background was not in law but in history. This aspect highlights both the absence of legal precision in British constitutionalism and the presence of its profound sense of tradition and gradual adaptation.

One of the most interesting traditions in British public administration is that civil servants have access to the papers of previous governments, but ministers do not. This surely helps them to develop the "departmental viewpoint," but it can also influence specific and politically charged decisions. Take, for example, the case of Sir Norman Brook (later Lord Normanbrook) as cabinet secretary for

Winston Churchill's government from 1951 to 1955. Brook was present at a meeting of the cabinet's Defence Committee, which had been called to discuss the extremely sensitive issue of whether Britain should manufacture the hydrogen bomb. Fearing opposition within his own cabinet, Churchill explored the possibility of making this decision without the approval of the full cabinet. Since Brook had been the cabinet secretary for Churchill's predecessor as prime minister, Clement Attlee, Churchill tried to coax Brook into confirming the rumor that Attlee had decided to make the atomic bomb without informing the full cabinet. Brook made no reply; he simply "stared out the window and said nothing."[32] Although he was known to be a firm supporter of Churchill and his policies, "there were some boundaries Brook would not cross."[33] Protecting the secrecy of previous government actions was one of them, even though, in doing so, he may have deprived Churchill of a politically useful precedent in an extremely sensitive matter of national defense.

Norman Brook's protection of a previous government's secrets shows how civil servants can take an active role in politics by their silence. They can also take an active role by speaking truth to power. In the years right after World War II, England had high hopes of regaining its prewar position as a great power. In the midst of the heady atmosphere that supported the development of a British atomic bomb and other measures suggesting prewar glories, Sir Henry Tizard, chief scientist adviser to the Ministry of Defence, provided his superiors with a bit of hardheaded and most unwelcome advice intended to give them a realistic assessment of Britain's diminished role in the world. He insisted that British leaders come to terms with the sober fact that "we are not a Great Power and never will be again. We are a great nation, but if we continue to behave like a Great Power, we shall soon cease to be a great nation." He paid dearly for his candor. His comment was treated "with the kind of horror one would expect if one made a disrespectful remark about the King."[34]

Unfortunately, however, the political role of civil servants is not always so edifying. Colin Campbell and Graham Wilson report that their extensive interviews with high-ranking civil servants during the Thatcher years revealed that "officials drew up over thirty changes in the definition of unemployment, all of which had the effect of making the government's economic record look better by making the rate of unemployment seem lower."[35]

A particularly insightful analysis of the proper role of civil servants appeared in 1979 in remarks by Richard Wilding, the deputy secretary of the Civil Service Department at that time. He recognized the likely conflict between the demands from the civil service for both a wholehearted commitment to the policies of the government of the day and a readiness to give no less dedication to the next government, which might well dismantle the very programs these same officials were putting in place. His advice was eloquent: "It is absolutely necessary to pursue today's policy with energy; it is almost equally necessary, in order to survive, to withhold from it the last ounce of commitment . . . and to invest that commitment in our particular institution, the Civil Service itself, with all its manifest imperfections."[36]

No minister can claim that "last ounce of commitment" that is wisely invested in "the Civil Service itself," thereby ensuring its capacity to give the next government all but that last ounce of commitment as well. The civil service must protect its own integrity precisely to enable it to support the goals of ministers.

To bring this discussion up to the present, consider the relatively harmonious relationship between the civil service and the then newly elected government of Tony Blair in spring 1997. While in opposition, many of Labour's shadow ministers worked hard at understanding the machinery of the ministries they would head if elected. Some of them even attended seminars "where former permanent secretaries inculcated them into Whitehall's mysteries."[37] These actions by busy men and women looking forward to being ministers show a clear recognition on their part that the civil service plays a crucial role in governing the United Kingdom. They knew that if they were to govern effectively, they would need the support of the civil service.

The governing role of the civil service, though indisputably crucial, is nevertheless at odds with the traditional norms of British public administration for two reasons. First, to the extent that civil servants really participate in governance, the principle of ministerial responsibility is in danger of becoming a morally and politically vacuous formality. It follows the path of the old navy rule that the captain is responsible if the ship runs aground. Such a rule has a certain value as an instrument of naval discipline insofar as it guides a Board of Inquiry in fixing blame, but it is of no moral significance if the guilty party was really a lazy operations officer. So also, to the extent that civil servants are the real source of government policy, there is no political merit in holding ministers accountable. Second, to the extent that civil servants really participate in governance, the principle of civil service anonymity is at war with the contemporary demand for "open government," which regards as intolerable the notion that those who really govern are screened from effective accountability by a misleading constitutional convention.

Richard Chapman reconciles practice with principle by de-emphasizing legal simplicities in favor of the de facto operation of the doctrine of ministerial responsibility that "permeates the day to day administrative work of all departments of state."[38] Acknowledging "that in recent times no minister has resigned simply because of errors by his officials," Chapman nevertheless discerns practical effects of the principle of ministerial responsibility in departmental attention to the ever-present possibility of parliamentary questions and to "the arrangements for financial accountability."[39] Other commentators, less generous than Chapman to constitutional traditions, describe the interrelated principles of ministerial responsibility and civil service anonymity as myth or fiction—a singularly penetrating myth and a very useful fiction, but myth and fiction nonetheless.[40]

One reason for the tarnished reputation of ministerial responsibility is a widespread misunderstanding of its true nature, resulting from the Crichel Down Affair of 1954. Crichel Down refers to an area where the government had acquired a tract of land for military purposes in World War II. The Ministry of Agriculture was accused of inordinate delays in returning the land to its rightful owners after the war. At the time, it appeared that the Minister of Agriculture, Sir Thomas Dugdale, had no knowledge of the failings of his wayward subordinates but felt, nonetheless, that the principle of ministerial responsibility demanded his resignation. Subsequent research has revealed that the entire affair was much more complicated than the diagrammatic simplicities of the case had originally suggested and that Dugdale was more personally involved than was thought at the time. Nevertheless, Crichel Down has become enshrined in the press as shorthand for the unrealistically lofty notion that blameless ministers must resign because of their subordinates' errors. When they fail to do so, the principle of ministerial responsibility is ridiculed as a cynical charade.

This is unfortunate, because Diana Woodhouse's painstaking research on ministerial responsibility shows that the convention has always involved some personal lapse in judgment or duty by ministers who have resigned over serious blunders in their departments. For example, Lord Carrington, the foreign secretary at the time of Argentina's invasion of the Falkland Islands, resigned for having badly misread the military situation in the South Atlantic. He clearly underestimated the threat. In resigning, he firmly and laudably defended subordinates in the Foreign Office against attacks from the parliamentary opposition, even though some of them had indeed given him very bad advice. Graciously and in full compliance with convention, he took the full responsibility upon himself. Lord Carrington, however, was not simply a victim of bad advice. He made some unwise decisions of his own and thus was partially responsible for the foreign policy disaster, not merely in the conventional sense of ministerial responsibility but also in a personal sense.[41]

Ministerial responsibility has also been criticized—and rightly so—when ministers mock the principle by blaming their subordinates in order to ward off criticism directed at themselves. Two cases involving spectacular prison breaks found ministers relying upon the discredited distinction between policy and administration to avoid resignation.

In 1983, thirty-eight Republican prisoners broke out of the Maze Prison in Northern Ireland. Several officers were injured, one of them fatally. James Prior, secretary of state for Northern Ireland, was the minister whose department was responsible for the prison. He refused to resign and, with the support of Prime Minister Thatcher, was able to remain in office. He defended himself on the ground that the prison policies of the government were sound, but the escape occurred because of subordinate officials' failure to carry out the policies properly. Although the distinction between policy and administration was well known in the United Kingdom, its appearance in a debate on ministerial responsibility was a bold constitutional innovation, vigorously denounced by the parliamentary opposition. Their main objection was: how was one to know where to draw the line dividing policy, and therefore ministerial responsibility, from administration? Prior to the breakout, the government had settled a hunger strike at the Maze Prison on terms the prison staff considered too lenient. An investigative report of the incident found a connection between lax security practices at the prison and the low morale of the staff. These were clearly administrative matters, but was the low morale caused by the policy decision that ended the hunger strike? Questions of this nature, though impossible to answer with any degree of certitude, revealed just how unworkable the distinction between policy and administration was for purposes of fixing ministerial responsibility.

The second breakout occurred at Brixton Prison in July 1991 when two IRA prisoners escaped by threatening a guard with a gun. The minister in charge, Home Secretary Kenneth Baker, laid the blame squarely on civil service subordinates—the director general of the prison service, the governor of Brixton Prison, and the head of the Directorate of Custody. Like Secretary of State Prior, Baker relied on the policy/administration distinction to parry calls for his resignation and again, like him, managed to remain in office. Although Baker was severely criticized by the opposition, his reliance on the policy/administration distinction surprisingly raised no questions in Parliament. Diana Woodhouse wonders if this means that members of Parliament now accept this distinction as part of the convention of ministerial responsibility. If so, she argues, that failure by Parliament to "question constitutional adjustments made by a minister" demonstrates "that constitutional change in Britain may occur not as a result of public debate but by default."[42]

Members of Parliament have long been dissatisfied with ministerial responsibility as an effective means of controlling the executive because of the tightly disciplined parties in the British Parliament. Ministers hold their positions because they belong to the parliamentary majority. Hence, responsibility of ministers to Parliament really means that they are responsible to their political allies. Consequently, ministers will be disciplined only if the members of their own party—and most notably the prime minister—want them disciplined. To enhance their influence on how government policies are carried out in this political milieu, members of Parliament in the late 1970s began to look to "select committees." The British Parliament has two types of committees—standing committees that examine proposed legislation and select committees that monitor the executive. Throughout most of the twentieth century, select committees were unimportant institutions, with the notable exception of the prestigious Public Accounts Committee. Under the leadership of Norman St. John-Stevas, Parliament began a serious effort to revitalize the select committees at the outset of the Thatcher era in 1979.

As provided by the Standing Orders of the House of Commons, select committees were appointed to "examine the expenditure, administration and policy of the principal government departments."[43] Thus a Select Committee on Agri-culture monitored the Ministry of Agriculture, Fisheries and Food; a Select Com-mittee on Defence monitored the Ministry of Defence, and so on. The specialization of these committees necessarily brought members of Parliament into close contact with civil servants who testified before them. By the mid-1980s, senior civil servants, contrary to earlier practice, had come to "accept committee appearances as a routine part of their job," and some of them have even "become public figures in their own right." Although these changes raised constitutional questions, they remain largely unresolved, no doubt because, as Gavin Drewry remarks, the direct connection between civil servants and parliamentary commit-tees "amounts to a dent rather than a gaping hole in official anonymity."[44]

The reason that select committees have made only a dent in official anonymity is that governments have drawn strict rules on just how officials are to conduct themselves before select committees. For example, they are reminded of "the need to preserve collective ministerial responsibility, which means that officials must not tell committees what advice they have given to their ministers, or about interdepartmental consultations, or about the nature and work of Cabi-net committees."[45] Furthermore, they are not to make any comments that are "politically contentious," and if they are urged by a select committee to go beyond the instructions from the government, "they should suggest that the ques-tion be addressed or referred to the minister."[46]

Clearly, the testimony of civil servants before select committees is far more measured than the comments American congressmen extract from civil servants appearing before them. Nevertheless, the select committees have matured into a serious element of contemporary British governance. Their sessions are fol-lowed by the media and lobbyists alike; and by publicly questioning civil ser-vants, the committees have gained information that otherwise would not be in the public record.

Potentially, select committees are powerful because they have the capacity "to send for persons, papers and records," but experience indicates "that a committee could do little in practice to enforce its considerable theoretical powers in this area if ministers flatly refuse to sanction disclosure of official documents."[47] Again, the difference between British and American constitutional practice is striking.

A serious constitutional-administrative challenge was raised by the latter-day Thatcher innovation of the "Next Steps," a management program that "trans-ferred many executive functions of central government departments to semi-independent agencies, headed by executives employed on short-term con-tracts—many of them having been recruited from outside the Civil Service."[48] Although agency staff still bear the increasingly amorphous title of "civil ser-vant," the diverse missions and management styles of the Next Steps agencies put considerable pressure on the traditional notion of a public service—notably in their decentralized recruitment patterns and in the erosion of nationally stan-dardized pay.[49] Helpful but less than convincing was the cheerful comment of

Cabinet Secretary Sir Robin Butler that the new British civil service was "uni-fied but not uniform." The same can be said of Prime Minister Thatcher's serene assurances that her Next Steps innovation would have no effect on the traditional principle of ministerial responsibility.

Next Steps agencies, which now employ over two-thirds of Britain's civil servants, are headed by chief executives whose roles certainly belie Margaret Thatcher's complaisance about ministerial responsibility. The precise role of each chief executive varies from one agency to another because each has a "framework document" that gives the details of the relationship between the chief executive and the minister to whose department the agency is—very loosely—attached. The Treasury and Civil Service Committee has referred to the "framework document" as a "contract" that specifies the authority of the chief executive vis-à-vis the minister—a development with far-reaching implications for ministerial responsibility. Indeed, Peter Kemp, whom Prime Minister Thatcher appointed as project manager of the Next Steps agencies, boldly stated that the framework document might empower a chief executive to resist minis-terial interference "even to the extent of saying, 'No, Minister!'"[50]

Since the Next Steps agencies were created to support new public manage-ment principles that maximize decentralized decision making, it is no wonder that commentators note that "the position of the chief executive requires a much higher public profile than that to which departmental civil servants have been accustomed." In a word, the agency head is "no longer a faceless civil servant."[51]

It is perhaps too early for comprehensive judgments on the extent to which Next Steps agencies have improved public management, but there can be no doubt that they have seriously influenced the meaning of ministerial responsibil-ity. They provide a powerful example of administrative reforms modifying con-stitutional principles.

DICEY'S GHOST AND ADMINISTRATIVE LAW

To continue the examination of the intimate connection between administration and constitutionalism, I turn now to the courts and the development of adminis-trative law. A recent biographer of Albert Venn Dicey states correctly and with-out qualification that his *Law of the Constitution* has remained the most influential constitutional textbook of the [nineteenth] century."[52] Despite Dicey's prominence as a great British constitutional scholar, he seldom merits more than an obscure footnote in contemporary American legal textbooks. If his name appears at all, it is most likely found in administrative law literature, where he is summarily dismissed as a bookish exotic who "effectively interred the idea of administrative law in England by denying its existence."[53]

True it is that Dicey did deny not only the existence but even the possibility of administrative law in England and all other countries that follow English law, but this is not the whole truth. Dicey's position is richer and more complex than bald assertions of his rejection of administrative law might suggest. More important, a careful examination of his curious position on administrative law might help us understand the origins and peculiar nature of the advanced administrative state we find in the United Kingdom today. Consequently, I shall first examine what Dicey actually had to say about administrative law and then use his ideas to analyze certain trends in contemporary administrative law in the United Kingdom.

Dicey's denial of the possibility of administrative law was not due to a failure to recognize the growth of administrative institutions in the world around him from 1885 to 1915, the years during which he worked on the first eight editions of his classic text. Rather, the denial flowed quite logically from his definition of law as "any rule which will be enforced by the courts."[54] Since administrative law is necessarily enforced by institutions other than a court, its status as law was doomed from the outset. Thus Dicey can assert so confidently that "the words 'administrative law' are unknown to English judges and counsel, and are in themselves hardly intelligible without further explanation." Conceding that "administrative law" is the "most natural rendering" of the French *droit administratif,* he finds this translation and any other translation fundamentally flawed because "the want of a name arises at bottom from our non-recognition of the thing itself."[55] Consequently, throughout the treatise he nearly always uses the untranslated (and for Dicey untranslatable) *droit administratif* rather than "administrative law." The constant use of the French term reinforces its foreign origin and its unsuitability for common law countries.

Dicey's jurisprudence rested on two fundamental principles that were closely related to each other: the sovereignty of Parliament and the rule of law. For Dicey the rule of law was crucial precisely because Parliament was sovereign. In practice, the rule of law meant the independence of English judges, which served as a safeguard against "the unscrupulous use of power by a Government which finds itself in command of a majority of the House of Commons."[56] Although the principle of parliamentary sovereignty precluded British courts from declaring acts of Parliament unconstitutional, Dicey looked to the independence of the judiciary as a practical way to reconcile the restraint on government implicit in the idea of the rule of law with the dangers of abuse implicit in parliamentary sovereignty itself. Hence, he sees administrative law as fundamentally at war with the principle of the rule of law because it permits adjudication by government officials who do not enjoy the independence of English judges.

Despite his denial of the existence of administrative law, this legal phantom haunted Dicey. In the early editions of *Law of the Constitution,* he devoted only part of a chapter on the rule of law to *droit administratif,* but by the eighth edition, the last one he worked on personally, this topic merited a full chapter by itself, which was substantially longer than any other chapter in the book. To a contemporary reader, the most striking aspect of Dicey's treatment of *droit administratif* is his lack of interest in the regulatory aspect of his topic. To be sure, he mentions in passing "the regulation of labour under the Factory Acts, and the supervision of public education under the Education Act,"[57] but only to absolve those who administer these laws from the taint of practicing the dark arts of *droit administratif.* This is because any English official "who exceeds the authority given him by the law incurs the common law responsibility for his wrongful act; he is amenable to the authority of the ordinary courts."[58] This point is thematic throughout the later editions of Dicey's great book. By 1915, he was well aware of the significant role played by administrative institutions in England, but he continued to insist that British officials had not succumbed to the blandishments of *droit administratif* because they could still be required to answer for their misdeeds before the ordinary courts of the realm.

For Dicey, the fundamental flaw in *droit administratif* was that French citizens, claiming to have been wronged by officials, brought their complaint to a special administrative jurisdiction from which there was no appeal to the ordinary courts in France. Nowhere is this clearer than in an article Dicey wrote in 1915 on the landmark decision of the House of Lords in *Local Government Board v. Arlidge,*[59] holding that an administrative body "in the exercise of statutory functions of a judicial character need not follow the procedure of a court of law, but could employ rules which appeared reasonable and fair for the conduct of its business."[60]

Although Dicey's private correspondence shows he was profoundly distressed by this decision and others that had preceded it,[61] he maintained a stiff upper lip in the 1915 article and even approved *Arlidge,* at least to the extent that if modern governments were to engage in activities traditionally reserved for commercial enterprises, "the servants of the Crown will be found to need that freedom of action necessarily possessed by every private person in the management of his own personal concerns."[62] He maintained it would be foolish to require a businessman "to conduct his own affairs in accordance with the rules which, quite properly, guide our judges in the administration of justice."[63] On the issue of *droit administratif,* however, Dicey wavered but ultimately held his ground. Acknowledging that *Arlidge* presented "a considerable step toward the introduction among us of something like the *droit administratif* of France,"[64] he noted that it did not exempt British officials from having to answer for their alleged misdeeds before the ordinary courts. Therefore England still preserved "that rule of law which is fatal to the existence of true *droit administratif.*"[65]

The facts of *Arlidge* make clear just how far Dicey had retreated from his earlier position denying the possibility of *droit administratif* in England. The Hampstead Borough Council had issued a closing order against Arlidge's house on the grounds that it was unfit for human habitation, a decision he appealed to the Local Government Board. Unsuccessful in his appeal, he then turned to the courts for relief, arguing that the board's decision should be overturned because it had denied him a fair hearing. He was not allowed to appear before the officer who made the decision against him or even to read the report of the inspector who conducted the inquiry initiated by Arlidge's appeal to the Local Government Board. Present-day commentators criticize several aspects of *Arlidge,* most notably the failure of the House of Lords to require disclosure of the report, noting that it "took over forty years for this mistake to be corrected."[66] Nevertheless, Dicey grudgingly acquiesced in this decision, maintaining that England still skirted the perilous shoals of *droit administratif,* but only because the administrators' decisions could still be reviewed by an English court. Thus, by 1915, Dicey's startling statements denying the possibility of *droit administratif* had come to mean no more than that English courts can still review the decisions of administrative agencies. On the more fundamental point that administrative agencies, which do not enjoy the independence of an English court, may nevertheless use clearly nonjudicial procedures to render a judicial decision, he strikes his colors.

This modest version of Dicey's rejection of *droit administratif* is quite consistent with statements he had made prior to his article on *Arlidge.* For example, he could be quite generous in assessing the contribution of *droit administratif* to the development of individual liberties in France.[67] He advises British jurists to study the fascinating story of how a "machinery invented to support a scheme of rational absolutism has in later times been used by legists and reformers for the promotion of legal liberty."[68] He gives high marks to the Council of State, the highest administrative court in France from which there is no appeal to the ordinary French courts, for taking the lead in this transformation.[69] He gives considerable attention to describing the similarities between *droit administratif* and the evolution of the rule of law in England, highlighting such matters as the central legal role played by the Crown and its servants "from the accession of the Tudors till the final expulsion of the Stuarts";[70] the fact that *"droit administratif* is, like the greater part of English law, 'case law,' or 'judge-made law,'" which, unlike ordinary French law, resembles English common law in resisting codification; and the striking similarities between *droit administratif* and certain aspects of England's equity jurisdiction as well as the jurisdiction of the Judicial Committee of the Privy Council for settling appeals from colonial courts to the Crown in Council.[71] Thus, a closer look at Dicey's work reveals not an implacable foe of *droit administratif* but a thoughtful critic, one who willingly acknowledges the benefits it has brought to France yet fears it will undermine fundamental principles of English law.

In view of the vast powers exercised by British administrative institutions throughout most of this century, including even the Thatcher and John Major years, one might wonder what relevance Dicey's position might have today. The short answer is that it remains of considerable relevance, provided one confines Dicey's teaching on administrative law to the minimalist position he had accepted by 1915, i.e., that England has no "true" *droit administratif* as long as ordinary courts continue to review the actions of administrative agencies. British judges have done this by the creative and aggressive development of two fundamental principles of administrative law: ultra vires and natural justice.

A leading contemporary textbook on British administrative law defines the doctrine of ultra vires as meaning "that a public authority may not act outside its powers" and then exalts it by saying it "might fitly be called the central principle of administrative law."[72] For a simple example of the doctrine in practice, consider an act of Parliament empowering a ministry to take land by compulsory purchase as long as it is not part of a park. If a dispute arises over a particular parcel of land, the court must decide whether the land in question is indeed part of a park. If it is, then the ministry cannot employ its powers of compulsory purchase to acquire it. To do so would be to act ultra vires, or beyond its powers.[73]

Since English courts cannot declare acts of Parliament unconstitutional, the ultra vires doctrine has enabled them to check administrative abuses by finding that the agencies in question have exceeded the powers granted them by Parliament, and therefore their actions cannot be legally enforced. In so doing, they have gone far beyond the simple example of determining whether a parcel of land is part of a park—an exercise based on specifically expressed statutory language. The most aggressive judicial use of ultra vires appears in the presumption that Parliament never intends to authorize abuses and therefore "that certain safeguards against abuse must be implied" in the statutes the courts construe. The safeguards are "matters of general principle, embodied in the rules of law which govern the interpretation of statutes." It is not necessary that Parliament state these principles expressly in every act it passes. They are considered as "implied conditions . . . which the courts extract by reading between the lines, or (it may be truer to say) insert by writing between the lines."[74] When the courts overturn administrative actions that violate these fundamental conditions, they simply affirm what Parliament really intended, even though it failed to say so expressly. This practice has the happy effect of marrying the rule of law to parliamentary sovereignty, a union that Dicey would surely bless.

To see how vigorously the courts have applied the ultra vires doctrine, consider the case of *Anisminic Ltd. v. Foreign Compensation Commission,*[75] which has aptly been called a "high-water mark of judicial review." The Foreign Compensation Act of 1950 provided that decisions of the Foreign Compensation Commission, a tribunal established to adjudicate compensation claims arising from expropriations of British property abroad, "shall not be called in question in any court of law." Nevertheless, the courts entertained a complaint from Anisminic Ltd., whose claim for compensation had been denied by the commission, a decision eventually reversed by the House of Lords on grounds of ultra vires. Their lordships ruled that the commission had erroneously interpreted an Order in Council taken pursuant to the act to mean that a claim for compensation for property already sold to a foreign buyer would not be allowed. That is, the commission erred in interpreting the Order in Council it had applied against Anisminic to mean that it was "required that the successor in title should have been of British nationality."[76] A majority of the law lords held that this error in interpreting the Order in Council on which the commission based its decision "destroyed the commission's jurisdiction and rendered their decision a nullity, since on a true view of the law they had no jurisdiction to take the successor in title's nationality into account."[77] The law lords made this decision in the face of the explicit statutory language to the effect that the rulings of the commission were not to be challenged in any court of law. According to Sir William Wade and Christopher Forsyth, this remarkable decision "shows clearly the great determination of the courts to uphold their long-standing policy of resisting attempts by Parliament to disarm them by enacting provisions which, if interpreted literally, would confer uncontrollable power upon subordinate tribunals."[78] Dicey lives!

Closely related to the ultra vires doctrine is the doctrine of natural justice, which might be considered as showing the procedural face of ultra vires. For example, natural justice requires that a person should be given a fair hearing before being penalized in any way, "for that is a duty lying upon everyone who decides anything"—as Lord Loreburn's oft-quoted maxim has it.[79] A fundamental element of a fair hearing is that the decision maker hear both sides of the story; *audi alteram partem* (hear the other side) is the term of art. This principle has been invoked in a wide variety of cases, including the "removal of a name from a list of approved foster parents or one of approved contractors, a ministerial order dissolving a municipal council, and a health review tribunal decision on the discharge of a mental patient."[80]

The courts justify their use of natural justice to reverse administrative decisions on the same grounds they use to support ultra vires, namely, the assumption that when Parliament confers power upon an administrative agency it expects that power to be used fairly, and natural justice is but another name for "acting fairly."[81]

Natural justice is closely akin to the American notion of due process of law, but the latter rests on positive language because of the written American Constitution. In practice, however, the due process clause has often been applied in such a way as to reflect the American judges' views of what the British would call natural justice. The due process clause has a somewhat narrower scope than natural justice because, in principle, it is applied only where life, liberty, or property is at stake.

Although the natural justice doctrine has deep roots in English legal history, it fell into disfavor for much of the twentieth century, notably in the immediate aftermath of World War II. It enjoyed a remarkable comeback, however, in the landmark 1963 decision, *Ridge v. Baldwin,*[82] a case involving the chief constable of Brighton, who had been fired by his city's Watch Committee without notice or hearing. The chief constable had been acquitted of a criminal charge of obstructing justice, but during the trial the judge had criticized his leadership of the Brighton police force. Shortly after the trial, the Brighton Watch Committee fired him. After exhausting his administrative appeals, the chief constable turned to the courts, claiming "that his dismissal was void since he had been given no notice of any charge against him and no opportunity of making his defense."[83] The House of Lords upheld his claim, relying on the statutory language permitting police authorities to dismiss any constable they deem to be "negligent in the discharge of his duty or otherwise unfit for the same."[84] Their lordships held that natural justice required the municipal authorities to grant a hearing in which the constable could respond to charges against him before they could possibly decide if he were negligent or otherwise unfit. *Ridge v. Baldwin* is particularly important because it rejected the notion that natural justice applied only to actions of administrative tribunals that were "judicial" but not to those that were "administrative." Their lordships found the judicial/administrative distinction meaningless in the context of applying the natural justice doctrine. Wade and Forsyth capture nicely the gist of the argument when they say "a power which affects rights must be exercised 'judicially,' i.e., fairly, and the fact that the power is administrative does not make it any the less judicial for this purpose."[85]

In his 1915 article on the *Arlidge* case, Dicey consoled himself with the thought that probably in some form or other the English courts would always find the means for correcting the injustice, if demonstrated, of any exercise by a government department of judicial or quasi-judicial authority.[86] The English courts did not disappoint him. Indeed, they surpassed his expectations by subjecting not just judicial or quasi-judicial authority to their supervision, but purely administrative authority as well. Through the creative use of natural justice, the courts have devised a canon of fair administrative procedure. By assuming that Parliament intends the power it delegates to be exercised fairly (so the argument goes), the courts do not undermine enacted law but fulfill it, thereby reaffirming the venerable doctrine that "the justice of the common law will supply the omission of the legislature."[87]

Thus far it is evident that the legal doctrines of ultra vires and natural justice have managed to safeguard the values Dicey had in mind when he launched his famous polemic against *droit administratif.* This is not the case, however, when one turns to the effects of British membership in the European Union upon the two cardinal principles of Dicey's jurisprudence: the sovereignty of Parliament and the rule of law.

Dicey would surely be displeased to learn that Blackstone's celebrated maxim that "what Parliament doth no authority on earth can undo" is no longer true. The *Economist* correctly asserts that "European membership has blown a hole through the middle of parliamentary sovereignty."[88] Nowhere is this clearer than in the famous 1990 *Factortame* case, in which the House of Lords found that the Merchant Shipping Act of 1988 and regulations issued pursuant to it "imposed on Spanish fishing vessels restrictions that were contrary to Community law" and therefore "had to give way."[89] Their lordships held that the traditional English principle prohibiting courts from enjoining the enforcement of a parliamentary statute had to be set aside when the statute was at odds with European Community (now European Union) law. If an English court found that but for a rule of national law injunctive relief would be granted, the national law must yield.[90]

The House of Lords revisited the *Factortame* doctrine in the Employment Opportunities Commission Case of 1994.[91] At issue was a European Economic Community (EEC) Council Directive prohibiting discrimination based on sex, "either directly or indirectly." The directive in turn was based on the EEC Treaty affirming "the principle that men and women should receive equal pay for equal work." Their lordships found that the act of Parliament making unemployment benefits more readily available to full-time than to part-time workers violated the Council Directive because full-time workers were far more likely to be men and part-time workers were far more likely to be women. Therefore, the statute fell under the Council Directive's ban on indirect discrimination based on sex. Particularly noteworthy is the fact that the House of Lords held that the act of Parliament had to yield to an administrative regulation. That is, the principles underlying the traditional doctrine of ultra vires whereby administrative regulations will be struck down if they exceed their statutory base was applied against an act of a once sovereign Parliament for violating an administrative regulation of the EEC. One can hardly imagine a more dramatic departure from Dicey's cherished principles. Parliament is no longer sovereign, and the rule of law is transformed in such a way that an act of Parliament is voided because it fails to conform to an administrative regulation of an international organization.[92]

Despite the vast differences between the constitutional traditions of France and the United Kingdom, they share the common trait of solidly integrating administrative practices into these traditions. They also share the common trait of being unitary states, although the recent devolution of power to parliaments in Scotland and Wales may eventually transform this aspect of the British Constitution. To expand the scope of my argument beyond unitary states, I now look to Canada for examples of administration within a vigorously federal regime.

3

Canada

Margaret Atwood, the distinguished Canadian novelist, captured the essence of her country's attitude toward government when, referring to the famous red-coated Mounties, she said, "Canada must be the only country in the world where a policeman is used as a national symbol."[1] Less catchy, but no less meaningful, were the remarks of Raymond Chrétien, Canada's ambassador to the United States, in his address "Canada @ 2000: America's Partner for the New Millennium." He reviewed for his American audience the strengths of the two countries, placing at the head of the list of Canada's accomplishments "our system of publicly financed health care," which has led to the happy state that "no one need fear that medical bills will result in financial disaster." And all the while, said the ambassador, "patients have complete freedom to choose their doctors."[2]

Law enforcement and government-sponsored health care are excellent examples of public administration in action. The importance of governance in Canadian culture finds clear expression in the British North America (BNA) Act of 1867, which served as Canada's Constitution until 1982. Whereas the U.S. Constitution defends "life, liberty and property" against government abuse, the BNA Act celebrates the Canadian Parliament's commitment to "peace, order and good government."[3]

The explanations for Canadians' positive attitude toward government are many and varied. Some trace it to Canada's achieving independence by gradual emancipation from England, unlike the Americans, who achieved it by revolution. Others point to the progovernment bias of the American Tories, who streamed into Nova Scotia as they fled the Revolution they abhorred in their own country. Another explanation looks to the strong-state tradition the French settlers brought to the New France in North America.

If one looks for a legal principle favorable to strong government, the prerogative powers of the Crown are quite relevant. The importance of these powers is often overlooked because they are easily confused with monarchical power, which has played an almost exclusively symbolic role throughout most of Canada's history. David E. Smith, in *The Invisible Crown: The First Principle of Canadian Government,* sets out to correct the neglect of the Crown in Canadian political science.[4] His first target is the nineteenth-century historian Walter Bagehot, whose distinction between the government as the "efficient" aspect of the Constitution and the Crown as its "dignified" aspect Smith finds too simple and even misleading. Conceding the rather murky meaning of the Crown in British and Canadian constitutional history[5]—a point stated by no less an authority than F. W. Maitland—Smith stresses the broad reservoir of executive powers derived from the Crown that Canadian prime ministers have used to their advantage for well over a century. For example, an order-in-council in 1896 "has enumerated as a special prerogative of the prime minister the right to make recommendations to council to dissolve and convoke Parliament" and to appoint a host of officers, including privy councillors, cabinet ministers, lieutenant-governors, and senators, to name but a few.[6] He also enjoys as part of his prerogative "other powers that adhere to the office as a result of constitutional convention and political practice."[7] These include his "privileged role in the determination of the budget and his absolute authority over the structure and membership of cabinet committees."[8] Smith goes on to enumerate other prime ministerial powers grounded in the prerogative power of the Crown and then concludes on this telling note: "All that is said in this and preceding paragraphs about the prerogative and the prime minister and his colleagues, it should be emphasized, applies with equal force to the provincial premiers and their colleagues."[9]

Thus the royal prerogative derived from the ancient principle of the Queen-in-Parliament as sovereign helps to explain the remarkably broad de facto powers of Canadian executives, not only at the federal level but also in the several provinces. These powers contributed substantially to the development of the modern Canadian administrative state, and their presence at both the federal and provincial levels contributed no less substantially to the endless tensions between these two levels, which have dominated Canadian politics since Confederation.

The most dramatic example of Canadians' faith in administrative institutions appeared in the aftermath of the Quebec sovereignty referendum of 30 October 1995, which failed by the narrowest of margins: 49.4 percent for Quebec sovereignty and 50.6 percent against. Prime Minister Chrétien was severely criticized for having failed to develop an effective strategy against the sovereigntists. His opponents charged that he had been "sleepwalking" during the long referendum campaign and that as a result he had "almost lost his country." In the midst of these postreferendum attacks, Chrétien replied that "the real problems in Canada are economic growth and the creation of jobs and good solid administration."[10] That Canada's prime minister would mention "good solid administration" as one of the nation's three "real" problems in the immediate aftermath of a referendum that nearly destroyed his country struck interested American observers as extraordinary and perhaps even as bizarre. Public administration is not prestigious activity in the United States. It is inconceivable that an American president in the midst of a great constitutional crisis would turn to administration—good and solid or otherwise—as the path to political salvation. Not so in Canada. Chrétien's remark was part of a national chorus that evoked the muse of administration to inspire politicians to achieve the high statesmanship needed to bind up the nation's wounds. Constitutional debates over the very survival of the regime moved effortlessly into detailed discussions of such classic administrative themes as environmental management, immigration policy, public finance, civil service pensions, education, manpower and training, unemployment benefits, control of natural resources, and, of course, that hardy perennial of Canadian federalism, equalization of payments.[11]

Federalists were not alone in enlisting administration to support their cause. Quebec separatists, most notably Premier Lucien Bouchard, frequently tempered the high rhetoric of sovereignty with the mundane details of education, employment, health care, civil service reform, and financial management—in a word, with all the practical consequences that would make independence worthwhile.[12]

To grasp the significance of Chrétien's remarks on administration healing constitutional ills, we must examine the place of administration in Canadian constitutional history. Before we look at specific administrative situations, however, a brief review of the highlights of Canadian constitutional history pertinent to our inquiry is in order.

For our purposes, the Confederation period of the 1860s is the most suitable starting point.[13] The BNA Act of 1867, although formally an act of the British Parliament, was primarily the work of statesmen from the North American colonies of New Brunswick, Nova Scotia, Newfoundland, Prince Edward Island, and "Canada," which at that time included both Ontario (Upper Canada or West Canada) and Quebec (Lower Canada or East Canada). The BNA Act created a new entity, "the Dominion of Canada," which originally comprised Ontario, Quebec, New Brunswick, and Nova Scotia. The BNA Act served as Canada's Constitution until it was replaced by the Constitution Act of 1982.[14] The latter, like the BNA Act, was technically an act of the British Parliament, but this time the full independence of Canada from the United Kingdom was formally recognized. Thus, Canadians refer to the "patriation" of their Constitution in 1982. Canada, of course, had been an independent country for all practical purposes at least since the 1920s. The patriation of the Constitution in 1982 made all this quite explicit, even though the Queen remains the head of state in Canada.

All the provinces of Canada except Quebec approved the new Constitution. Since the 1960s there had been a strong nationalist movement in Quebec pledged to gain independence from the rest of Canada. Indeed, the "sovereigntist" government of Premier René Lévesque's *Parti Québecois* had sponsored an unsuccessful referendum on independence in 1980. With the patriated Constitution in hand, the federal government in Ottawa undertook a series of initiatives aimed at winning Quebec's approval. The two most important ones were called the Meech Lake and Charlottetown Accords, after the locations in which they were fashioned. Quebec accepted the Meech Lake Accord, but Manitoba and Newfoundland did not, thereby defeating it since unanimity was required. The Charlottetown Accord was submitted to a national referendum in 1992 and was decisively defeated, with six (including Quebec) of the ten provinces voting against it. Relations between Quebec and the rest of Canada grew increasingly hostile, and three years later, in October 1995, Quebec held the independence referendum that prompted Chrétien's comment on the remedial powers of "good solid administration." With this background in mind, I examine in some detail the relationship between constitutionalism and administration, first in the Confederation Debates of 1865, then in the constitutional conflict over the powers of administrative officers known as lieutenant-governors in the late nineteenth century, and finally, in the current Quebec crisis.

THE CONFEDERATION DEBATES

The Confederation Debates refer to the debates of the Eighth Provincial Parliament of Canada, held during February and March 1865 in the City of Quebec. They took place in the two chambers of the Provincial Parliament, the Legislative Assembly (the lower house) and the Legislative Council (the upper house). These debates focused on a set of resolutions adopted by delegates from Canada (Upper and Lower), Nova Scotia, New Brunswick, Prince Edward Island, and Newfoundland at a conference also held in Quebec City during the previous October. These Quebec Resolutions led eventually to the BNA Act of 1867. Prince Edward Island joined the Dominion in 1873, but Newfoundland waited until 1949 to do so.

During the 1860s, confederation gradually emerged as an idea whose time had come. British imperial policy favored consolidating the colonies scattered across North America into a manageable union. The Maritime Provinces of New Brunswick, Nova Scotia, and Prince Edward Island looked forward to closer economic and commercial integration. The two Canadas chafed under the uneasy and obviously artificial union that brought them together in one legislature. The differences between the francophone Catholics of Quebec and the English-speaking Protestants of Ontario were deep and abiding. John A. Macdonald, who became the first prime minister of the Dominion of Canada, used his position as leader of the Conservative Party of Upper Canada to further his grand vision of a union of many colonies as a welcome alternative to the unsatisfactory union of the two Canadas. Such prominent Quebecers as George-Etienne Cartier and Etienne-Pascal Taché believed such a federated union would provide greater protection for the language, law, and religion they cherished. Military considerations also pushed the British colonists toward confederation, notably the dark shadow cast by the United States on the Confederation Debates of 1865, which took place during the closing months of the American Civil War. One of the major arguments for confederation was the need to prepare for a possible attack from the United States once that war was over. Canadian statesmen of all persuasions knew that the U.S. government was greatly displeased with the sympathetic position of the British Empire toward the southern states throughout the war. Several minor but exceedingly unpleasant border skirmishes had not escaped the attention of thoughtful Canadians. The record of the debates reveals a serious concern that the victorious Union armies might soon invade Canada to settle some scores with the British Empire and even to annex certain sections of British North America. For example, after noting the rapid march of recent events in the American Civil War, Thomas Ryan declared:

> Already we hear the great anticipated successes of the North. If the news be true that Charleston has been evacuated, it will be a severe blow to the cause of the South; and if the South be conquered, we know what have been the sentiments toward Canada expressed in the United States for the last three years. They will, perhaps, turn north for further conquests, and try to humble a power which has not in every way met their wishes. We should, at all events, be prepared to meet such a contingency, prepared to repel attack, prepared to defend our homes and the free Constitution under which we live.[15]

John Rose expressed his hopes that peaceful relations could be maintained with the United States, yet then warned: "But at the same time we cannot conceal from ourselves the fact that within the last three or four years we have several times been seriously threatened. It is not in the power of any man to say when the cloud, which so darkly overshadows us, may burst in full fury on our heads, and those who have the direction of the destinies of this country ought to be prepared to do all that in them lies to place it in a position to meet that event."[16]

Recalling past military glories, William McGiverin assured his listeners that, if the proper precautions were taken, "we are in quite as good a position to hold our own as those who successfully resisted the invader in the war of 1812."[17] Joseph Blanchet echoed these patriotic sentiments with his own pledge that if "we are ever invaded by the United States, I shall ever be ready to take up arms to drive the invaders out of the country."[18] J. Beaubien linked military preparedness specifically to confederation by asserting that the proximity of the British colonies to the United States required that they "unite together in order to form a stronger nation, and one more able to withstand the onslaught of an enemy."[19] Thomas Ferguson saw the situation as grim indeed, for the Americans "are at this moment a war-making and war-loving people."[20]

With these forces—economic, imperial, political, and military—counseling confederation, the parliamentarians began in earnest in February 1865 to debate the Quebec Resolutions adopted by representatives from the several colonies four months earlier in October 1864. The purpose of the debate was to decide if

Canada should approve the resolutions and join the other colonies in petitioning the British Parliament to grant them the new form of government. The first few minutes of the debate sounded a dire warning whose echo can be heard today. The first speaker in the Legislative Council, Etienne-Pascal Taché, addressed his colleagues in French. John Ross arose at once and asked him to speak in English. Luc Lettelier said the speaker should continue in French, but the diplomatic Taché "concluded that as there were English members who did not understand French at all, while the French members all understood English, it would be best for him to speak in the latter language, and proceeded to do so."[21] Thus the divisive issue of language asserted itself in the opening minutes of the Confederation debates and has never gone away.

Fortunately, language was not the only issue before Parliament. The debates covered a broad range of topics, including the distinctive character of Quebec, the possibility of amending the Quebec Resolutions, the feasibility of submitting the text before them to a popular referendum, the appropriateness of an elected as opposed to an appointed senate, religious liberty, the dangers of American republicanism, and the advantages of a federation vis-à-vis a "legislative union," which would bind the colonies together in a unitary state.[22]

For our purposes, it is important to observe that amid these high questions of state, the members of Parliament found time and energy to give extraordinary attention to the details of public administration under the new regime. The topics ranged from broad generalizations on the hopes for improved administration from the stable institutions confederation was expected to provide, to more focused attention to public works, and, finally, to specific discussions on canals and schools.[23] Woven into the fabric of these arguments was a curious debate over the provision in Resolution 64 that the "General Parliament" would make "an annual grant in aid" to each province "equal to eighty cents per head of the population, as established by the census of 1861." Subsequent resolutions provided special benefits for New Brunswick, Newfoundland, and Prince Edward Island.[24] These provisions triggered debates foreshadowing later controversies over the equalization payments among the provinces that would play so important a role in the administration of Canadian federalism.[25]

Among the many administrative questions debated in 1865, however, none can match the importance of the Intercolonial Railway. In reviewing the debates over this immensely controversial innovation, I have no intention of weighing the merits of the issue. I examine the railroad question, which was to dominate the early development of administration in the Dominion of Canada, only to give a specific example of the salience of administration in the Confederation debates. I do this to establish the link between then and now, thereby suggesting that when contemporary Canadians, like Prime Minister Chrétien, link mundane questions of administration to the high statesmanship of saving a great nation, they echo sentiments harking back to the beginnings of confederation.

Quebec Resolution 68 proposed an Intercolonial Railway to extend "from

Rivière du Loup, through New Brunswick, to Truro in Nova Scotia." Its importance in the debates for friend and foe alike of the resolutions is textually demonstrable. Speaking before the Legislative Council, William Macmaster, an opponent of confederation, denounced the proposed railroad as "a very questionable part of the project" and then elevated its importance by adding, "indeed to my mind it is the most objectionable of the whole."[26] Echoing these sentiments, anticonfederationist Matthew Cameron saw the railroad as nothing less than the "leading feature" of the proposed constitutional change and one of the main reasons why it should be rejected.[27]

Not to be outdone, the friends of confederation were no less outspoken in supporting the railroad than their adversaries were in condemning it. For Antoine Harwood, "the building of the Intercolonial Railway" was "the most important consideration of all for everyone, and one which would of itself be sufficient to make us desire the union of the provinces."[28]

Raising his sights beyond the railway proposed in the text before him, Colonel Arthur Rankin proclaimed it but the first step toward "that still more important and magnificent project, the Atlantic and Pacific Railway." Seeing the embryo of this grander project in the proposed Intercolonial Railway, Rankin assured his colleagues that "it would be impossible to overestimate the advantages which any country must derive from being possessed of a line of communication destined to become the highway from Europe to Asia."[29]

With such strong statements both in its favor and against it, the Intercolonial Railway became the subject of considerable controversy. At the very outset of the debates in the Legislative Assembly, Luther Holton, a prominent anticonfederationist, went to the heart of the matter when he registered his surprise at finding in a constitutional text a proposal to build a railway. He ridiculed this provision as "a novelty that, perhaps might not be found in the constitution of any country."[30] To this John A. Macdonald replied, "The railroad was not, as stated by Mr. Holton, a portion of the Constitution, but was one of the conditions on which the Lower Provinces [New Brunswick and Nova Scotia] agreed to enter into the constitutional agreement with us."[31]

Macdonald's distinction between "a portion of the Constitution" and a "condition" for accepting the constitution was no shallow legalism. It produced an immediate and most unwelcome reaction in New Brunswick, where the friends of confederation were facing an imminent election that focused on the Quebec Resolutions. For Samuel Tilley, the leading New Brunswick confederationist, the Intercolonial Railway was absolutely essential. It was, as Donald Creighton puts it, "Tilley's biggest political asset."[32] Albert J. Smith, Tilley's principal opponent, seized on Macdonald's unfortunate comment that the railway was not a "portion of the Constitution" to argue that the commitments in the Quebec Resolutions most favorable to New Brunswick, above all the Intercolonial Railway, meant nothing at all. Frantically, Macdonald sent a telegram to Tilley assuring him that the provision for the railway—regardless of its status as part of the constitution—would appear in the text of the imperial act, which was the ultimate goal of the Quebec Resolutions. His remarks helped to reassure the "terrified Unionists" in New Brunswick, but mistrust and hard feelings remained.[33]

The prominent place given to the railway provision in the proposed constitution brought a technical dimension to the Confederation debates conspicuously absent from the comparable debates in the United States in 1787 or in France in 1958. The railroad clause prompted extremely lengthy and detailed discussions of what we might call today financial management. The wearisome detail in these two excerpts captures nicely the technical flavor of much of the debate over the railroad:

HON. MR. RYAN (speaking in favor of the resolutions on 20 February): I want to shew by this [a lengthy discussion he had just finished on the economics of transporting a barrel of flour] that the carrying of flour over the Intercolonial Railway will not be so difficult of accomplishment as people who have not gone into the calculation closely may be disposed to imagine. (Hear, hear.) I have here, too, a statement of the imports of flour into New Brunswick, Nova Scotia, and Newfoundland. It is as follows:

Imports of Flour	Barrels
New Brunswick	243,000
Nova Scotia	328,000
Newfoundland	226,000
[Total]	797,000

MR. A. MACKENZIE (speaking against the resolutions on 23 February): Major Robinson estimates the cost of the road at about £7,000 pounds per mile, or about £2,800,000 altogether. I do not think, judging from the statement he gives of the grades in the road, the bridges to be built, and the material to be found along the line, that it is a fair inference that the cost would equal the amount he sets down. The character of the ground over which the road will pass is very similar to the railways of Canada. It is represented to be very much of the nature of the country through which the Great Western runs westward of Hamilton over a great portion of the line. The best portion of the line is equal to the worst portions of the Great Western. Even at the cost of £7,000 per mile the expense of constructing the entire road would be a little over fifteen millions of dollars.[34]

Statements of this nature abound throughout the Confederation debates.[35] As noted above, there is nothing like them in the French or American debates. Luther Holton was right. To insert a clause about a specifically named railroad into a constitution was an innovation, but it underscores a blending of administration and constitutionalism in a distinctively Canadian way.[36]

The debate over the railroad serves not only as an example of administration in the Confederation debates, but also highlights the theme of technology driving constitutional reform. Central to this argument is a report issued in 1839 by Lord Durham, who had been appointed "governor-in-chief of the British North American colonies" and sent there to report on governance in the wake of several outbreaks of violence.[37] In English-speaking Canada, Durham's *Report* is often hailed as "one of the great documents of both Canadian and British Colonial history."[38] Quebecers, however, are likely to denounce Durham as a bigot because of what they see as his determination to destroy French culture through assimilation.[39] Lord Durham's famous (or infamous) *Report* was invoked by John Ross, who rose to speak in favor of the railroad. He cited passages from the *Report* in which Durham had argued that a railroad "between Halifax and Quebec would, in fact, produce relations between these provinces which would render a general union absolutely necessary."[40] This very same passage was cited by Anselme Paquet, an opponent of confederation, as a reason for rejecting the Quebec Resolutions.[41] The curious fact that the same author is cited verbatim, first for confederation and then against it, is explained by the diametrically opposed memories of Lord Durham held by residents of the two Canadas as of 1865. Generally loved and admired in Ontario, in Quebec he was, quite simply, despised.[42] Interestingly, both his friends and foes agree with his prediction that an Intercolonial Railway would be a particularly apt means for achieving political unity. Logically enough, Ross and Paquet cite Lord Durham's argument, each to his own end of bringing about confederation (for Ross) or of stopping it (for Paquet). For the latter, the railroad should be opposed because it would lead to political union as the *mal aimé* Durham had correctly surmised. For the former, the railroad should be supported for precisely the same reason. For our study of the administrative-constitutional link, the important point, however, is that Lord Durham had the wit to foresee technological innovation as a sure path to constitutional reform and that men on both sides of the 1865 debate recognized that he was right.

The Confederation fathers of 1865 had no need of promptings from Lord Durham to see the connection between the Intercolonial Railway and confederation. Thus, anticonfederationist James Currie, noting that "some leading men in Halifax had said 'the Railway first, and Confederation next,'" argued that the simplest way to defeat confederation would be to reject the railway proposal. He was satisfied that "if the Intercolonial Railway project were taken out of the scheme [i.e., the proposed constitution,] we would not hear much about it afterwards."[43] Although Currie, like Lord Durham, saw a close connection between the railway and confederation, he did not fear the railway as simply a means to confederation. His argument was that the confederationists in the Maritime Provinces cared only about the railway but would cynically embrace confederation as a necessary evil. This position was expanded by A. A. Dorion, who attributed to Samuel Tilley, the prominent New Brunswick confederationist, the sentiment "no railway, no confederation." Indeed, Dorion went on to denounce the entire confederation plan as nothing but an elaborate scheme to rescue the financially troubled Grand Trunk Railroad.[44]

Confederationist Hector-Louis Langevin candidly acknowledges that his cause would be doomed without the Intercolonial Railway, "for it is almost impossible that so great an enterprise [as the railway] should succeed unless it is in the hands of a great central power."[45] Thus Langevin joins his opponents Currie and Dorion in recognizing, albeit for very different reasons, the close link between the proposed railroad and confederation itself. Langevin seems to reverse Lord Durham's timetable, however, because he envisions confederation ("a great central power") preceding the railroad. Langevin's priorities differ sharply from those of his fellow confederationist A. M. Smith, who, rather surprisingly, concedes that "as a commercial undertaking, the Intercolonial Railway presents no attraction." But he then adds that "for the establishing of those intimate social and commercial relations indispensable to political unity between ourselves and the sister provinces, the railway is a necessity."[46]

Although there are many variations on it, the theme is clear and unambiguous.[47] Regardless of how they might differ on the merits of the Quebec Resolutions, the men of 1865 were at one in seeing a close connection between confederation and the great public enterprise of the Intercolonial Railway. That is, they found in railroads, the high tech of their day, a path to meaningful compromise that created a great nation. Today there is no dearth of technological innovation; it is the hallmark of our time. Perhaps some bright statesmen in Quebec City or Ottawa will seize upon it to preserve that nation.

ORIGINAL INTENT AND THE LIEUTENANT-GOVERNORS

The Confederation debates focused on a federal regime that was an innovation in the British tradition of parliamentary government. Some sort of federalism was deemed necessary, not only to accommodate the vast territorial expanse of the united colonies but also to guarantee a safe haven for the language, law, and religion of Quebec within a larger political unit. The 1860s, however, were not a particularly propitious time for Canadians to draft a constitution committed to federalism, in view of the tragic collapse of that principle into bloody civil war among their neighbors to the south. A wise commentator on the Canadian Constitution astutely observes: "If the Canadian Fathers of Confederation held any truth to be self-evident, it was that the architects of the U.S. Constitution had made a fundamental constitutional mistake in 1787, the terrible consequences of which were being played out at that very moment . . . on the battlefield."[48]

John A. Macdonald, the prime mover toward confederation, might best be described as a Canadian nationalist masquerading as a federalist. In today's political climate, when a respected journalist can write of "the unbearable lightness of being Canadian,"[49] it may seem inappropriate to juxtapose the words *Cana-*

dian and *nationalist;* but if ever there was a Canadian nationalist, it was surely John A. Macdonald. Although the official text approved by the British Parliament in 1867 described the original provinces (Ontario, Quebec, New Brunswick, and Nova Scotia) as "federally united into One Dominion," Macdonald showed his true colors during the debates on confederation in early 1865 when he stated, "We thereby . . . make the Confederation one people and one government, instead of five peoples and five governments . . . one united province, with the local governments and legislatures subordinate to the General Government and Legislature."[50]

Like Alexander Hamilton in 1787, Macdonald had a sweeping nationalistic vision for his country far in advance of the overwhelming majority of its citizens. Unlike Hamilton, however, Macdonald and his close allies succeeded in translating many of their principles into law. Although the BNA Act created a nominally federal regime, its unadorned text, unfettered by history and judicial interpretation, makes a far more nationalistic statement than the Constitution of the United States.

Like the American Constitution, the BNA Act explicitly confers an impressive array of powers on the federal Parliament, but the specifically enumerated powers follow a sweeping grant of power to Ottawa "to make Laws for the Peace, Order, and Good Government of Canada, in relation to all Matters not coming within the Classes of Subjects by this Act assigned exclusively to the Legislatures of the Provinces."

In other words, under the BNA Act all powers not assigned exclusively to the provinces belong to the federal government, thereby inverting the order of the American Constitution, wherein "the powers not delegated to the United States by the Constitution . . . are reserved to the States respectively or to the people."[51] After granting the federal Parliament a broad power to legislate for the peace, order, and good government of Canada, the BNA Act confers a long list of twenty-nine specific powers on Parliament, but only "for greater certainty" and "not as to restrict the Generality of the foregoing terms of this Section," i.e., peace, order, and good government.

Thus, the text of the BNA Act makes doubly sure that the federal government will have the upper hand in its dealings with the provinces, first by granting it a general power to legislate for peace, order, and good government and then by explicitly granting that same body exclusive constitutional jurisdiction over a long list of such important matters as the regulation of trade and commerce, the power to tax and borrow on the public credit, "the Militia, Military and Naval Service, and Defence," banking, "currency and coinage," "marriage and divorce," "Indians, and lands reserved for the Indians," and "the criminal law."[52]

These impressive powers were reinforced by additional federal powers of "reservation" and "disallowance." The former permitted the lieutenant-governor, who represented the Crown in each of the provinces, to withhold his assent from a bill passed by a provincial legislature in order to "reserve" it for the further consideration of the federal cabinet. If a full year passed without the cabinet instructing the lieutenant-governor to sign it, the bill would die. "Disallowance" was simply a veto "under which the federal government could render null and void any provincial law within a year of its passage by the provincial legislature."[53] It corresponded roughly with the "Council of Revision" that James Madison and James Wilson tried unsuccessfully to insert into the Constitution of the United States. This council would have had authority to nullify acts passed by the legislatures of the several states. Since this power could have been exercised on policy as well as constitutional grounds, it would have made the U.S. Constitution a far more explicitly nationalistic document.

As Peter Russell observes, the powers of reservation and disallowance "derived from an imperial rather than a federal structure."[54] The imperial Parliament in London exercised similar powers over the federal Parliament in Ottawa. This symmetry accurately reflects Macdonald's unorthodox view of federalism—a view based on his belief that "the relation between Ottawa and the provinces would replicate the relation between the sovereign imperial parliament and the colonial legislatures."[55]

The most remarkable aspect of Canadian constitutional history is that the provinces have remained so powerful vis-à-vis the federal government, despite these textual provisions we have just examined. Although the deck was stacked against them, the provinces always seemed to hold the trumps. In a certain sense, the constitutional histories of Canada and the United States are mirror images of each other. A person unencumbered with any knowledge of the history of the two countries and familiar only with their constitutional texts would surely be forgiven for erroneously surmising that Canada would have a far more centralized government than the United States. How all this came about is too vast a topic to treat here, but a brief glimpse at one early aspect of the Canadian part of the story provides an interesting example of the clash between political practice and authoritative texts.

The example centers on *Citizens Insurance Company v. Parsons,* a landmark judicial decision in 1881 on the validity of an Ontario statute imposing uniform conditions on fire insurance contracts issued in that province.[56] Parsons initiated the litigation by suing Citizens Insurance for failing to compensate him for losses he had suffered in a warehouse fire. The company denied his claim on the grounds that he had failed to comply with conditions specified in his policy. Parsons maintained that the conditions in question violated Ontario's Fire Insurance Policy Act, to which the company replied that the Ontario law was invalid because it regulated a subject reserved exclusively to the federal government by the BNA Act.

The case eventually wound its way to the Judicial Committee of the Privy Council (JCPC) in London, where it was decided in 1881. (Although the Ottawa Parliament had established a Supreme Court of Canada in 1875, it was supreme only in name; the real judicial supremacy lay with the JCPC until 1949.) The case presented JCPC with a difficult problem. Parsons maintained that the Ontario law was clearly valid because the BNA Act explicitly conferred upon the provinces the exclusive power to make laws relating to "Property and Civil Rights in the Province," a category surely broad enough to include the regulation of fire insurance policies. The insurance company countered by citing the BNA Act language no less clearly conferring upon the federal Parliament exclusive jurisdiction over "the regulation of Trade and Commerce," an expression sufficiently broad to encompass the insurance plan in question. Did the regulation of insurance policies fall under property and civil rights or under trade and commerce? Clearly, it fell under both.

Sir Montague Smith, who delivered the Judicial Committee's opinion, rejected the easy solution of resolving all conflicts of jurisdiction in favor of the federal Parliament. At first blush, this would seem to have been the correct interpretation because of the sweeping language with which the BNA Act empowered the federal government. The JCPC rejected this approach, however, because it would prove too much. The committee's examination of the text revealed a good number of apparent textual conflicts, e.g., between Ottawa's control over "marriage and divorce" and the provinces' control over "the solemnization of marriage." If all such apparent conflicts were to be resolved in favor of the federal Parliament, there would be precious little left for the provinces to do. The JCPC held that the authors of the BNA Act "could not have intended that the powers exclusively granted to the provincial legislature should be absorbed in those given to the domain of parliament."[57] Hence, the JCPC reasoned that the authors of the BNA Act must not have intended that conflicts should exist between the powers distributed between the provinces and Ottawa, "and in order to prevent such a result, the two sections must be read together, and the language of one interpreted, and, where necessary, modified, by that of the other."[58] Having announced its hermeneutic principle, the JCPC then pondered the competing texts—civil rights and property on the one hand and trade and commerce on the other—and eventually concluded that Ontario had not exceeded its constitutional powers.

This decision yields two important insights into Canadian federalism. First, in what we might call today a bold act of judicial activism, the JCPC took upon itself the task of demarcating the limits of the federal and the provincial governments, a task the authors of the BNA Act might have thought they had themselves settled definitively in 1867 to the advantage of Ottawa. As a result, JCPC became a major player in Canadian federalism, usually to the advantage of the provinces. If it is difficult to square the JCPC's provincial orientation with "the intent of the framers" of the BNA Act, it is easier to see in its jurisprudence a faithful reflection of the political sentiment for decentralization in late-nineteenth-century Canada. Despite the authoritative character of the BNA Act as a quasi constitution, its centralizing tendencies had been viewed with considerable suspicion from the outset—a suspicion reinforced by its legal character as an enactment of an imperial Parliament that could not be submitted to the people of Canada for popular ratification.

Second, in the course of developing its argument that the regulation of fire insurance policies belongs to the provinces and not to the federal government, the JCPC had to give some examples of the sorts of activities that would fall within the federal jurisdiction over trade and commerce. Americans will be interested to note that the Judicial Committee confined this federal power to "matters of interprovincial concern: and it may . . . include general regulations of trade affecting the whole Dominion."[59] This bears a striking resemblance to the American constitutional provision limiting congressional power to commerce "among the states"—a limitation that from the time of the New Deal until 1995 offered little resistance to federal power. Peter Russell notes that "ironically, the express restrictions in the American Constitution have proved to be far less of a barrier to the development of national economic policies than have the judicially created restrictions in Canada."[60]

The judicial activism of the Judicial Committee of the Privy Council played a major role in the curious tale of the lieutenant-governors, administrative officers who served as the queen's representative in each of the provinces. Today, the office is quite obscure, meriting only a few lines in contemporary accounts of Canadian government and politics;[61] but this was not so in the period immediately after Confederation, when Prime Minister John A. Macdonald "supposed that the lieutenant governor would act as an agent of the federal government in Ottawa's efforts to control the provinces."[62]

In reading Macdonald's view of the role of the lieutenant-governor, one is reminded of the French prefect, the national officer stationed in a department to represent the national authority in Paris and to establish a line of communication between local officials and the central government. Although French prefects and Canadian lieutenant-governors shared the ambiguities of a bifurcated role, the latter's situation was far more complicated, for a variety of reasons.

First, a Canadian province is—and always has been—far more independent of Ottawa than a French department is of Paris. French departments are creatures of the central government in a unitary state, an institutional arrangement far different from Canadian federalism. Second, at least two decades before Confederation, the British colonies in North America had won for themselves the same principle of "responsible government" that prevailed in England. That is, "the Representative of the Sovereign, can act only on the advice of his ministers, those ministers being responsible to the people through Parliament."[63] This principle carried over into the new institutional arrangement created by Confederation, whereby former British colonies that had enjoyed considerable autonomy in regulating their domestic affairs were brought together into one Dominion of Canada. Offices filled by colonial governors representing the Crown prior to Confederation were now filled by lieutenant-governors, and a governor-general in Ottawa represented the queen at the newly created federal level.

The new circumstances promoted a lively debate on whether the lieutenant-governors represented the queen or the governor-general; but regardless of the position one took on this issue, there was no doubt that in accordance with the principle of responsible government he was to be the compliant instrument of the provincial legislature. This, of course, led to an irreconcilable conflict with his role as Ottawa's man in the province. Prior to Confederation, the same conflict had arisen for the governors who represented the Crown in each of the colonies. On the one hand, the governor was to follow the lead of the colonial legislatures under the principle of responsible government, and on the other, he was to enforce imperial policy in the colony. A practical accommodation was reached by distinguishing local from imperial affairs, making the governor subordinate to the colonial legislature in the former and independent in the latter. Certainly there was no bright line to distinguish local from imperial affairs, but the system was tolerable despite its lack of conceptual rigor. The most difficult problem for the colonials lay in the governor's power to reserve his assent from a measure voted by the legislatures until imperial authorities in London had had a chance either to approve or reject it. The point of the objection was not their subordination to the imperial authorities; as colonials, they had made their peace with that. Their objection was that the governor, the very symbol of responsible government, was the one who initiated the process by which the will of the colonial legislature would be thwarted.

This unsettled state of affairs resurfaced in the context of Confederation after 1867. Applying an imperial analogy to the Confederation wherein the federal government would be to the provinces as the British government was to the colonies, Macdonald looked to the lieutenant-governors to use their powers to reserve their assent to questionable provincial legislation in order to keep the provinces in their proper constitutional place, which, for Macdonald, was one of subordination to Ottawa. Again, following the imperial analogy, Macdonald agreed that the lieutenant-governors should reserve their assent only when questions of jurisdiction arose. That is, the lieutenant-governors were not to exercise this power on substantive grounds of policy but only to curb efforts by the provinces to legislate in any of the areas falling under federal jurisdiction. Thus, the distinction between local and imperial affairs that had been salient before Confederation was transformed into a jurisdictional distinction between federal and provincial affairs as specified in the BNA Act.

This arrangement proved unsatisfactory for most "provincial autonomists," as Robert Vipond aptly dubs the opponents of Macdonald's centralizing plans. They could not abide the notion that the lieutenant-governor, who, according to the principle of responsible government, was the compliant instrument of the provincial legislature, should have authority to withhold his assent from bills duly enacted. This, of course, was the same fault the preconfederation colonials had found with the royal governors in the several colonies.

While the advocates of greater provincial autonomy criticized the reservation power of the lieutenant-governors on the principled grounds of its incom-

patibility with responsible government, the authorities in Ottawa, including Macdonald himself, gradually began to look upon the reservation power as a nuisance
that brought unwelcome provincial political squabbles to their doorstep. By
1882, Macdonald had grown sufficiently disenchanted with the lieutenant-governors' reservation power as to instruct them henceforward to use it only at the
behest of the governor-general in Ottawa. Since the principle of responsible government at the federal level placed the governor-general squarely under the
thumb of the federal Parliament and its cabinet, the new directive meant, in practice, that the lieutenant-governors' reservation powers could come into play only
at the direction of the government in Ottawa. From here, it was but a small step
to the collapse of the reservation power into desuetude. Because the federal government already enjoyed the power to disallow provincial legislation—that is, to
nullify it within one year after it had come into effect—the lieutenant-governors'
power to reserve assent was meaningless if it could be exercised only at the federal government's behest. The purpose of the lieutenant-governors' reservation
power was simply to suspend approval of a provincial law until the federal government had a chance to review it. To exercise such a power only with permission in advance from a federal government endowed with the power of disallowance was utterly superfluous. Thus, the principle of responsible government advocated by the friends of provincial autonomy joined forces with the
practical misgivings of the leadership in Ottawa to render inoperative an explicit
constitutional power of the lieutenant-governors.

Having neutralized the lieutenant-governor as a threat from Ottawa, the
provincial autonomists then set out to capture him as a trophy for their cause.
They did so by arguing that he was the queen's representative in a province, just
as the governor-general was her representative in Ottawa. The purpose of this
argument was to enhance the credentials of the lieutenant-governor (once he had
been reined in by the principle of responsible government) in order to establish
parity between the provinces and Ottawa in their relationship with the Crown.
That is, where federal questions were concerned, the queen was directly represented in Ottawa by the governor-general; and when it came to provincial questions, she was, according to the provincial autonomists, no less directly
represented by the lieutenant-governor. This line of argument was intended to
head off the federalist idea that the lieutenant-governors were simply the representatives of the federal government, despite clear statements in the BNA Act to
the effect that the governor-general "carr[ies] on the government of Canada on
behalf and in the name of the Queen" and that the lieutenant-governor shall be
"appointed by the Governor General in Council," i.e., at the direction of the cabinet in Ottawa.[64] These texts seemed to suggest that the provinces were subordinate levels of government "akin to municipal councils"—an idea altogether
repugnant to the provincial autonomists.[65]

The issue crystallized on a debate over the power of the lieutenant-governors
to appoint queen's counsel in the various provinces. The office of queen's coun-

sel carried certain rights of preferred treatment in legal proceedings and was looked upon as a desirable patronage appointment that brought a certain honor and recognition. Far more important than the office itself, however, was the question of whether this office was the lieutenant-governor's to give, because the appointment was grounded in the royal prerogative. The federalists who would deny this power to the lieutenant-governor were hunting bigger game than queen's counsel. They wanted to deny any share in the royal prerogative to the lieutenant-governor in order to reinforce their point on the subordination of the provinces to Ottawa. The provincial autonomists argued just the opposite. They saw in their effort to preserve a share in the royal prerogative for their lieutenant-governors an indispensable means of maintaining their direct link with the Crown, which was an essential element of their political identity. Through the principle of responsible government they could say that "our system is the English constitutional system . . . free but also monarchical."[66] Having achieved "almost complete colonial autonomy before Confederation without having to sever their connection to the Crown," the provincial autonomists were not about to sacrifice all this on the altar of federal supremacy. Since British constitutional doctrine as expounded by Dicey, Bagehot, and Maitland had definitively subordinated the royal prerogative to ministerial control, there was no fear among the autonomists that a rogue lieutenant-governor would use the prerogative power against the provincial government. In their view, the denial of this power to the lieutenant-governors would fatally compromise their cherished political identity.

The argument over the prerogative powers of the lieutenant-governor became inextricably entwined in larger aspects of the prerogative question until the Judicial Committee of the Privy Council issued a definitive ruling in 1892 upholding prerogative powers for the provinces—in this particular litigation, New Brunswick's reliance upon prerogative power to claim priority over other creditors seeking to recover funds from the liquidators of a failed bank.[67] In this case, the JCPC expressed a conception of Canadian federalism extremely favorable to the provinces and one that "underlies most of the Judicial Committee's decisions on the Canadian Constitution."[68] The controversy over the powers of lieutenant-governors, midlevel colonial administrative officers destined for constitutional obscurity, laid the foundation for this landmark constitutional decision in the steady retreat of the practice of Canadian federalism from its centralized constitutional text.

THE QUEBEC CRISIS

The defeat of the Meech Lake Accord, an effort by the federal government primarily to win Quebec's support for the patriated Constitution of 1982, was unfortunate because its text contained language referring to Quebec as a "distinct society," a symbolic statement of enormous importance to Quebecers deeply involved in the always volatile politics of identity. Political orthodoxy in Quebec has long insisted that the origins of the Canadian Confederation lay in a great compact between two founding peoples—the French and the English. The historical evidence to support this interpretation is rather meager, but this takes nothing from the idea's power in Quebec, where it has assumed mythic proportions. It provides the foundation for rejecting the argument that Quebec is simply one of ten provinces and, as such, has no special place in the Confederation. If the "two founding peoples" theory is historically suspect, the notion that Quebec is just another Canadian province is utterly preposterous. If anything is obvious in Canadian history, it is the distinct character of Quebec. The distinct society formula, though sharply criticized by many non-Quebecers, seemed to hold the best promise of stating a middle ground acceptable to Quebecers and the "rest of Canada" (as the other provinces have come to be called).

In addition to the distinct society clause, the Meech Lake Accord also contained important constitutional changes concerning the Supreme Court, the provinces' role in immigration policy, and certain limitations on federal spending—all of which were intended to accommodate Quebec and, in some cases, other provinces as well. The Constitution of 1982 provides several formulas for amendments, depending on the nature of the amendment in question.[69] Because the Meech Lake Accord required the consent of the ten provinces, when Manitoba and Newfoundland failed to approve it before the deadline of 23 June 1990, it was doomed.

This was a bitter outcome for Quebecers who sought reconciliation with the rest of Canada and for the federal government of Prime Minister Brian Mulroney, himself a Quebecer, who had made Meech Lake a centerpiece of his administration. The bitterness was compounded by the fact that when the accord was originally drafted in 1987, the ten premiers had approved it, but political changes between the drafting of the accord and the deadline for its approval had kept the legislatures of Manitoba and Newfoundland from granting their consent.

One of the major events leading to the accord's defeat focused on Quebec's language law, which forbade the use of any language but French on commercial signs. On 15 December 1988, the Supreme Court of Canada struck down this law on the grounds that it violated the Canadian Charter of Rights and Freedoms, which was part of the patriated Constitution of 1982. Quebec Premier Robert Bourassa retaliated by successfully urging the National Assembly—as Quebecers significantly call their provincial legislature—to invoke the remarkable "notwithstanding" clause of the Constitution to restore the key provisions of the law voided by the Supreme Court. The notwithstanding clause appears in section 33 of the Constitution: "Parliament or the legislature of a province may expressly declare in an Act of Parliament or of the legislature, as the case may be, that the Act or a provision thereof shall operate notwithstanding a provision included in section 2 or sections 7 to 15 of this Charter."

This means just what it says. It gives Parliament and each provincial legislature the authority to pass laws that violate certain sections of the Charter of Rights and Freedoms touching on such important matters as "freedom of conscience and religion," "freedom of thought, belief, opinion and expression," "the right to be secure against unreasonable search or seizure," and so forth. A statute based on the notwithstanding clause remains in effect for five years, when it can be renewed for another five years.

Bourassa's decision to invoke the notwithstanding clause to reinstate the essential provisions of Quebec's odious language law ignited a firestorm of protest throughout anglophone Canada. Premier Gary Filmon of Manitoba withdrew his support for Meech Lake, thereby beginning the process that eventually unraveled the fragile consensus supporting the accord. Things went from bad to worse when, in 1992, Prime Minister Mulroney's Conservative government sponsored a disastrous nationwide referendum on the Charlottetown Accord, which tried in vain to bridge the ever-widening gap between Quebec and the rest of Canada.

Jean Chrétien's Liberal government came into office in 1993 with the profound conviction that "it was time for a moratorium on constitutional discussions." The new policy was that federal-provincial relations in general and relations with Quebec in particular "could be dealt with by administrative arrangements outside the Constitution."[70] Hence, when the Quebec referendum on independence was narrowly defeated in October 1995, Chrétien was ready with his comment on "good, solid administration" as the road to constitutional salvation. Chrétien's commitment to administrative solutions to constitutional problems was not an empty slogan; it has been a matter of high priority throughout his years as prime minster. He frequently speaks—indeed, boasts—of his "step-by-step" approach to reforming and redefining ever so gradually the nature of Canadian federalism with regard to Quebec and to the other provinces as well.

Since the wake-up call Chrétien's government received in the 1995 referendum, his government has developed a two-pronged attack, sometimes called Plan A and Plan B. Plan A, avoiding specific constitutional questions in favor of administrative reform, folds the Quebec question into broader questions of federalism throughout Canada. Nearly all the reforms aim in one way or another at "devolving" upon the provinces powers hitherto exercised in whole or in part by Ottawa. This strategy masks the salience of the Quebec issue while exploiting the advantage of linking the perennial cry from Quebec for greater provincial autonomy to the interests of other provinces desiring greater autonomy for themselves—notably wealthy ones controlled by political conservatives, like Alberta and Ontario. Plan B favors a policy of tough love intended to specify the precise rules Quebec must follow in any future referendum and to bring home to Quebecers the severe economic and political consequences that would follow the establishment of Quebec as a sovereign state.

A good example of Plan A emerged in the immediate aftermath of the 1995 referendum when the cabinet committee on national unity, chaired by Treasury

Board president Marcel Massé, presented the prime minister with a "multi-step package of nonconstitutional changes" that included a proposal enabling the provinces to "exercise exclusive control over such areas as mining and forestry." The plan also envisaged granting the provinces "the right to work with Ottawa to set up national standards for social programs such as medicare."[71] Although Massé's plan was not released to the public, *Maclean's* confidently relied on insiders to report additional details. From a public administration perspective, it is interesting to note that Marcel Massé reportedly relied on the European Union's "subsidiarity rule" to determine which policy areas could be most appropriately turned over to the provinces and "consulted all fifteen members to devise his criteria for efficiency." With careful attention to administrative detail, the report provided that "Ottawa is prepared to relinquish its powers over forestry to the provinces, but it will continue its research into such problems as the spruce budworm control because it does not make sense for individual provinces to spend money on identical work."[72]

The link between minute details of forest management and the Quebec constitutional crisis recalls the debate in 1865 linking the high politics of Confederation to the mundane price of shipping a barrel of flour. This time around, the spruce budworm replaced the Intercolonial Railway.[73]

The Speech from the Throne delivered on 27 February 1996 confirmed the accuracy of *Maclean's* report on the government's plan to turn over significant powers to the provinces. (The Speech from the Throne is read by the governor-general of Canada as the queen's representative, but it is written by the government of the day to announce its policies for the coming year.) In a section of the text entitled "A Modern and United Country," the governor-general stated that the "government is prepared to withdraw from its functions in such areas as labor market training, forestry, mining, and recreation, that are more appropriately the responsibility of others, including provincial governments, local authorities or the private sector."[74] In the same section, the government pledged that "it will not use its spending power to create new shared-cost programs in areas of exclusive provincial jurisdiction without the consent of a majority of the provinces."[75] It then proposed the following major concession: "Any new program will be designed so that non-participating provinces will be compensated, provided they establish equivalent or comparable initiatives."[76] Although no mention was made of Quebec explicitly, this initiative closely followed an administrative reform that province had favored for years. In still another initiative, the Chrétien government promised to "propose to the provinces a much strengthened process to work in partnership, focusing on such priorities as food inspection, environmental management, social housing, tourism, and freshwater fish habitat."[77]

Clearly Plan A was under way. Although the Quebec crisis formed the background for this devolution of power to the provinces, it was artfully hidden behind the rhetoric of modernizing Canada to meet the challenges of the twenty-first century. Significantly, however, the Speech from the Throne acknowledged that "this modernization must be respectful of our diversity [read Quebec] and based on partnership and dialogue." No less significant was the closing paragraph of this section, which offered a word of welcome to the "new government of Quebec"—headed by the staunch sovereigntist Lucien Bouchard—and its pledge to "work in collaboration with the Government of Quebec and all provincial governments on an agenda of economic renewal and job creation."[78] The juxtaposition of Quebec and "all provincial governments" clearly implied the government's recognition of Quebec's special status as something other than merely one province among nine others.

Throughout the latter half of the 1990s, the Chrétien government has continued to follow its plan of administrative reform through the devolution of some powers to the provinces and the sharing of other powers with them. Particularly significant have been the initiatives on environmental affairs, manpower and training, and "social policy"—a catchall term that includes such matters as health care, unemployment insurance, seasonal workers, the disabled, child poverty, postsecondary education, and youth employment. Addressing an international conference on federalism in 1999, Intergovernmental Affairs minister Stéphane Dion stressed the importance of "senior bureaucrats" in negotiating these agreements.[79]

While offering the carrot of Plan A, the Chrétien government did not neglect the stick of Plan B, the tough love policy intended to clarify the rules for any possible secession efforts by Quebec in the future and to remind Quebecers of the serious consequences of secession. The most important action in support of Plan B was the government's controversial decision to submit a "reference" to the Supreme Court of Canada to determine the constitutional principles governing any future referenda on secession.[80] The government's reference posed three questions for the justices:

1. Under the Constitution of Canada, can the National Assembly, legislature or government of Quebec effect the secession of Quebec from Canada unilaterally?
2. Does international law give the National Assembly, legislature or government of Quebec the right to effect the secession of Quebec from Canada unilaterally? In this regard, is there a right to self-determination under international law that would give the National Assembly, legislature or government of Quebec the right to effect the secession of Quebec from Canada unilaterally?
3. In the event of a conflict between domestic and international law on the right of the National Assembly, legislature or government of Quebec to effect the secession of Quebec from Canada unilaterally, which would take precedence in Canada?[81]

Reduced to simpler terms, the first two questions asked if either Canadian or international law permits Quebec to secede from Canada unilaterally. The answer from the nine-judge court was a unanimous no, and therefore there was no need for the court to address the third question as to which law—Canadian or international—would take precedence in the event of a conflict between them. As might be expected, the importance and complexity of the questions required the court to explain its decision fully. Although Quebec had no right to secede unilaterally, this finding was not the end of the matter. In a careful and remarkably thoughtful analysis, the court concluded that "a clear majority vote in Quebec on a clear question in favor of secession would confer legitimacy on the initiative which all of the other participants in Confederation would have to recognize."[82] That is, the federal government and the other provinces would be obliged to enter into negotiations with Quebec over "the potential act of secession as well as its possible terms should in fact secession proceed."[83]

Thus, the Supreme Court held that, in principle, Canada, unlike the American Republic, is divisible, provided a "clear majority" of Quebecers votes in favor of secession on a "clear question." This, of course, was a major victory for the Quebec sovereigntists. The court's emphasis, however, on the clarity of both the question posed and the majority supporting it favored the federalists. They had argued that the only reason so many Quebecers had voted yes in the 1995 referendum was that the Quebec government had cynically confused them with a needlessly complex question. Polls taken in Quebec over the years showed that the majority of Quebecers would always vote against a referendum stating the question in stark terms of whether the voter wanted Quebec to remain within Canada or to leave it. Further, the reference to a "clear majority" suggested that 50 percent of the voters plus 1 might not suffice to carry the day for secession— an idea utterly anathema to most Quebecers, including those who favored remaining in Canada. Wisely, the court left it to the political authorities to determine just when a question and a majority were clear.

Also left to the political authorities was the staggering task of negotiating the precise terms of secession should a clear majority of Quebecers ever vote yes on a clear question in favor of secession. Surely the court belabored the obvious by adding that "no one suggests that it would be an easy set of negotiations."[84] Should such negotiations ever come to pass, the negotiators would be faced with such seemingly intractable issues as the borders of Quebec, the rights of aboriginal peoples within these borders, the rights of English-speaking Quebecers who wish to retain their Canadian citizenship, the apportionment of the national debt—to say nothing of such mundane matters as the new currency, passports, and retirement benefits for federal military and civilian personnel. The court did not exaggerate when it said, "The devil would be in the details."[85] Not only would the devil be there, but so, perforce, would public administrators with the expertise they bring to such questions. The court recognized that in such negotiations there "would be no conclusions predetermined by law on any issue."[86] The field would be open for a judicious blending of statesmanlike wisdom and technical administrative expertise. In such high matters of state, public administration does not simply apply the law. It shapes it.

Part I of this book has provided abundant empirical evidence to support the constitutional-administrative nexus so conspicuously absent in even the best of the New Public Management literature. I have grounded my argument in space (three countries) and time (three centuries) as well as in a variety of constitutional orders. For example, I have examined one country with separation of powers, France, and two without, the United Kingdom and Canada. I have also examined two unitary states, France and the United Kingdom, and one federal regime, Canada. Part II extends my argument to the United States, a country endowed with a constitutional foundation based on both federalism and separation of powers as well as on a deep commitment to the defense of individual rights. At first it might seem that the decentralizing tendencies of federalism and separation of powers combined with the individualism of a rights-driven society would not provide a fertile field for administrative institutions to take root and flourish. In the chapters that follow on American separation of powers, rights, and federalism, I shall show that the constitutional-administrative nexus we have seen in France, the United Kingdom, and Canada has trumped a hostile institutional environment and played a central role in the constitutional drama of the United States.

PART II
The Constitution of the United States

4

Separation of Powers

In the preface to this book I cited James Q. Wilson's sage observation that persons interested in learning about American bureaucracy would do well to begin with James Madison's brilliant discussion of separation of powers in *Federalist* no. 51.[1] This is sound advice, not only because separation of powers is the fundamental organizing principle of the American political order but also because it is the principal structural element in the preservation of American liberty as manifested in this country's commitment to individual rights and federalism. These three characteristics define the American constitutional experience, and so, to pursue the purpose of this book, in the next three chapters I shall examine the importance of administration, first, in expressing concretely the principle of separation of powers; then in defending and, alas, at times impinging upon individual rights; and finally, in following the vagaries of federalism.

AN OVERVIEW

To grasp the pervasive character of separation of powers in public administration, let us consider its impact in four very different administrative settings: constitutional texts, the judicial image of administration, administrative theory and practice, and the fascinating institution of the federal magistrate.

Constitutional Texts

We have it on no less an authority than Publius himself that the "administration of government . . . falls peculiarly within the province of the executive department." And yet the text of the Constitution vests some traditionally executive powers dealing with administration in Congress rather than in the president. For example, Article 2, section 2, states that all offices must be created "by law," i.e., by Congress, thereby transferring to the legislature a power that had been vested in the Crown prior to the Revolution. Although Congress cannot appoint officers of the executive branch, it can determine who the appointing authority will be for "inferior officers" whose form of appointment is not stated in the Constitution itself: "But the Congress may by law vest the Appointment of such inferior Officers, as they think proper, in the President alone, in the Courts of Law, or in the Heads of Departments."[2] The explicit constitutional power of Congress to vest the appointing power in "the Courts of Law" was the basis of Kenneth Starr's appointment as independent counsel, which eventually led to the impeachment of President Bill Clinton. These texts have given Congress a constitutional basis for the aggressive role it has always taken in investigating and, in some cases, in managing the activities of the executive departments.

Presidents and Congress have jousted over the limits of their respective powers from the earliest days of the Republic. The most important battlefield in this perennial struggle is the seemingly straightforward statement at the very beginning of Article 2: "The executive Power shall be vested in a President of the United States of America." This language contrasts markedly with the opening words of Article 1: "All legislative powers herein granted shall be vested in a Congress of the United States, which shall consist of a Senate and House of Representatives." Champions of a strong executive have always emphasized the absence of the qualifying words "herein granted" in Article 2. This absence, they maintain, means that *the* executive power (presumably all of it) is vested in the president. Congress possesses all those legislative powers that are granted in the Constitution itself, but it does not possess all legislative power. That is, there are many areas of life in which Congress may not legislate; it may legislate only in those areas in which the Constitution permits it to do so. To be sure, Congress possesses all legislative powers in the sense that other institutions created by the Constitution have no explicit authorization to legislate. But the legislative powers of Congress are confined to the written document.

The practical import of these exegetical niceties is that they serve as a launching pad for a constitutional argument in support of inherent executive powers that are not confined by the text of the Constitution. This argument sees in the executive power clause a positive grant of power to the president to do whatever any political executive can do. Activist presidents, like Andrew Jackson, Abraham Lincoln, and Theodore Roosevelt, made skillful use of this argument. Theodore Roosevelt, for example, used this clause to support the robust theory of presidential power that led him to conclude that "it was not only [the president's] right but his duty to do anything that the needs of the nation demanded unless such action was forbidden by the Constitution or by the laws."[3]

Critics of presidential power have responded in a variety of ways. One line of argument admits that the president does indeed possess all executive power without qualification, but it maintains that this does not justify the far-reaching conclusions of presidential apologists. What is executive power, they ask. It is simply the power to execute law. The president may execute only that which the Congress has legislated. It was perfectly logical for the framers to omit the "herein granted" qualification from the grant of the executive power to the president, because, having provided that Congress has only those legislative powers "herein granted," there was no need to repeat the same language in the article establishing the executive. Executive power cannot outstrip legislative power, for there would be nothing for the executive to execute. Hence the limitations on the scope of congressional power necessarily encumber the executive power of the president as well.

This argument is reinforced by explicit constitutional grants of power to the president to command the armed forces of the nation, to grant reprieves and pardons, to share in the power to make treaties and to appoint officers, to convene either or both houses of Congress, to receive ambassadors, and so forth. The fact that these powers are explicitly granted in the Constitution undercuts the argument that the executive power clause confers inherent executive powers on the president. If the executive power clause did this, what would be the purpose of spelling out all these other powers that are traditionally associated with the executive? These additional powers would be redundant and could be found in the teeming womb of the executive power clause. Clearly, the argument goes, the framers intended that the executive power clause should give the president nothing more than the power to execute laws passed by Congress. Whatever other powers he might possess are explicitly stated in Article 2. The president has no powers other than the sum of the powers resulting from these two sources.

Another argument against inherent executive power in the first section of Article 2 draws from sections 2, 3, and 4 of the same article. Here the argument differs from the preceding considerations, which conceded that the executive power clause does indeed grant complete executive power to the president. Having made this concession, the thrust of that argument was to limit the scope of executive power by confining the meaning of the word to executing the will of the Congress and thereby to deny any additional, inherent powers to the president. The argument here maintains that the other sections of Article 2 cannot be reconciled with the claim that the executive power clause gives *all* executive power to the president—no matter how narrowly one defines executive power.

The most important constitutional clause in support of this position states that the president "shall take care that the laws be faithfully executed, and shall commission all the officers of the United States." This language makes it rather clear that the president himself is not to execute the laws but is to see to it that others do so; and to assist him in doing just this, the Constitution empowers the president to commission officers. These constitutional provisions are followed immediately by the impeachment clauses, which clearly describe the president as a legally accountable officer who "presides" (as a *president* should) over an executive establishment that carries out the laws mandated by Congress.

This point is reinforced by the explicit constitutional provision for "executive departments," each of which will be headed by a single "principal officer." This language casts a shadow over the interpretation of the executive power clause that maintains that the framers meant to give *the* executive power (i.e., all of it) to the president alone. Surely a constitutional provision for a principal officer in each of the several executive departments implies that these high officials hold some sort of executive power in their own right. But if they hold any executive power at all, the president cannot hold all of it.

These considerations will suffice to support the point that at the time of the founding of the Republic, there was considerable ambiguity and confusion over the meaning of executive power. This ambiguity and confusion came from the framers' unresolved tension in desiring an executive that was strong and independent, but not too strong and independent. Not surprisingly, this ambiguity and confusion spilled over into the text of the Constitution itself and is still with us today.[4]

Judicializing Administration

In sharp contrast to the French Council of State, from which there is no appeal to the ordinary courts, is the Anglo-American practice where, as Dicey maintained, the principle of the rule of law requires judicial review of agency action. In the United States, this means review by a court created under Article 3 of the Constitution, which vests "the judicial Power of the United States . . . in one Supreme Court and in such inferior courts as the Congress may from time to time ordain and establish." Not surprisingly, when courts review agency action, they tend to impose judicial standards on administrators, especially those involved in adjudicating disputes between their agency and disgruntled citizens. This tendency is often called the "judicialization" of administration, a process by which courts tend to shape administrative agencies in their own image and likeness.

A good example of this tendency occurred in the famous *Morgan* litigation in which the same parties, Morgan, a Kansas City Stockyard broker, and the United States Department of Agriculture (USDA), appeared four times before the Supreme Court between 1936 and 1941.[5] The case involved Morgan's challenge to the procedure followed by the secretary of agriculture in issuing a commodity rate order, i.e., an order "fixing the maximum rates to be charged by market agencies for buying and selling livestock at the Kansas City Stock Yards."[6]

The secretary had issued the commodity rate order under the Packers and Stockyards Act of 1921, which provided that such orders could be issued only after a "full hearing." The plaintiffs alleged that the secretary of agriculture, the official decision maker named in the statute, "had not personally heard or read any of the evidence presented at any hearing in connection with the proceeding" and that therefore they had not received the "full hearing" the statute required.[7] The federal district court in Kansas City dismissed this complaint, but the

Supreme Court reversed, holding that if the allegations were true, the full hearing had not been granted and the commodity rate order would therefore be illegal. Consequently, the case was remanded to the federal district court in Kansas City to determine the extent to which the secretary of agriculture was familiar with the evidence supporting the order he had issued.

Chief Justice Charles Evans Hughes delivered the opinion of the Court in which he used a pithy sentence that has become a consecrated phrase in the literature: "The one who decides must hear."[8] He supported this aphorism by stating explicitly that the obligation for the administrator to hear the evidence supporting his decision is "a duty akin to that of a judge."[9] It would be absurd for one judge to hear the evidence and another one to decide the outcome; the same holds for the administrative process. The statutorily designated decision maker, in this case the secretary of agriculture, cannot make a decision on evidence heard and read by his subordinates but not by the secretary himself.

Although "the one who decides must hear" is often cited as a classic example of judicializing administration, Chief Justice Hughes's opinion put the maxim in a broader context. He added that this standard "does not preclude practicable administrative procedure in obtaining the aid of assistants in the department." The secretary of agriculture may make use of a hearing examiner and may rely on "competent subordinates" to sift and analyze the evidence. "The requirements are not technical. But there must be a hearing in a substantial sense." This means that "the officer who makes the determinations must consider and approve the evidence which justifies them."[10] This pragmatic qualification of the stern rule that the one who decides must hear was absolutely crucial for the survival of the administrative state. Interpreted literally, the judicial maxim would make it impossible for the Department of Agriculture or any other executive department to conduct its affairs. There are not enough days in the year to permit the secretary of agriculture to hear all the evidence supporting the myriad decisions issued formally over his signature.

Upon remand, the district court directed interrogatories to the secretary, which he answered. Although he had neither heard the oral argument nor read the entire record, which exceeded ten thousand pages, he assured the court that he had studied the briefs, conferred with knowledgeable subordinates, and "dipped into" the bulky record "from time to time to get its drift." This satisfied the district court and, upon appeal, the Supreme Court agreed. On this second round, however, the Supreme Court found another flaw that led to the ruling that the USDA's procedure still fell short of a full hearing. This time the problem was that the secretary's subordinates had failed to give plaintiffs notice of the proposed findings and recommendations they had forwarded to the secretary. This deprived the plaintiffs of "a reasonable opportunity to know the claims of the opposing party and to meet them."[11] Relying explicitly on the judicial analogy, Chief Justice Hughes held that when Congress required a full hearing, it had judicial standards in mind—"not in any technical sense but with respect to those fundamental requirements of fairness which are of the essence of due process in a proceeding of a judicial nature."[12] Lest there be any doubt of the Court's effort to judicialize the administrative process, Chief Justice Hughes closed his opinion (written in 1938 in the midst of the New Deal), with this solemn warning: "If these multiplying agencies deemed to be necessary in our complex society are to serve the purposes for which they are created and endowed with vast powers, they must accredit themselves by acting in accordance with the cherished judicial tradition embodying the basic concepts of fair play."[13]

The third *Morgan* appearance before the Supreme Court raised no issues relevant here, but *Morgan IV* revisited the judicialization issue from a very different angle. Decided in 1941, *Morgan IV* was heard by a Supreme Court dominated by appointees of President Franklin Roosevelt, who were much more favorably disposed toward the administrative state. One of the significant events in the prolonged *Morgan* litigation in the federal district court in Kansas City "was the appearance in person of the Secretary who was questioned at length regarding the process by which he reached his conclusions."[14] The precise issue in *Morgan IV* concerned the distribution of funds impounded during the litigation, which the Court resolved in favor of the government. For our purposes, however, the important aspect of the case was a gratuitous comment in Justice Felix Frankfurter's opinion of the Court. After having settled the legal issue, Frankfurter reached out to express his disapproval of the district court's decision to depose the secretary of agriculture over the government's objection. Maintaining that "it was not the function of the court to probe the mental processes of the Secretary," Frankfurter continued:

> But the short of the business is that the Secretary should never have been subjected to this examination. The proceeding before the Secretary "has a quality resembling that of a judicial proceeding." Such an examination of judge would be destructive of judicial responsibility. . . . Just as a judge cannot be subjected to such a scrutiny, . . . so the integrity of the administrative process must be respected. . . . It will bear repeating that although the administrative process has had a different development and pursues somewhat different ways from those of courts, they are to be deemed collaborative instrumentalities of justice and the appropriate independence of each should be respected by the other.[15]

Here is an eloquent defense of the administrative process based on its judicialization. Thus the judiciary's efforts to shape the administrative process in its own image and likeness is a two-edged sword. It can restrain, structure, and refine administrative power when it says the one who decides must hear; but it can also uphold the "appropriate independence," expertise, and integrity of agencies when it asserts that courts must not probe the mental processes of the administrator. Wisely, the Court avoided the hard question of just how to put these two standards together. How can a court know that the one who decided really did hear (or at least read) the evidence, if it does not probe the mental processes of the administrator?

Administrative Theory and Practice

Administrative theory is presently one of the most intellectually engaging sub-fields in public administration. It boasts an energetic national association, the Public Administration Theory Network, with its own refereed journal and an annual national conference. Its members analyze the broader implications of such current and traditional topics as leadership, organizations, privatization, downsizing, the public-private divide, and the new public management. Since separation of powers pervades public administration, it is not surprising to find it taking its rightful place in the theoretical literature as well. The most important recent contribution to this literature is David Rosenbloom's argument that American administration should be looked upon as an *extension* of the *legislative* power of Congress rather than as simply an *agent* of the executive.[16] Rosenbloom suggests that a long string of congressional enactments, starting with the frequently amended Administrative Procedure Act of 1946, views administrative agencies as "almost seamless extensions of the legislature for supplementing legislation through rulemaking."[17] As extensions of Congress, the agencies are "fused to the legislature" and "exercise its core constitutional responsibility—legislation."[18]

The legislative character of administration becomes manifest in the participation, transparency, accountability, and protection of individual rights that infuse the American administrative process through such statutes as the Administrative Procedure Act, the Federal Advisory Committee Act, the Negotiated Rulemaking Act, and the Small Business Regulatory Fairness Enforcement Act, which encourage participation in rulemaking; the Freedom of Information Act and the Government in the Sunshine Act, which promote transparency; the Federal Tort Claims Act, which enhances accountability; and the Privacy Act and the adjudication sections of the Administrative Procedure Act, which protect individual rights. These attributes—especially participation, transparency, and accountability—are legislative characteristics that set a tone quite different from efficiency, effectiveness, and economy, the traditional hallmarks of administrative orthodoxy. The latter dwell more easily in the precincts of the executive, where vigor, secrecy, and dispatch hold sway.

Rosenbloom puts particular emphasis on the year 1946 when Congress passed not only the Administrative Procedure Act but also the Legislative Reorganization Act, the Federal Tort Claims Act, and the Employment Act. This was no coincidence. World War II had postponed Congress's initial efforts in 1940 and 1941 to redefine its constitutional role vis-à-vis the burgeoning administrative state of the New Deal. Recognizing that the administrative state with its dominant executive was here to stay, Congress sought to penetrate the bureau-

cracy with its "legislative values of representation, participation and open information."[19] Congressional efforts along these lines expressed not only its traditional competition with the executive over the scope of institutional powers but
also, as Rosenbloom puts it, the "core values" of the legislature.[20]

Rosenbloom's argument calls to mind the British practice of using the terms
"secondary legislation" and "legislative instruments" to describe what Americans call "rules and regulations." The principle of separation of powers precludes
our adopting the British nomenclature, but this should not blind us to the fact that
American public administration is, to a considerable extent, legislative activity.

To reduce the administrative theory of separation of powers to practice, we
can do no better than to examine the Government Performance and Results Act
(GPRA) of 1993. Strongly influenced by new public management ideas, Vice-
President Gore's National Performance Review, and the well-known management best-seller, *Reinventing Government,*[21] the GPRA enacts into law a
performance-based management and budget system. Its centerpiece is a bold
innovation requiring a gradual phasing in of a series of consultations between
Congress and the agencies in the executive branch of government as the latter
develop "strategic plans," "annual performance plans," and "annual performance
results," pursuant to the statute. Although already well under way, the new system has had more than its share of growing pains, and this, despite having been
created by a Democratic Congress in 1993 and warmly embraced by the Republicans, who gained control of Congress in the 1994 elections. Not even the enthu-
siastic support of President Bush in 2001 could mask the GPRA's problems,
which are more deeply rooted in the abiding institutional conflicts between the
executive and the legislature than in strictly partisan strife.

Knowledgeable observers have seriously doubted that the GPRA would
meet all its statutorily imposed deadlines. If its timetable is too optimistic, it is
only because the statute itself is so bold. By law it requires nothing less than
close cooperation between executive branch agencies and congressional subcommittees, first in developing goals and plans and then in evaluating performance measured against these same goals and plans. This process is tightly
integrated into the budgetary processes. If the GPRA realizes its considerable
potential, it will do yeoman work in bringing the venerable constitutional principle of separation of powers into the twenty-first century. As a practical matter,
the most serious work goes on in the trenches, where career civil servants from
the executive branch bargain and negotiate with congressional staffers. The final
product, of course, requires the blessing of their political masters—key representatives and senators on the one hand, and the presidentially appointed heads
of the executive departments on the other. The act promises to enable congressional committees and subcommittees to operationalize such vague statutory language as the "public interest" and "to the extent feasible" by interacting directly
with agency personnel as they formulate strategic plans to carry out their legislative mandates.

For our purposes, however, the cloud on the GPRA horizon is that those individuals who are most familiar with its inner workings seem oblivious of the constitutional dimensions of what they are about. Consider, for example, a fine symposium on the GPRA presented in a recent issue of the *Public Manager*.[22] Here one finds brief but insightful articles from seasoned experts in such agencies as the Office of Management and Budget, the General Accounting Office, the Office of Personnel Management, and the Department of the Treasury. Their combined efforts provide an invaluable source for practitioners and academics interested in following the GPRA's intricacies. Unfortunately, however, neither the word *Constitution* nor the expression *separation of powers* appears in the thirty-eight double-columned pages devoted to the symposium. This strikes me as a "forest and trees" problem of the first order. The dazzling managerial potential of the GPRA seems to have blinded these experts to its constitutional meaning. Indeed, if viewed as more than simply a tool of public management, the GPRA offers conscientious civil servants and congressional staffers a high-minded opportunity to operationalize their oath of office.

The *Public Manager* was not alone in ignoring the GPRA's constitutional dimension. A comprehensive study of the act, supplemented with crucial documentation, was undertaken by the prestigious National Academy of Public Administration (NAPA).[23] Herein readers find but one reference to the Constitution in the thirty-page report and six-page executive summary. The report was excellent as far as it went, but its failure to address constitutional issues was a serious omission. For example, the study would have been considerably strengthened if it had grounded its references to inspectors general and the General Accounting Office in the constitutional history of these institutions. Both of them were established to address separation of powers problems. An awareness of their backgrounds might have prompted the authors of the report to place the GPRA in a tradition of constitutionally based administrative reform. More specifically, the favorable comments on the GPRA's training efforts for executive and legislative personnel might have been strengthened by a suggestion that career personnel and congressional staffers receive their training together instead of separately, as is now the case. To make such a suggestion, however, one must first be schooled to think of the GPRA in constitutional terms. To invite practicing administrators to do just this contributes directly to the purpose of this book.

The NAPA report did not entirely ignore the Constitution. The last page admonishes Congress "to respect the constitutional boundaries between it and the executive agencies."[24] This is sound advice and accurately reflects the well-founded fear of executive branch personnel of being micromanaged by Congress. The report might have presented the GPRA in a more evenhanded fashion, however, if it had also reminded executive branch personnel of the textually explicit constitutional language inviting Congress to play a vigorous role in overseeing administration. I refer to the provisions in Article 2, section 2, stating that federal offices can be created only "by law," i.e., by Congress, and that Congress has the

constitutional authority to decide whether the power to appoint "inferior officers" will be vested in the president with the advice and consent of the Senate,
"in the President alone, in the Courts of Law or in the Heads of Departments."

Attention to such matters might give those implementing the GPRA a
grander vision of their work. If successful, the act could go a long way toward
sparing the United States the political trauma of another government shutdown
and threats thereof grounded in inexcusable abuses of separation of powers both
by Congress and the president.

Federal Magistrate Judges

Federal magistrate judges embody an interesting institutional expression of the
principle of separation of powers. If one sees them at work in a federal courtroom,
one would have trouble explaining how they differ in any way from ordinary federal judges in any federal district court. They wear black robes. The audience is
told to rise upon their arrival and departure. Counsel respectfully address them as
"your honor," and the magistrate judges, following judicial tradition, refer to
themselves as "the court." The courtrooms in which they preside have all the customary trappings—the flag, a clerk, security officers, and that intangible aura of
dignity one expects in a federal courtroom. To the untrained eye, there is no difference between a magistrate judge and an Article 3 judge, i.e., a judge exercising "the judicial power of the United States" mentioned at the beginning of that
article and enjoying the constitutional protections specified therein.

Magistrate judges exercise "the judicial power of the United States" insofar
as they are authorized by Congress to preside over any federal civil trial and federal criminal trials for misdemeanors but not for felonies.[25] The litigants, however, must consent to having their cases heard by a magistrate judge rather than
by an Article 3 judge.[26] This consent is usually given because of the time litigants
can save and the excellent reputation of the magistrate judges.[27]

The most important differences between magistrate judges and Article 3
judges concern appointment and removal. Article 3 judges are appointed by the
president by and with the advice and consent of the Senate, and they hold office
during "good behavior," which means they can be removed only by impeachment by the House of Representatives and conviction by the Senate. Magistrate
judges are appointed by federal district judges to eight-year renewable terms and
can be removed by the judges of the court where they serve before the expiration
of their term but "only for incompetence, misconduct, neglect of duty or physical or mental disability."[28]

Constitutional questions have been raised about magistrate judges exercising judicial power without the constitutional protections enjoyed by Article 3
judges. Congress gave careful attention to this matter when it debated the Federal Magistrate Act of 1968 and found three safeguards sufficient to lay to rest
any constitutional qualms: the parties' right to a full and automatic appeal to an

Article 3 judge is preserved under the legislation; the magistrate acts as an adjunct under the supervision of the Article 3 district court; and the parties freely consent to a magistrate's jurisdiction over their case by specifically waiving their statutory right to a trial by an Article 3 district court judge in the first instance.[29]

The fundamental basis for the institution of the magistrate judge looks more to practice than to doctrine. Federal judges have always needed help in managing their crowded dockets. This is especially true today because of Congress's decision in recent years to criminalize such serious social problems as drug abuse, gun control, and "deadbeat dads." In many jurisdictions federal district judges have been so overwhelmed with felony cases, which they alone can hear, that they have turned over nearly all their civil cases to the magistrate judges.

The need for magistrate judges, however, is not a recent development. In 1793 Congress authorized federal circuit courts to appoint "discreet persons learned in the law" to handle matters relating to bail in federal criminal cases. In 1817 these discreet persons came to be known as "commissioners," and their authority gradually expanded until Congress renamed them "magistrates" in 1968 and heightened their role within the judicial system. In 1990, to the chagrin of some Article 3 judges, their title was upgraded to magistrate judge "to reflect more accurately the responsibilities and duties of the office."[30] This recognition was reinforced by the current practice of appeals from magistrate judges' decisions going directly to a federal court of appeals instead of to the district court in which the magistrate judge sits, as had been the practice. This suggests a departure from the hierarchical notion of the magistrate judge as simply the subordinate of Article 3 judges.

For our purposes, the most interesting aspect of magistrate judges is that their office, though clearly a judicial one, has often been justified on the same grounds customarily invoked to support the creation of administrative agencies. For example, Peter McCabe begins his frequently cited article, "The Federal Magistrate Act of 1979," with the assertion that the legislation in question "provides a method for litigants to dispose of their cases voluntarily in a less formal, less expensive, and less time-consuming manner."[31] Later he states that the Magistrates Act was intended "to improve access to the federal courts . . . by giving additional flexibility to the courts and to the litigants to dispose of cases expeditiously." The same legislation, he writes, will "decrease the expense of litigation and improve the quality of the federal judiciary."[32] With a little historical imagination, one might think McCabe had borrowed a page from the Progressive reformers of the early twentieth century, who used similar language to support the case for independent regulatory commissions as expeditious alternatives to the ordinary courts; they promised improved public service that was cheaper, faster, less formal, and more flexible than what the ordinary courts and traditional executive departments could offer.

McCabe is not alone in borrowing the traditional language of administrative reform. Philip Pro and Thomas Hnatowski describe the "mission of the magis-

trate judges system" as one of providing "the federal district courts with supportive and flexible supplemental judicial resources." It will thereby improve
"public access to the courts, promoting prompt and efficient case resolution and
preserving scarce Article 3 resources."[33] For an administrative translation, consider efficiency, economy, and effectiveness.

Administrative agencies have often been justified on the grounds of their
specialized expertise, which contrasts with the broad range of activities legislators and judges must necessarily address. A major study of the magistrates undertaken by the Federal Judicial Center identifies one of the principal roles they play
as that of "specialists who become experts in a demanding and ongoing area of
the docket."[34] An earlier study by the Federal Judicial Center had identified
social security cases and prison petitions as areas in which magistrates had
become highly specialized.[35] Once again, one sees the link between magistrate
judges who are clearly judicial officers and traditional public administration.

The link to public administration extends to the Article 3 judges who super-
vise the magistrate judges. The Federal Magistrates Act of 1968 gave the task of
administering the magistrate system to the Judicial Conference of the United
States, a body composed of judges selected from every circuit and presided over
by the chief justice of the United States. Its duties include the clearly administrative responsibility of "determining the number of magistrates, as well as the
type, location, and salary of each magistrate position."[36] Although the Administrative Office of the U.S. Courts handles most of the day-to-day routine matters
concerning magistrate judges, the duties of the Judicial Conference provide a
clear example of federal judges exercising significant administrative responsibilities. When these responsibilities are linked to those of the Article 3 judges, who
exercise the administrative responsibility of appointing magistrate judges and
assigning their precise tasks for the district courts in which they serve, we can
readily see why the office of magistrate judge highlights the close connection
between judicial and administrative behavior that enriches our awareness of
administration as constitutional practice.

DELEGATION

When Congress delegates legislative authority to the president, the constitutional
issue centers on how closely the president and Congress may cooperate without
violating the principle of separation of powers. On rare occasions the Supreme
Court has found the cooperation excessive. Delegation presents a further problem when Congress grants authority not to the president but to executive departments, independent regulatory agencies, or to the motley assortment of admin-
istrations, offices, and corporations that are neither executive departments nor
independent agencies. Presidents interested in controlling delegated powers of
this sort must rely on influence and persuasion rather than on command. They

must spend political capital if they care about how these delegated powers affect public policy.[37]

Congressional Delegation of Legislative Authority

The constitutional foundation for congressional delegation of legislative authority comes from the necessary and proper clause of Article 1, section 8. This section enumerates the various powers of Congress (to borrow money, to regulate commerce, to provide and maintain a navy) and concludes by providing that Congress has the power "to make all Laws which shall be necessary and proper for carrying into execution the foregoing powers, and all other powers vested by this Constitution in the government of the United States, or in any department or officer thereof."

The Supreme Court has held that, because of this clause, any specific power granted to Congress "implies a power of delegation of authority under it sufficient to effect its purposes."[38] Commentators traditionally distinguish two types of delegation: interstitial administrative action and contingent legislation. The Supreme Court upheld both forms of congressional delegation during the era of Chief Justice John Marshall (1801–1835).

Interstitial administrative action allows Congress to delegate authority to fill in the gaps in legislation that have not been specifically provided for. In 1825 the Supreme Court upheld a congressional delegation of authority to the Court itself that enabled the justices to use their own discretion to modify procedural rules established by Congress for the federal judiciary. In upholding this delegation of legislative authority to the judiciary, Chief Justice Marshall said, "A federal provision may be made, and power given to those who are to act under such general provisions to fill up the details."[39]

Contingent legislation is congressional action that permits a statute to take effect only after an administrative officer has found that a certain factual situation exists. For example, toward the end of the nineteenth century Congress directed the president to suspend the free importation of specific commodities from abroad whenever he believed that other countries had imposed unfair burdens on American exports.[40] The Supreme Court upheld delegation through contingent legislation as early as 1813 in the *Brig Aurora* case, which involved a statute authorizing the president to impose restrictions on British shipping if he found that certain events described in the statute were actually taking place in the conduct of international affairs.[41]

The constitutional problem with the delegation of congressional authority lies in its potential threat to the doctrine of separation of powers. Delegation permits the executive or the judiciary to exercise what would appear to be legislative powers. In the 1932 *Shreveport* case, the Supreme Court stated, "That the legislative power of Congress cannot be delegated is, of course clear."[42] If anything is clear, it is that the legislative power of Congress had been delegated many times before 1932 and would be delegated many more times afterward. By 1932 Congress had already delegated its authority to make rules for judicial proceedings, to impose tariffs on imports, and to embargo shipping to an unfriendly nation. Moreover, the Supreme Court had upheld congressional delegation of its power to make rules "governing the use of forest reservations; permitting reasonable variations and tolerances in the marking of food packages to disclose their contents; . . . establishing priorities for the transportation of freight during a period of emergency; . . . and prescribing methods of accounting for carriers in interstate commerce."[43] Thus the Court's assertion in 1932 that legislative authority could not be delegated was more a sentiment of wishful thinking than a statement of fact. Delegation of authority from Congress to the president or to an administrative agency was in 1932—and still is today—a sensible technique of modern government, but it is bound to founder on the shoals of a strict interpretation of separation of powers. This is why the Court announced the "doctrine of nondelegability [*sic*],"[44] despite all the factual evidence to the contrary.

Judicial unrest in the face of congressional delegation of legislative authority can be traced to causes that predate the Constitution and are more properly associated with political philosophy than with constitutional law. John Locke borrowed from the private law of agency the maxim *delegata potestas non potest delegari* (delegated power cannot be delegated) and made it a principle of political science. Locke borrowed wisely, for the maxim accommodated nicely his doctrine of natural rights and a prepolitical state of nature:

> The legislative cannot transfer the power of making laws to any other hands; for it being but a delegated power from the people, they who have it cannot pass it over to others. The people alone can appoint the form of the commonwealth, which is by constituting the legislative and appointing in whose hands that shall be. And when the people have said, we will submit to rules and be governed by laws made by such men, and in such forms, nobody else can say other men shall make laws for them; nor can the people be bound by any laws but such as are enacted by those whom they have chosen and authorized to make laws for them. The power of the legislative, being derived from the people by a positive voluntary grant and institution, can be no other than what that positive grant conveyed, which being only to make laws, and not to make legislators, the legislative can have no power to transfer their authority of making laws and place it in other hands.[45]

The key point in Locke's teaching is that legislative power is "derived from the people by a positive voluntary grant and institution." People are governed because they choose to be governed and not because it is natural for them to live in this way. On the contrary, it is natural for people to live outside of civil society in a prepolitical state of nature. It is therefore altogether fitting that Locke should find a principle of political science in the private law of agency. His radical individualism encouraged this easy transit between public and private spheres.

Locke's teaching also implies that people delegate political power to legislators just as they delegate authority over their private affairs to agents, trustees, or executors of their own choosing. With this analogy in mind, legal commentators at the end of the nineteenth century criticized the growing tendency in both state and national government for legislatures to delegate their authority to administrative agencies in order to regulate railroads and other aspects of a burgeoning industrial economy. Trustees, brokers, and testators did not delegate their delegated powers, and legislators should likewise follow this wholesome private law practice.

The force of the argument comes from the Lockean presumption that legislative power is the result of a prior, positive, voluntary delegation and not the result of human nature. If it were natural for people to live under some form of government, there would be no need to turn to the private law of agency for suitable exemplars of political power. The utter irrelevance of the law of agency for politics would be quite apparent, and there would be no need to fret over the sensible tendency of legislatures to delegate authority as practical considerations warranted. Because Locke maintained that legislative power was not the result of human nature but instead a voluntary delegation, he established a principled basis for distress at the prospect of legislatures delegating what were believed to be delegated powers. This distress manifests itself even in the face of compellingly practical reasons in support of broad delegations. This is the origin of what has come to be known as the nondelegation doctrine.

Only twice in American history has the Supreme Court relied primarily on this doctrine to declare unconstitutional a congressional delegation of legislative authority: in *Panama Refining Company v. Ryan* (1935) and *Schechter Poultry Corporation v. U.S.* (1935).[45] In both cases, the authority was delegated to the president, not to an administrative agency. And in both cases, the president was Franklin D. Roosevelt and the statute was the National Industrial Recovery Act of 1933. *Schechter* is usually considered the most important decision on excessive congressional delegation.

The National Industrial Recovery Act authorized the creation of comprehensive codes for virtually every aspect of the nation's economy. These codes, which had the force of law, were drawn up by industry and trade associations and submitted to the president for approval. The Schechter Poultry Corporation had violated several provisions of the live-poultry code and appealed its conviction on the grounds that the codes had been created by an unconstitutional delegation of legislative authority.

In a unanimous opinion, the Supreme Court agreed. Chief Justice Charles Evans Hughes's opinion of the Court stressed the salience of regulated industries in formulating their own regulations. He insisted that no one would seriously contend that "Congress could delegate its legislative authority to trade or industrial associations or groups so as to empower them to enact the laws they deem to be wise and beneficent for the rehabilitation and expansion of their trade or industries." A delegation of this sort "is unknown to our law and is utterly inconsistent with the constitutional prerogative and duties of Congress."[47] *Schechter* is often presented as an attack by the Supreme Court on the administrative state. This interpretation ignores the fact that a crucial element in Chief Justice Hughes's argument was that Congress had given too much power to the private sector.

Hughes also argued that if the delegation was constitutionally permissible, it was only because of the president's role in approving the codes submitted by the regulated industries. On this point, however, he found that the delegation to the president was far too broad. The statute offered him no meaningful standards to decide which code provisions should be approved and which ones rejected. In effect, Congress had delegated "legislative power to the President to exercise an unfettered discretion to make whatever laws he thinks may be needed or advisable for the rehabilitation and expansion of trade or industry." According to the chief justice, this amounted to abdication by Congress of its legislative duty to see that delegations of authority were accompanied by meaningful standards. In the colorful language of Justice Benjamin Cardozo's concurring opinion, it was "delegation run riot."[48] Critics of the administrative state often overstate the Court's rejection of the delegation at issue in *Schechter.* The Court did not declare delegation itself unconstitutional but only delegation without meaningful standards.

For our purposes, the most interesting part of the opinion came in Hughes's handling of the government lawyers' efforts to draw analogies between the delegation to the president under the National Industrial Recovery Act and delegations to administrative agencies such as the Interstate Commerce Commission and the Federal Radio Commission. These delegations had been approved by the courts in cases prior to *Schechter,* but the Court rejected these analogies on several grounds. The administrative agencies had narrowly limited jurisdictions, such as railroads and broadcasting frequencies, but the National Industrial Recovery Act authorized the president to approve codes for virtually every aspect of the nation's economy. The administrative agencies were "expert bod[ies]," dealing with technical questions, and the authority delegated to these agencies by Congress was accompanied by fixed procedures for notice, hearings, findings, and evidence. Such provisions were conspicuously absent from the National Industrial Recovery Act's delegation to the president. The statute mentioned findings to be made by the president, but the Court found these to be "but a statement of an opinion as to the general effect upon the promotion of trade or industry of a scheme of laws."[49]

The most telling statement of the Court's view on the relationship between the president and administrative subordinates came when the justices noted the National Industrial Recovery Act's provision "for the creation by the President of administrative agencies to assist him." These agencies did nothing to limit the president's unfettered discretion and therefore were of no help in healing the act's constitutional infirmities: "But the action or reports of such agencies, or of [the President's] other assistants,—their recommendations and findings in relation to the making of codes—have no sanction beyond the will of the President, who may accept, modify or reject them as he pleases. Such recommendations or findings in no way limit the authority which §3 [of the National Industrial Recovery Act] undertakes to vest in the president."[50]

Significantly, the Court suggested that it would have looked more favorably on the act's delegation to the president if the statute had created agencies "to assist him," provided that the assistance was rendered in such a way as to enable the agencies to exercise some control over the unfettered discretion of the president. This is a significant point. In the most important delegation case in American constitutional history, the Supreme Court suggested that a constitutionally defective delegation of authority might have been corrected had Congress created administrative agencies to limit the president's authority.

The idea of subordinate agencies limiting the president's power may be startling to contemporary Americans, who have grown accustomed to thinking about the presidency in managerial and hierarchical terms. However, the *Schechter* Court's idea of an agency that at once assists the president and limits his authority bears a distinguished American pedigree. George Mason, one of the leading framers of the Constitution at the Philadelphia Convention in 1787, had argued strenuously for an executive council that would perform precisely this twofold function. Mason failed in this effort. The absence of an executive council in the Constitution was one of the major reasons for his decision to refuse to sign the Constitution. When the convention ended, Mason became a leading Anti-Federalist in the great ratification debate of 1787 and 1788.[51]

The Legislative Veto

Despite the Supreme Court's ruling in *Schechter,* Congress showed no reluctance in delegating extremely broad powers to both FDR and his subordinates during the later years of the New Deal and throughout World War II. For example, the Agricultural Marketing Agreement Act of 1937 empowered the secretary of agriculture to fix the price of milk in various marketing areas. The legislative standard imposed on the secretary was merely to set a price that would "provide adequate quantities of wholesome milk and be in the public interest." Similarly, during World War II, the Emergency Price Control Act authorized the administrator of the Office of Price Administration to fix prices for a wide range of commodities, which "in his judgment will be duly fair and equitable and will effectuate the purposes of this Act." The purposes of the act were quite general. They included such praiseworthy but nebulous goals as "to stabilize prices, . . . to eliminate and prevent profiteering, . . . [and] to protect . . . wage earners from undue impairment of their standard of living."[52]

The Supreme Court upheld the constitutionality of both these delegations of congressional authority. It also upheld some remarkably broad delegations that predated *Schechter.* For example, in 1947 the Court sustained a 1933 statute that had given the Federal Home Loan Bank Board extensive powers over "the reorganization, consolidation, merger, or liquidation" of savings associations. These powers included an authorization "to appoint a conservator or receiver to take charge of the affairs of any such association." The board could exercise its significant power to appoint a conservator on nothing more than a finding that a savings association was "in an unsound or unsafe condition."[53]

Edward Corwin, writing in 1957, was so impressed with the pattern of judicial acquiescence in the face of broad congressional delegations of authority that he dismissed the *Schechter* case as nothing more than a "judicial curiosity."[54] Today, no commentator would treat *Schechter* in a manner quite so cavalier. The *Schechter* ruling has enjoyed a rebirth, notably in several important opinions of Chief Justice William Rehnquist. This renewed interest in *Schechter* peaked in 1999 when a federal court of appeals struck down a section of the Clean Air Act as an unconstitutional delegation of authority. The offending statute empowered the administrator of EPA to set air quality standards "the attainment of which . . . are requisite to protect the public health" with "an adequate margin of safety." In a unanimous decision, the Supreme Court reversed the court of appeals, finding that the EPA administrator's delegated authority "fits comfortably within the scope of discretion permitted by our precedents."[55]

Another reason for the interest in *Schechter* in recent years can be traced to an extremely important Supreme Court decision in 1983 declaring the legislative veto unconstitutional. Prior to 1983, the legislative veto had been looked upon as a practical arrangement to allow Congress to maintain some control over authority it had delegated to the president, the executive departments, or to independent agencies. This control could be exercised despite the extremely relaxed interpretation of *Schechter* that had rendered that decision all but meaningless. Thus, the legislative veto served as a surrogate for *Schechter,* and its constitutional demise in 1983 signaled renewed attention to that case.

In its broadest sense, the legislative veto is a statutory provision that conditions the exercise of delegated authority on a subsequent congressional judgment. The judgment may be made by either or both houses of Congress. At times, even a congressional committee can make the judgment. The judgment itself can be one of approval or disapproval; that is, a statute may provide that executive actions cannot go into effect without the approval of one or both houses of Congress. Conversely, a statute may permit an executive action to become effective within a certain fixed period (for example, sixty days), unless one or both houses disapprove. The origin of the legislative veto is usually traced to the Executive Reorganization Act of 1932. This act authorized the president to reorganize the executive branch of government by submitting a reorganization plan to Congress. If neither house of Congress disapproved of the plan within sixty days, the plan would become law. This arrangement came to be known as the one-house veto, because either house of Congress could refuse assent to the president's plan. Over the next half century, Congress passed more than two hundred laws with some form of legislative veto. These laws ran the gamut of public policy: reorganization plans, arms sales, foreign aid, presidential impounding of appropriated funds, deployment of troops in hostile areas, the governing of the District of Columbia, and rules promulgated by a host of administrative agencies.

The veto came to be viewed as a practical expression of the principle of separation of powers in the contemporary administrative state. Its proponents argued that the meaningful standards doctrine of *Schechter* was unrealistic and that the courts, wisely, had no intention of enforcing it. The legislative veto would fill the constitutional gap created by a moribund *Schechter* rule. Congress, they argued, lacked the technical expertise (and at times the political courage) to write detailed standards into its broad delegations of authority. It was not the part of wisdom to require Congress to do the impossible or even the impolitic. The legislative veto gave Congress an after-the-fact check on agencies prone to abuse their authority. In this way the people's elected representatives would maintain important controls over the modern administrative state. With the legislative veto in place, the *Schechter* rule could be safely dismissed as a judicial curiosity.

This line of reasoning was not without its critics, notably presidents who reluctantly signed into law bills with legislative vetoes that they maintained threatened their constitutional powers. Presidents frequently regarded the legislative veto as impermissible congressional meddling in the execution of public law. Lacking an item veto, however, presidents usually approved bills with legislative vetoes as the lesser of two evils—better arms sales legislation with a veto than no arms sales legislation at all, for example.

In 1983 the Supreme Court declared the legislative veto unconstitutional, in *Immigration and Naturalization Service v. Chadha.*[56] Although the facts of the case did not extend beyond narrow issues of immigration law, the Court's sweeping opinion clearly implied that all forms of the legislative veto were unconstitutional. As one commentator observed, "In that single decision, the Court implied the unconstitutionality of more provisions in more federal laws than in all its earlier decisions combined since 1789."[57]

Jagdish Rai Chadha was an alien who had been lawfully admitted to the United States on a nonimmigrant student visa. After his visa had expired, the Immigration and Naturalization Service ordered him to show cause why he should not be deported, in accordance with the Immigration and Nationality Act. The same act conferred discretion on the attorney general to suspend deportation if an alien met certain statutory criteria, for example, at least seven years residence in the United States, good moral character, and extreme hardship. The Immigration Act also provided a one-house veto to enable either the House or the Senate to overturn a decision by the attorney general to suspend the deportation of a particular alien. In Chadha's case, the attorney general decided to suspend deportation, but the House of Representatives exercised its veto over this decision and thereby returned Chadha to the status of a deportable alien.

Chadha brought a suit, contending that the legislative veto was unconstitutional and therefore the attorney general's decision to suspend his deportation should be reinstated.

The Supreme Court agreed with Chadha. Writing for a six-member majority, Chief Justice Warren Burger maintained that when the House of Representatives overturned the attorney general's decision to suspend Chadha's deportation, it performed a legislative act. Legislation was involved because Chadha's legal status had been changed; "absent the House action, Chadha would remain in the United States." The chief justice then made the textbook argument that the Constitution did not permit legislation by one house of Congress alone. Article 1, section 7, made it unmistakably clear that legislation required favorable action by both houses. Thus, the one-house veto was clearly unconstitutional. A veto requiring action by both houses was also unconstitutional because before a bill can become law, it had to be presented to the president. A two-house veto violated this "presentment" clause. A one-house veto was unconstitutional because it violated both the presentment and the bicameral clauses.

In a long and thoughtful dissent, Justice Byron White sharply criticized the majority opinion for upsetting the practical accommodation that the legislative veto had brought about between Congress and the executive, finding the Court's understanding of separation of powers excessively rigid and formalistic. He was particularly critical of the Court's argument that the veto was a form of legislation because it changed Chadha's legal status, and that because it was legislation, it therefore had to conform to the constitutional demands of bicameralism and presentment to the president. White argued persuasively that whenever legislative authority was delegated to an executive agency, the agency could change the legal status of persons subject to its jurisdiction without worrying about the bicameral and presentment clauses of the Constitution. If Congress could delegate legislative power without violating the Constitution, "it is most difficult to understand Article I as forbidding Congress from also reserving a check on legislative power for itself." Thus, for White, the legislative veto was not a form of legislation but simply a legislative check on the way executive agencies used power delegated to them by Congress. If Congress could delegate legislative authority to an administrative agency, why could it not delegate to one of its own houses the authority to monitor the agency's use of its delegated authority? White maintained that the *Chadha* decision presented Congress with a Hobson's choice: "either to refrain from delegating the necessary authority, leaving itself with a hopeless task of writing laws with the requisite specificity to cover the endless special circumstances across the entire policy landscape, or in the alternative, to abdicate its lawmaking function to the executive branch and independent agencies. To choose the former leaves major national problems unresolved; to opt for the latter risks unaccountable policymaking by those not elected to fill that role."[58]

Commentators on the *Chadha* case followed White's lead but softened the harshness of the dilemma he posed. They discussed the likelihood of reinvigorating the nondelegation doctrine in such a way as to avoid the legislative nightmare envisioned in White's extreme and polemical predictions of a "hopeless task" and a need to consider "endless special circumstances across the entire policy landscape." If Congress could no longer use the legislative veto to control the exercise of the authority it had delegated, then it would have to be more cautious in delegating its authority.

Despite its intuitive appeal, the case for narrowly drafted statutes encountered some serious difficulties. The propriety of highly specific statutes varies from one policy area to another. A delegation to the president to effect arms sales is not a likely candidate for statutory precision, because the vagaries of international affairs discourage specificity prior to the sale. Where arms sales are concerned, it is quite likely that the president's decisions will be influenced by events hidden from Congress at the time of the original delegation of authority. Indeed, the same could be said about most questions of foreign and military affairs. To the extent that the president needs delegated authority in such matters, it would seem that his authority should be broad enough to provide a flexibility suited to the uncertain terrain of foreign policy.

Rule making by administrative agencies offers a more hospitable environment for specific standards to accompany delegations of authority. In matters such as environmental or safety regulations, there are, of course, severe technical limitations on congressional specificity. Perhaps as important as the technical considerations, however, are the political dangers for members of Congress who support or oppose highly specific statutory standards. Quite understandably, Congress often prefers to postpone (and possibly to avoid indefinitely) a difficult political decision by the simple expedient of giving an agency a very general mandate and then relying on the legislative veto to correct abuses. Without the legislative veto, Congress must at times choose between making a politically difficult decision or losing control over a specific policy area. This is a serious choice—and not a foregone conclusion. It is by no means certain Congress will always choose to make the difficult decision that would be politically risky. To abdicate authority is not always unattractive.

Chadha has cast a long constitutional shadow. It served as the principal precedent for the Supreme Court's decision in 1998 to strike down the line-item veto, a complicated legislative maneuver whereby Congress empowered the president, under certain carefully stated conditions, to cancel a "limited tax benefit" or an "item of new direct spending" in a duly enacted statute.[59] The Court considered the president's power to cancel part of a statute as nothing other than a power to amend that statute by repealing a part of it. Citing *Chadha* explicitly, Justice Stevens's opinion of the Court found the exercise of such power by the president to be a form of legislation and therefore in violation of the only acceptable procedure for legislating stated in Article 1 of the Constitution. Journalistic commentary tended to stress the unusual politics of the line-item veto because the Republican 104th Congress had granted this extraordinary power to Democratic president Bill Clinton. Intriguing as the politics of the case might be, the more interesting point for our purposes is that the Supreme Court would not let Congress yield to the president certain powers over spending even when the administrative imperatives of economy and efficiency surely favored his having them.

The actual response of Congress to the *Chadha* case in the mid-1980s improved considerably on simplistic calls for stricter delegation and illustrates how separation of powers works in practice. Louis Fisher of the Congressional Research Service reported that in "the sixteen months between *Chadha* and the end of the ninety-eighth Congress, an additional fifty-three legislative vetoes were added to the books."[60] For example, a post-*Chadha* statute provided that before the Environmental Protection Agency can give a construction grant, it must first get the approval of the appropriations committees in the House and in the Senate. Similar provisions conferring post-*Chadha* vetoes on committees appeared in legislation affecting foreign aid and the District of Columbia.

A full year after the *Chadha* case, President Reagan was still receiving bills from Congress with legislative vetoes attached. In signing one of these bills he announced that he would implement it "in a manner consistent with the *Chadha* decision," that is, he would ignore the veto provision. The appropriations committees retaliated by revoking an agreement they had reached with the National Aeronautics and Space Administration (NASA) some years earlier that allowed the agency to exceed spending ceilings with committee approval. The committees took this action reluctantly, because they would lose their option to veto NASA proposals. NASA was displeased with the committees' action because it would no longer be able to exceed spending ceilings without the enactment of a separate appropriations bill. NASA administrator James Beggs wrote a letter to the two congressional committees, outlining a creative strategy to accommodate the mutual interests of NASA and the committees in a post-*Chadha* environment. He reviewed the cooperation that had characterized NASA's dealings with the committee prior to *Chadha* and proposed a way to restore something akin to the status quo ante. If NASA could not exceed spending ceilings, it would be subject to "inflexible, binding funding limitations," Beggs maintained.

> Without some procedure for adjustment, other than a subsequent separate legislative enactment, these ceilings could seriously impact the ability of NASA to meet unforeseen technical changes or problems that are inherent in challenging R&D programs. We believe that the present legislative procedure could be converted by this letter into an informal agreement by NASA not to exceed amounts for Committee designated programs without the approval of the Committees on Appropriations. This agreement would assume that both the statutory funding ceilings and the Committee approval mechanisms would be deleted from the FY 1985 legislation, and that it would not be the normal practice to include either mechanism in future appropriation bills. Further, the agreement would assume that future pro-

gram ceiling amounts would be identified by the Committees in the Conference Report accompanying NASA's annual appropriations act and confirmed by NASA in its submission of the annual operating plan. NASA would not expend any funds over the ceilings identified in the Conference Report for these programs without the prior approval of the Committees.[61]

In commenting on this remarkable proposal, Louis Fisher aptly noted that it "reveals the pragmatic sense of give-and-take that is customary between executive agencies and congressional committees." In essence, Beggs proposed that NASA continue to honor a legislative veto that would be "informal rather than statutory" and that therefore would not run afoul of *Chadha*.[62]

The General Services Administration developed a policy that accomplishes many of the same results as the legislative veto without triggering the constitutional objections to the veto. This agency has a statutory obligation to notify several congressional committees before it can authorize the sale of surplus government property worth more than ten thousand dollars. This is not a legislative veto but simply a "report and wait" procedure that gives Congress the opportunity to enact legislation prohibiting the proposed sale. Such legislation would fully comply with *Chadha* because it would pass both houses and would be presented to the president for his signature, but it is a cumbersome way for Congress to express its displeasure with proposed agency action.

To solve this problem, the General Services Administration promulgated regulations of its own that permitted the proposed sale to proceed after thirty-five days, provided there was no "adverse comment" from any of the committees to which the agency had reported. In other words, by its own regulations the agency conferred a legislative veto on several congressional committees. This procedure was upheld by the U.S. Court of Appeals for the Federal Circuit. The court's hardheaded realism reveals the salience of fundamental constitutional principles in fashioning a solution to a serious administrative problem:

> Committee chairmen and members naturally develop interest and expertise in the subjects entrusted to their continuing surveillance. Officials in the executive branch have to take these committees into account and keep them informed, respond to their inquiries, and it may be, flatter and please them when necessary. Committees do not need even the type of "report and wait" provision we have here to develop enormous influence over executive branch doings. There is nothing unconstitutional about this: indeed, our separation of powers makes such informal cooperation much more necessary than it would be in a pure system of parliamentary government.[63]

The shrewd maneuvering by agencies like NASA and the General Services Administration takes place in the engine room of the ship of state. They contrast sharply with Chief Justice Burger's view from the bridge in *Chadha*. Burger's recitation of textbook simplicities is confounded by the complexity of interbranch relations. Justice Holmes surely had it right when he said that a page of history is worth a volume of logic. History reveals a thicket of informal networks tying congressional committees and administrative agencies together in a way no abstract constitutional doctrine can tear asunder.

In 1996, the Republican 104th Congress found a way to reject administrative rules it disliked without agency cooperation and without violating *Chadha.* The Congressional Review Act of that year, which slipped into law beneath the political radar of all but the most indefatigable government watchers, enables Congress to adopt a joint "resolution of disapproval" of a proposed rule within sixty days after the General Accounting Office shall have certified it as having sufficient economic impact as to be considered a "major" rule. The statute places the joint resolution squarely on an extremely fast legislative track that bypasses the customary committee hearings, severely limits debate, and forbids amendments. If passed by both houses (thereby satisfying the constitutional requirement of bicameralism), the resolution is presented to the president to satisfy the presentment clause.

This obscure legislation had no impact during the Clinton years because it was quite unlikely that President Clinton would support Republican initiatives aimed at overturning regulations coming from agencies headed by Democrats. With President George W. Bush in the White House, however, Congress lost no time in using the expedited procedures of the little-known Congressional Review Act to pass a joint resolution of disapproval of a Clinton-era Occupational Safety and Health Administration (OSHA) regulation intended to provide workers relief from repetitive motion injuries—the ergonomics rule, as it was commonly known. Fearing the regulation's provisions would impose prohibitive costs on small business, the Republican Congress joined forces with the Bush White House to overturn the regulation in less than four days. This was truly a legislative tour de force that promised to be a useful instrument for congressional control over agency rule making as long as the same political party controls Congress and the White House.

SERVING TWO MASTERS

The struggle for control of administrative agencies has been an abiding feature in the long history of the relationship between the president and Congress.[64] From George Washington to George W. Bush, presidents have faced difficulties, embarrassments, and conflicts from actions taken by their subordinates. Albert Gallatin, Thomas Jefferson's treasury secretary, had an extraordinarily close relationship with the House Committee on Ways and Means, which he had helped to establish as an opposition congressman during the Washington presidency. Both John Adams and his son John Quincy Adams had great difficulty as presidents in maintaining the allegiance of the heads of their executive departments vis-à-vis unfriendly congressional cliques that tried to capture them. President James Monroe complained that he was not shown the expenditure estimates his treasury secretary had submitted to Congress. During the period after the Civil War, there was serious discussion of amending the Constitution to permit cabinet officers to take seats in Congress. President William Howard Taft's efforts to prepare an executive budget met stiff congressional opposition in the early part of the twentieth century. Just before World War II, an isolationist Congress conferred upon Admiral Harold Stark, chief of Naval Operations, extraordinary powers over President Roosevelt's authority to negotiate with Winston Churchill on how the U.S. Navy might deliver badly needed destroyers to the hard-pressed Royal Navy. Congressional investigation of suspected Communists in government agencies had a profound impact on federal personnel management during the Joseph McCarthy era. Health, Education and Welfare Secretary Joseph Califano incurred President Carter's intense displeasure with his interpretation of an act of Congress authorizing federal funding of abortions under certain narrowly defined circumstances. More recently, congressional committees have encouraged federal employees to blow the whistle on irregularities in defense contracting and in the enforcement of environmental laws.

At the heart of the struggle between Congress and the president for control of administrative agencies is the long-standing congressional practice of driving a wedge between the president and his subordinates in the executive branch of government. Congress does so by conferring broad discretionary powers on these officers, thus providing them with an independence from the president in specific situations defined by statute. In some cases it imposes a certain legal independence upon reluctant officers. Regardless of whether the officers welcome the independence or not, they have it, and they, not the president, must answer to Congress for the results of their actions. This accountability to Congress severs the hierarchical chain of command in the executive branch and exposes the subordinate to the full force of Congress's impressive powers to investigate the public administration and to subject it to the rigors of legislative oversight. We have it on good authority that "no man can serve two masters," but this is precisely what high-ranking administrative officers are called upon to do, because they must carry out their duties in a regime of separation of powers.

One of the most dramatic examples of this problem took place in the midst of President Andrew Jackson's monumental struggle with the Second Bank of the United States, or the "hydra," as he preferred to call it. The struggle culminated in Jackson's decision in 1834 to remove U.S. assets from that bank and to place them in selected state banks. Jackson's most comprehensive biographer, Robert V. Remini, maintains that removal of the assets "became the central issue of the decade. No other approached it in importance."[65] At the center of the controversy was Jackson's treasury secretary William J. Duane, who flatly refused to carry out the president's order to remove the government's deposits from the Bank of the United States.

The Bank of the United States traced its origins to the Washington administration, when its original chartering was the subject of a celebrated constitutional debate between Alexander Hamilton and Thomas Jefferson. The bank was rechartered in 1816, and in 1832 its supporters urged Congress to renew the charter again, even though it still had four years to run. Congress did so, but Jackson vetoed the measure. The bank then became the central issue in the presidential election of 1832, in which Jackson won his second term in office.

The bitterness of the 1832 campaign reinforced Jackson's hostility toward the Bank. Early in 1833 he decided to remove the government's deposits and to place them in state banks (or "pet banks," as Jackson's critics called them). Removal of the deposits from the Bank of the United States would "slay the monster," even though the charter would keep it formally in existence for a few years. This plan was complicated by a congressional provision that vested the authority to remove the deposits in the secretary of the treasury. The secretary at that time, Louis McLane, was known to oppose removal of the deposits, especially since the House of Representatives in the previous year had conducted a careful investigation of the Bank and concluded that the government's money was safe.

A solution to this problem presented itself when Jackson's secretary of state, Edward Livingston, expressed an interest in becoming ambassador to France. Jackson took this opportunity to move McLane from the Treasury Department to the State Department. Having gone to this trouble, Jackson might have been expected to take extraordinary precautions in selecting McLane's replacement. Unfortunately, he did not. In a manner that was somewhat characteristic of Jackson in making personnel selections, he acted quite precipitously, selecting William J. Duane of Pennsylvania, a man who had worked for the Girard banking interests of Philadelphia and was known to be a foe of the Bank of the United States. Duane's chief political asset was a father who had served as editor of *Aurora,* a newspaper that had supported Thomas Jefferson many years earlier. Apparently, Jackson wanted to forge a link between old-fashioned Jeffersonians and contemporary Jacksonians in the grand strategy of bringing the Bank to its knees.

Duane took office on 1 June 1833. On his second day on the job he was visited by Amos Kendall, who was one of his subordinates in the Treasury Department and, far more important, a close adviser and personal friend of the president. The new secretary was told that the president had decided to remove the government's assets from the Bank of the United States and that Duane would soon receive instructions on how to proceed. Duane immediately complained to the president that he was being reduced "to a mere cipher in the administration."[66]

Jackson was about to leave on a tour of New England and told Duane he would discuss the matter in a letter he would write while he was traveling. In the letter Jackson declared that he did indeed want the government's deposits removed and suggested that Amos Kendall be sent around the country to find new banks to receive the deposits. Nevertheless, the president assured Duane that his comments were only "suggestions" and that he had no desire "to interfere with the independent exercise of the discretion committed to you by law over the subject."[67] Duane advised the president that, although he was no friend of the Bank, he opposed the plan to remove the deposits. He believed the renewal of the Bank's charter should be opposed when the time came, but removing the deposits was an entirely different matter.

As the tension mounted throughout summer 1833, Duane assured Jackson that if directly ordered to remove the deposits, he would resign rather than block the president's plan. He began to reconsider this promise, however, when he saw the banks Kendall had chosen to receive the government's money; he did not think they were safe. Toward the end of the summer, the crisis came to a head. Jackson offered Duane the post of ambassador to Russia, but Duane had decided to stay at Treasury and fulfill his statutory duties to safeguard the government's assets.

At an important cabinet meeting in September 1833, Jackson discovered that only Attorney General Roger B. Taney and Postmaster General William Berry supported him unequivocally. Secretary of State McLane and Secretary of War Lewis Cass joined Duane in opposing the policy of removing the assets. Navy Secretary Levi Woodbury said he opposed the plan but promised to support the president.

Taney prepared a paper defending the president's position, which was read to the entire cabinet at a meeting later in September. Duane asked the president directly if he were being ordered to remove the deposits. Jackson said yes, but that he would make it clear that the responsibility was his own and not that of the secretary of the treasury. Duane remained dissatisfied because he knew that he was the only officer who could remove the deposits, and it had become his firm conviction that this action should be taken only if Congress directly ordered him to do so. Otherwise, he believed the government's money was much safer with the Bank of the United States than in the state banks Jackson and Kendall had chosen. Duane told Jackson of his decision, assured him it was final, and stated that he would not resign.

Jackson considered Duane's intransigence a form of insubordination and decided to remove the secretary from office. Attorney General Taney was appointed as the new secretary of the treasury and immediately executed the asset removal plan. The decision to remove Duane from office triggered a tremendous political furor. Cass and McLane came close to resigning. They were persuaded to remain only by Jackson's promise to make it clear to the public that the decision to remove Duane had not been a cabinet decision but the president's alone.

Although an act of Congress in 1789 gave legal support to Jackson's decision, his action as a matter of fact was without precedent. No president had ever before removed the head of an executive department from office. The Senate took the equally unprecedented action of formally censuring the president for his action, and Jackson replied with his famous "protest" message. This document announced the startling doctrine that "the President is the direct representative of

the American people" who possesses "the entire executive power of this government," thus justifying the removal of Duane because of the president's constitutional duty to "take care that the Laws be faithfully executed." Jackson's critics
replied that he had transformed his duty to "take care" that the laws were executed into a spurious duty to execute them as he saw fit.

Shortly after President Jackson left office in 1837, the Supreme Court decided an
important case that addressed the main constitutional issue in the controversy over
Treasury Secretary Duane's refusal to abdicate his statutory obligation to enforce
the law as he saw fit and not as the president wanted it enforced. Fortunately, the
facts of the case involved nothing more than a contractual dispute with a disgruntled postal contractor; therefore the highly charged politics of the Bank controversy did not distract the Court from the narrow issue before it. That issue was
whether a judicial writ of mandamus could direct a subordinate of the president to
fulfill a statutory obligation imposed by Congress directly on that subordinate.
The question, despite its technical flavor, was of enormous constitutional significance. At issue was the constitutionality of the long-standing congressional practice of bypassing the president in order to impose a duty on the head of an
executive department or on an inferior officer—the precise issue at stake in Treasury Secretary Duane's struggle with President Jackson. This practice was—and
still is—one of the most important congressional instruments for influencing public administration because it gives Congress direct access to the bureaucracy.

The case began during Jackson's administration; as might be expected, he
resisted congressional incursions into his department. To understand the Court's
ruling, it is necessary to review the circumstances that triggered the litigation,
Kendall v. U.S. ex rel. Stokes (1838).[68] William B. Stokes, a contractor with the
Post Office, claimed that that agency owed him a substantial sum of money. Congress agreed and passed a law directing the solicitor of the treasury to investigate
the matter and determine a suitable sum "according to the principles of equity."[69]
Congress further directed the postmaster general to award the sum fixed by the
solicitor, which came to $161,563.89. Jackson's postmaster general, Amos
Kendall, whom we have already met as a Treasury Department officer during the
bank controversy, was suspicious of Stokes. He found the award excessive and
certified the release of only $122,102.46.

Stokes appealed to President Jackson for the remaining funds, which came
to nearly $40,000. Jackson shared Kendall's suspicion of Stokes and offered him
no help. Instead, Jackson suggested that Stokes take his troubles back to Congress. There was nothing more that Congress could do since it had already passed
an act on Stokes's behalf, which the postmaster had defied. Stokes's only
recourse was to sue. The circuit court for the District of Columbia issued a writ
of mandamus directing Postmaster General Kendall to obey the act of Congress
and to give Stokes the full sum as determined by the solicitor of the treasury.
Kendall then appealed to the U.S. Supreme Court.

The postmaster general argued that Congress could not fix a statutory responsibility on a subordinate of the president because it would undercut the president's control over the executive branch of government. The Constitution placed on the president the duty to "take Care that the Laws be faithfully executed." If Congress could designate a presidential subordinate as the officer responsible for executing a law, the unity of the executive branch would be undermined, and the president would not be able to ensure the faithful execution of the laws, Kendall concluded.

No Supreme Court justice accepted this argument. The decision of the Court was six-to-three against the postmaster general, with the three dissenters basing their position on a technical question about the jurisdiction of the lower court in issuing a writ of mandamus. All the justices agreed that Congress could impose statutory responsibilities on presidential subordinates. In delivering the opinion of the Court, Justice Smith Thompson noted that although the executive power was directly vested in the president. "it by no means follows that every officer in every branch of that department is under the exclusive direction of the President." Thompson granted that there were "certain political duties imposed upon many officers in the executive department, the discharge of which is under the direction of the President." He followed this concession with the most important sentence in the opinion on the relationship between the president and executive subordinates: "But it would be an alarming doctrine that Congress cannot impose upon any executive officer any duty they may think proper, which is not repugnant to any rights secured and protected by the Constitution; and in such cases, the duty and responsibility grow out of and are subject to the control of the law, and not to the direction of the President."[70] The *Kendall* decision made it clear that as a matter of constitutional law it was incorrect to maintain that the executive officers were "all the president's men." They were preeminently officers of the law.

The principles announced in *Kendall v. Stokes* were invoked by Congress during a bitter dispute with the Reagan administration in the 1980s. President Reagan used the Office of Management and Budget (OMB) quite effectively to discipline administrative agencies tempted to wander from the path of his administration's policy. Agency personnel, notably career civil servants in the Environmental Protection Agency (EPA), often complained that Reagan administration policies could not be squared with the environmental laws their agency had a legal obligation to enforce. Two executive orders conferred remarkably broad powers on the OMB to encourage agencies to exercise their regulatory powers in accordance with the priorities of the Reagan administration. Under these executive orders, all proposed rules from the agencies were to be submitted to the Office of Information and Regulatory Affairs, a subsidiary of the OMB. The most important rules were to be accompanied by a regulatory impact analysis, which had to show how the benefits of the proposed rule would outweigh its costs. If the Office of Information and Regulatory Affairs found the analysis inadequate, it could order a delay in publication of the proposed rule.

There was no time limit on the OMB's reviewing process, which led to complaints that the executive orders enabled the office to delay proposed regulations indefinitely. When these powers were combined with the OMB's power over agency budgets, agency personnel ceilings, and agency communications with Congress, there emerged "an integrated process for presidential review and control of agency development of rules, from initial conception and formulation to final promulgation."[71]

Champions of executive authority applauded this arrangement as long overdue. Members of Congress, quite predictably, saw it as a sinister conspiracy to keep agencies from exercising the statutory rule-making powers that Congress has conferred on them—and not on the OMB—a modern version of the constitutional issue addressed in *Kendall v. Stokes* a century and a half earlier. One congressional committee report charged that the Office of Management and Budget thwarted or delayed important environmental regulations in response to importunities from favored industrial interests. The view from Capitol Hill was grim indeed:

> OMB's interference with EPA's asbestos rulemakings is not an isolated incident. The public record is now replete with evidence of a pervasive and persistent pattern of intrusion and interference that has shifted the locus of discretionary decision-making authority from the agencies designated by Congress to OMB. Congressional investigations and court litigation have brought to light instances of arbitrary delays in the OMB review process forcing violations of statutorily prescribed or court-ordered deadlines; the modification or complete displacement of technical, scientific, and policy judgments of agency officials as a result of OMB pressure; OMB imposition of cost-benefit criteria in agency rulemakings in contravention of specific Congressional mandates; OMB substitution of political considerations for the economic analyses required by the Order; secret meetings between OMB officials and affected industry representatives; OMB transmission of industry views to agency decision-makers without identification; and failure to record OMB input in the public docket of an agency's rulemaking.[72]

This congressional report was issued in October 1985. Within a year Congress had made considerable progress in getting the OMB to agree to open its regulatory review procedures to public scrutiny. The issue continued to spark controversy throughout the Bush administration and led President Clinton to issue a somewhat conciliatory executive order in September 1993.

And so it goes. Presidents, senators, and representatives continue to speak the lines Publius wrote for them two centuries ago when he argued that "the interest of the man must be connected with the constitutional rights of the place."[73] Presidents, senators, and representatives jealously protect their offices

—jealously and rightfully. There will be more pulling and tugging between the president and Congress over the OMB's effort to control and coordinate agency rule making from the Executive Office of the President. It is a new variation on a fine old theme that places administration center stage in a great constitutional drama of the Republic.

PRESERVING ADMINISTRATIVE INTEGRITY

Albert V. Dicey believed that common law countries could avoid the perils of *droit administratif* as long as their administrators were accountable to the ordinary courts for their quasi-judicial activities. American administrative law not only meets this criterion,[74] but it surpasses it by structuring safeguards to protect the integrity of administrative decision making—both rule making and adjudication—before unhappy litigants take their appeals to the ordinary courts. This long-standing policy of Congress and the courts is of considerable practical importance because, given the crowded dockets of most federal judges, relatively few administrative decisions will actually be reviewed by the courts. If Dicey's standard is to have any practical effect on public administration as a whole, something akin to the spirit of judicial independence and fundamental fairness must permeate the administrative process itself.

For an instructive example of a judicial effort to build safeguards into the administrative process, consider the case of *PATCO v. FLRA,* which came before the U.S. Court of Appeals for the District of Columbia in 1982.[75] This case presented the legal face of the great political controversy triggered by President Reagan's spectacular decision in August 1981 to fire air traffic controllers who had participated in an illegal strike. The Civil Service Reform Act of 1978 had created the Federal Labor Relations Authority (FLRA) and empowered it to revoke the "exclusive recognition status" of a union calling such a strike. This revocation, which union leaders correctly labeled a death sentence, was imposed by the three members of the FLRA when they unanimously upheld a decision by their Administrative Law Judge (ALJ), holding that revocation was the appropriate punishment for the Professional Air Traffic Controllers Organization (PATCO). The union challenged this decision before the D.C. Court of Appeals.

On the day before oral argument was to begin, the Department of Justice alerted the court that the FBI had been investigating allegations of seriously improper contacts between Albert Shanker, a prominent labor leader, and Leon Applewhaite, one of the three members of the FLRA. This prompted the court to arrange for the appointment of a special ALJ from outside the FLRA to hold an evidentiary hearing on the allegedly improper contacts. The purpose of the hearing was to enable the court to determine whether it should remand the case to the FLRA before hearing PATCO's appeal. This matter was quite serious because under the Administrative Procedure Act (APA), a person making an ex parte communication to an officer performing a quasi-judicial function could be required "to show cause why his claim or interest in the proceeding should not be dismissed, denied, disregarded, or otherwise adversely affected on account of such violations."[76] The same statute permitted an agency to impose the milder punishment of requiring the offending party simply to disclose the improper communication, which then would become part of the record.

John Vittone, an ALJ at the Civil Aeronautics Board, was appointed as the special ALJ charged with investigating the nature and extent of the communication between Shanker and Applewhaite. He conducted a thorough inquiry that unearthed several questionable communications between interested parties and the FLRA. Shanker's was the most flagrant because he had invited Applewhaite, a personal friend, to dinner and expressed his opinion on the merits of the PATCO case pending before his guest. Shanker's remarks in support of PATCO lasted about fifteen minutes, with no effort by Applewhaite to stop him.

Less flagrant but still questionable was Judge Vittone's finding that Transportation Secretary Andrew Lewis, whose department included the Federal Aviation Administration, had called Applewhaite and FLRA member Henry Frazier to express his concern that the PATCO case be settled speedily. He explicitly disavowed any intention to discuss the merits of the case, but Frazier found the call unusual because he had never heard from a cabinet-level officer before. The Administrative Procedure Act explicitly exempts "requests for status reports" from ex parte prohibitions, and Secretary Lewis maintained his query as to the progress of the case fell within this exemption. The exemption Lewis invoked was inserted to enable members of Congress to make status report inquiries to administrative agencies without running into ex parte problems. Lewis's reliance on this clause was an interesting illustration of the complexities of public administration under a regime of separation of powers—the executive uses a clause clearly intended to benefit the legislature. Whatever irregularity the secretary's call might have involved was considerably mitigated by Applewhaite's advice to him to file a written request for an expedited procedure that would be part of the record, to which PATCO could then reply. Secretary Lewis followed this advice.

A third questionable situation arose during a meeting between Stephen Gordon, the FLRA's general counsel, and Applewhaite in the latter's office. Although Gordon was the FLRA official responsible for prosecuting PATCO, the meeting in question dealt with the FLRA's budget and had nothing to do with the PATCO case. The focus of the meeting changed, however, with the arrival of Ellen Stern, an FLRA staff attorney, who had prepared a memorandum interpreting the statute on decertifying unions—a matter of considerable relevance to the PATCO case. Applewhaite and Stern freely discussed the memo in Gordon's presence, and Gordon himself joined in the conversation without, however, advising Applewhaite on how he should decide the PATCO litigation.

Despite these irregularities, ALJ Vittone found that whatever ex parte communications might have taken place, they "did not have any effect on the final decision of the members of the FLRA in the PATCO case." The court of appeals accepted Judge Vittone's findings and therefore decided not to remand the case to the FLRA for reconsideration. Judge Harry T. Edwards, writing for the court of appeals, explained that upon remand, the FLRA "might produce a new record free from procedural defects," but "it would serve no other purpose."[77] Since there was no reason to think any member of the FLRA would change his decision, the court proceeded to the merits of the case, which led to a decision against PATCO.

Just how seriously should one take these ex parte communications, especially since, at the end of the day, the specially appointed ALJ and the court of appeals agreed that not enough harm was done to remand the case to the agency? After all, what is so bad about two old friends discussing matters of mutual interest over dinner when no threats are made, no bribes are offered, and nothing is said that had not already been said in public? What is so bad about the secretary of transportation calling FLRA members merely to express his concern that a decision be reached quickly while carefully avoiding any discussion of what he thinks that decision should be? What is so bad about three high-ranking civil servants discussing briefly a statute relevant to the PATCO case during a meeting called for another purpose? Perhaps most people will see in all three cases nothing more than trivial bureaucratic peccadilloes, but the judges who heard the case saw them quite differently. Although acknowledging that none of the ex parte contacts changed anyone's decision, they nevertheless condemned the FLRA's administrative behavior in no uncertain terms. In so doing, they reveal judicial expectations of what sound public administration requires. This judicial concern goes far beyond Dicey's standard that agency decisions be reviewed by the courts. In this case, the judges were trying to insert principles of fairness into the administrative process itself, a goal Dicey never considered. Let us look at each judge's opinion—Judge Edwards writing for the court and Judges Spottswood Robinson and George E. MacKinnon concurring.

Judge Edwards's opinion candidly recognizes that Congress established commonsense guidelines rather than rigid rules to govern questions of ex parte communications. Thus, Congress clearly did not intend that administrators and judges impose the maximum penalty of dismissing a claim for every violation. The APA explicitly directs administrators who discover ex parte communications to temper their reaction by imposing penalties only "to the extent consistent with the interests of justice and the policy of the underlying statutes."[78] Although Judge Edwards allows for some flexibility within the administrative process, he clearly sees it as part of his role to look "to the protection of the integrity of the administrative and judicial decisionmaking processes"[79] and to see to it that "public officials are held to high standards of behavior."[80] Addressing the specific communications at issue in this case, he is "astonished" at Albert Shanker's "claim that he did nothing wrong." To put the record straight, he comments:

> *It is simply unacceptable behavior for any person directly to attempt to influ-*
> *ence the decision of a judicial officer in a pending case outside of the for-*
> *mal, public proceedings.* This is true for the general public, for "interested
> persons," and for the formal parties to the case. This rule applies to admin-
> istrative adjudications as well as to cases in Article III courts.[81]

It is particularly significant that he applies the same standard to administrative adjudications as to ordinary courts. Where Dicey would rest content
with an appeal to a court, Judge Edwards imposes judicial standards on the
agency itself—a step Dicey shrunk from taking in his commentary on the
Arlidge case. Judge Edwards does not fault Applewhaite for accepting
Shanker's dinner invitation but states that once "the conversation turned to the
discipline appropriate for a striking union like PATCO, Member Applewhaite
should have promptly terminated the discussion."[82] As to Transportation Secretary Lewis's phone call on the FLRA's decision-making timetable, Judge
Edwards simply notes that "even a procedural inquiry may be a subtle effort to
influence an agency decision."[83]

Perhaps the most interesting aspect of Edwards's opinion focused on
Stephen Gordon, the FLRA's general counsel and, as such, the person primarily
responsible for prosecuting PATCO before the FLRA's ALJ and the Authority
itself. The prohibitions in the APA against ex parte communications apply only
to "interested persons outside the agency."[84] As prosecutor, Gordon was clearly
an interested person, but Judge Edwards found that he was also "outside the
agency" for ex parte communications purposes, despite his status as an employee
of the FLRA. This is a strong statement of the court's willingness to weigh more
heavily the function one plays in the administrative process than one's position
on the agency's organizational chart.

Judge Robinson agrees with Edwards that General Counsel Gordon was "an
interested person outside the agency" but finds the meeting he attended in Applewhaite's office more sinister than his judicial colleague. As Robinson sees the
three-way discussion among Gordon, Applewhaite, and staff attorney Stern, the
prosecutor was "permitted to witness an internal discussion during which the
legal analysis of the decisionmaking on a key issue is evolving" and therefore
"enjoys an obvious advantage even if he cannot discern exactly how the deci-
sionmaker will vote."[85] Particularly offensive was Applewhaite's turning to Gordon to ask his opinion on the decertification statute he and Stern were discussing.
Robinson found this conversation "not merely indiscreet or undesirable" but
"purely and simply a prohibited ex parte contact that never should have
occurred." Applewhaite was "grossly at fault in soliciting Gordon's opinion on
the issue." Because of the easy access between prosecutors and adjudicators in
administrative agencies, Judge Robinson calls for "a heightened degree of vigi-
lance—a particularly keen scrupulousness—on the part of agency personnel."[86]

Judge Robinson found Secretary Lewis's phone call "exceedingly troubling"

because his interpretation of prohibited conversations on the "merits of the proceeding" was not confined to the discussion of the facts of the case. Robinson
found that "the Secretary's insistence that the case was very important to the
Government and therefore needed to be dealt with rapidly was a communication
on the merits of that issue."[87]

Robinson's harshest judgment was reserved for the Shanker-Applewhaite
dinner conversation. Of Shanker's behavior, he says: "His deliberate crusade to
sway through private importunity the decision of one acting as judge in a pending case is so far beyond the pale of legally tolerable activity that even the most
caustic criticism could not overstate the magnitude of the impropriety."[88] As for
Applewhaite:

> This court should not hesitate to allocate blame squarely where it belongs:
> at the doorstep of one acting as a judicial officer who, with a solemn respon-
> sibility to preserve both the fact and appearance of complete impartiality,
> first subjected himself to a palpable risk of contamination, and then made no
> effort to arrest advocacy when it came. . . . While it may be possible to
> attribute Applewhaite's actions in placing himself in a compromising posi-
> tion to thoughtless imprudence, his unprotesting submission to blatant *ex
> parte* advocacy on the merits of the case defies explanation.[89]

Judge MacKinnon's opinion was shorter but no less severe. He finds the num-
bers of ex parte contacts "appalling" and puts "union officials, cabinet officers and
all citizens" on notice that "officials of the administrative agencies engaged in
adjudicating rights and interests are *not* their handmaidens."[90] He calls attention to
the relationship between ex parte contacts and possible criminal indictments if one
"corruptly . . . *endeavors to influence,* obstruct, or impede the due and proper
administration of the law under which [a] proceeding is being held before [an]
agency of the United States."[91]

The PATCO case is but one of many examples of how Congress and the
courts have tried to enhance the integrity of administrative decision making by
protecting administrators from improper influences. This protection addresses
one of Dicey's principal objections to *droit administratif,* the fear that administrative decisions will not be independent of government officials. For Dicey, the
independence of British judges was one of the glories of the common law. For a
distinctively American approach to the problem of protecting the integrity of the
administrative process, one must look to the distinctively American understanding of separation of powers for examples of how administrators are protected
from the president, the Congress, and the courts.

As we saw in *PATCO,* the APA forbids an "interested person outside the
agency" from making an ex parte contact with any administrative officers
involved in agency adjudication. *Portland Audubon Society v. Endangered
Species Committee*[92] raised the question of whether the president of the United
States is an "interested person" in decisions made by the Endangered Species

Committee and, if so, whether he is "outside the agency." The Endangered Species Committee, also known as the God Squad, is an extraordinary seven-person body comprising two cabinet secretaries, the administrator of the EPA, the chairman of the Council of Economic Advisers, and other high-ranking officials whose duties include deciding whether to make exceptions to the Endangered Species Act. The Portland Audubon Society challenged the God Squad's decision to grant an exemption to the Bureau of Land Management that would permit timber cutting likely to threaten the northern spotted owl.

During the litigation, the Associated Press reported that several members of the God Squad had "been summoned to White House meetings to discuss coming decisions on the owl." The Portland Audubon Society filed a motion for leave to conduct discovery into these allegations of improper ex parte communications. The government argued that the ex parte prohibitions did not apply to the president and his staff.

The court found that the president and members of the White House staff are "interested persons," not only because as "the head of the government and chief executive officer, the president necessarily has an interest in every agency proceeding," but also because "no communication from any other person is more likely to deprive the parties and the public of the right to effective participation in a key governmental decision at a most crucial time."[93] Although the court relied on the president's position as "head of the government" to make him an "interested person," he still remained "outside the agency" because "the Endangered Species Act explicitly vests discretion to make exemptions in the Committee and does not contemplate that the President or the White House will become involved in Committee deliberations."[94] Therefore the court remanded the case to the committee for an evidentiary hearing before an ALJ on the precise effect of the White House communication on the committee.[95]

Interestingly, the court distinguished this case from *Sierra Club v. Costle,*[96] wherein the D.C. Court of Appeals had taken a very different view of a meeting between EPA officials and President Carter on the limits to be imposed on sulfur dioxide emissions. In holding that this meeting did not involve an ex parte communication, the court found that "an overworked administrator exposed on a twenty-four-hour basis to a dedicated but zealous staff needs to know the arguments and ideas of policymakers in other agencies as well as in the White House."[97] Writing for the court, Judge Patricia Wald acknowledged that "undisclosed presidential prodding" could lead to a situation in which "the political process did affect the outcome in a way the courts could not police."[98] Such, however, are the risks we take to avoid converting "informal rulemaking into a rarified technocratic process."[99]

The *Portland Audubon* court distinguished its decision from Judge Wald's *Sierra Club* opinion on the grounds that the God Squad was involved in adjudication, whereas the limits EPA would impose on sulfuric dioxide emissions would be settled by the more relaxed procedure of rule making, which did not fall under the APA's strictures against ex parte communications. Thus the court recognizes a greater scope for legitimate political influence in rule making that is quasi-legislative action than it does in adjudication, its quasi-judicial counterpart.

The distinction between rule making and adjudication played a major role in *Pillsbury v. FTC*,[100] a decision providing a telling example of inappropriate congressional influence on administrative adjudication.[101] The case involved a petition by Pillsbury requesting the court of appeals for the Fifth Circuit to set aside a Federal Trade Commission (FTC) order requiring the company to divest itself of certain assets of competitors it had acquired. The time line of the case was quite important. It began in 1953 before a hearing examiner (the old title for those we call ALJs today) whose decision in favor of the company was reversed by the FTC, his parent agency. The examiner then spent several years taking additional evidence as to whether the acquisition violated anticompetitive prohibitions in Title 7 of the Clayton Anti-Trust Act, as interpreted by the FTC. In 1959 he ruled against Pillsbury, and his decision was adopted virtually unchanged by the FTC in 1960.

Pillsbury then brought its suit, charging it had been denied due process because of inappropriate congressional interference with the FTC's decision-making process while its case was pending before that agency. Pillsbury could not base its complaint on the ex parte prohibitions because they were not added to the APA until 1976, hence, the reliance on the more general grounds of due process. The court of appeals found for Pillsbury in 1966—thirteen years after the affair had first come before the FTC examiner.

The specific interference of which Pillsbury complained occurred in 1955 during hearings before several congressional subcommittees concerned with antitrust questions. Senator Estes Kefauver took the lead in criticizing FTC chairman Howrey's interpretation of the Clayton Act as applied to Pillsbury's acquisition of its competitors' assets. The senator's remarks were quite detailed and clearly revealed his displeasure with Howrey's interpretation, which Kefauver feared would lead to an FTC decision favorable to the company. Kefauver's incessant probing into just how Howrey had reached his decision finally led the chairman to complain: "Well, I think the question you are asking about the Pillsbury decision is a much greater challenge to judicial processes, because I am sitting as a quasi-judicial officer in that case. . . . I think I will disqualify myself in the Pillsbury case for the rest of the case because of the inquiry which you have made about my mental process in it. . . . I think you have delved too deeply into the quasi-judicial mind in the Pillsbury matter."[102]

Pillsbury cited this comment and others like it as the basis of its complaint about improper congressional interference in the FTC adjudication. Although five years had elapsed between Kefauver's intervention and the FTC's decision against Pillsbury in 1960, the company noted that three of the commissioners who participated in the 1960 decision had been associated with the FTC in 1955 and therefore were likely to have been influenced by the congressional pressure at issue in the case. Chairman Howrey had left the FTC by 1960, but his successor, Earl Kintner, had been general counsel at the time and, as such, had felt the full force of the congressional cues on how the case should be decided. Interestingly, however, the FTC did not accept the interpretation of the Clayton Act Senator Kefauver had urged upon it, even though it eventually did rule against Pillsbury on other grounds.

In deciding the Pillsbury case, the Court of Appeals for the Fifth Circuit quoted generously from the congressional hearings in question before concluding "that the proceedings just outlined constituted an improper intrusion into the adjudicatory processes of the Commission."[103] Because of "the inordinate lapse of time in this proceeding," the court was "naturally loathe to frustrate the proceedings at this late date." Nevertheless, "common justice to a litigant requires that we invalidate the order entered by a quasi-judicial tribunal that was importuned by a member of the United States Senate, however innocent they intended their conduct to be, to arrive at the ultimate conclusion which they did reach."[104]

The court then directed that the FTC order to which Pillsbury had objected "be remanded to the Commission," which could then decide what steps should "appropriately be taken in view of both the lapse of time and the present state of the case law applying Section 7 [of the Clayton Act.]" On remand, the FTC dismissed the case it had originally brought against Pillsbury, "declaring that the record (now fourteen years old) was too stale and the effects of the merger were too entrenched, to make divestiture a realistic possibility."[105]

The most significant aspect of the court's opinion was its effort to distinguish the inappropriate congressional interference in this case from the clearly legitimate congressional duty of legislative oversight. Noting that agencies exercise their quasi-legislative (as opposed to their quasi-judicial) authority when they issue "interpretive rules" to inform the public of their official position on the statutes they administer, the court found no problem in congressional objections that the interpretations in question fail to adhere to "the intent of Congress." These interpretations are a form of rule making and, as such, are fair game for congressional criticism. When, however, a congressional investigation "focuses directly and substantially upon the mental decisional process of a Commission *in a case which is pending before it,* Congress is no longer intervening in the agency's *legislative* function, but rather in its *judicial* function." When the judicial function is in play, the court becomes "concerned with the right of private litigants to a fair trial . . . which cannot be maintained unless those who exercise the judicial function are free from powerful external influences"[106]

By distinguishing the rule-making and adjudicative functions, even when the "rules" are interpretations of statutory language, the court gives ample scope for interventions by democratically elected officials while protecting administrators from congressional interference in cases actually before them. The rule-making/adjudication distinction, though often difficult to apply in practice, provides a helpful conceptual framework for protecting Dicey's concern for judicial independence without sacrificing the imperatives of a democratic administrative state.

The courts have protected the independence of administrative adjudication not only from the president and Congress but also from the judges. In *Grant v. Shalala,*[107] the Court of Appeals for the Third Circuit examined the question of whether a federal district court should have granted a plaintiff's request for discovery into the decision-making processes of an ALJ who had denied her claim for disability benefits. ALJ Russell Rowell had denied Lois Grant's application, which alleged that an injury to her knee had caused her lasting pain and rendered her incapable of working for a living. Judge Rowell rejected both these claims, finding that Grant could do sedentary work and that her complaints about lasting pain were not credible.

Grant "amended her complaint to convert it to a class action, consisting of claimants whose cases had been or would be assigned to Judge Rowell."[108] She maintained that Rowell would not give disability claimants a fair hearing because he was biased against them, and to this end she successfully petitioned the district court "to conduct extensive discovery in support of her claims."[109]

Writing for the court of appeals, Judge Samuel A. Alito provided a long list of the intrusive questions Grant's counsel raised during the discovery proceedings. By deposing an opinion writer who had worked with Rowell for five years, counsel delved into such matters as his "use of 'stock' language," "differences between his work procedures and views and those of other ALJs," "his consultation of law books," "his familiarity with views about particular rules of law," "whether he ever uttered racial or ethnic epithets," "complaints about him from typists and secretaries," "the number of hours he worked," "his views regarding alcoholism and obesity," and so forth.

Recalling that the Supreme Court has held that "the role of the modern ALJ is 'functionally comparable' to that of a judge," the appeals court found the district court had erred seriously in permitting discovery. "Such efforts to probe the mind of an ALJ, if allowed, would pose a substantial threat to the administrative process."[110] Noting further that the Social Security Administration had adequate procedures in place for reviewing complaints of bias on the part of ALJs and that the results of these procedures were themselves subject to judicial review, Judge Alito remanded the case to the district court with a firm directive to avoid discovery in the future. In a ringing affirmation of the need to protect the independence of ALJs from Article III judges—or judges of the ordinary courts, as Dicey would say—Judge Alito reviewed the pernicious character of subjecting ALJs to discovery:

Every ALJ would work under the threat of being subjected to such treatment [as ALJ Rowell had undergone] if his or her pattern of decisions displeased any administrative litigant or group with the resources to put together a suit charging bias. Every ALJ would know that his or her staff members could be deposed and questioned in detail about the ALJ's decision-making and thought processes, that co-workers could be subpoenaed and questioned about social conversations, that the ALJ's notes and papers could be ordered produced in discovery, and that any evidence gathered by these means could be used, in essence, to put the ALJ on trial in district court to determine if he or she should be barred from performing the core functions of his or her office. This would seriously interfere with the ability of many ALJs to decide the cases that come before them based on the evidence and the law.[111]

In this chapter I have covered a broad range of topics from such formal institutions as the federal magistrate-judge, to lofty constitutional debates over delegation, to bare-knuckled political infighting between Congress and the president, with many stops along the way. The unifying theme has been the salience of administration across the broad band of law and politics. Particular attention was given to the judiciary, first in its early efforts to shape administration in its own image and, more recently, in its commitment to preserve the integrity of the administrative process from improper interference by the president, the Congress, and the judiciary itself.

5

Civil Servants' Rights and Powers

Separation of powers deals with institutional arrangements. I now examine the rights and powers of the men and women who manage these separated powers of the state—or, as Woodrow Wilson would say, the ones who "run" the Constitution. The broad powers exercised by administrators can usually be traced to such statutory generalities as "the public interest, convenience, or necessity," or "fair and orderly markets," or "unfair methods of competition." Statutory expressions like "adequate," "appropriate," "expedient," "practicable, "reasonable," and so forth also enhance the powers of administrative agencies and of those who staff them.

This malleable statutory language forms the legal basis for the considerable discretionary powers exercised by administrators. Although statutes ordinarily vest these powers in high-ranking officials, like the heads of the executive departments, these officials, as a practical matter, routinely delegate their statutory powers to their civil service subordinates, both political appointees and career personnel. In this way, administrators play an impressive role in governing the Republic.

With these powers come certain legal disabilities. Civil servants are legitimately subjected to forms of discipline that could not be constitutionally imposed on ordinary citizens—e.g., limitations on political activities, restrictions on the sorts of positions they can fill after leaving government service, obligations to file financial disclosure statements, grooming standards, residency requirements, dress codes, and so forth. No single individual is subjected to all these restrictions, but most civil servants are covered by some of them. These restrictions raise important questions about the constitutional rights of civil servants. In this chapter I look first at the rights of civil servants as government employees and then at their power to share in governing the United States.

RIGHTS

A substantial body of constitutional law has developed around the problematic position of civil servants, problematic because of their dual role as employees and citizens.[1] As employees, they are the hierarchical inferiors of their political masters and, as such, should do their bidding. This is true of all employees. As citizens, however, they are the superiors of elected officials and, like all citizens, have a civic duty to see to it that elected officials serve the people faithfully. It is not always easy to reconcile these conflicting roles. Two of the most important areas concerning civil servants' constitutional rights are freedom of speech and patronage.

Freedom of Speech

The story of the constitutional position of civil servants begins, like almost all constitutional stories, with the founding of the Republic when the first Congress debated the question of whether federal office was a form of property.[2] To examine freedom of speech, however, the starting point is an often quoted maxim of Justice Holmes: "The petitioner may have a constitutional right to talk politics, but he has no constitutional right to be a policeman."[3] This pithy sentence arose in the context of a complaint brought by a policeman who had been fired by the city of New Bedford, Massachusetts, for violating a regulation forbidding partisan comments by policemen and other public servants. Written in 1892 when Holmes was a judge on the Supreme Court of Massachusetts, the maxim took on a life of its own as its author gained increasing prominence, first as chief justice of the Supreme Court of Massachusetts and later during his thirty-year tenure as an associate justice of the Supreme Court of the United States.

Unfortunately, Holmes's memorable sentence slipped the bonds of the prosaic context in which he had originally placed it by carefully stating that "the city may impose any reasonable condition upon holding office within its control" and then concluding that the political neutrality ordinance "seems to us reasonable." Holmes's appeal to reasonableness was often overlooked during the first half of the twentieth century, when the legal principle denying a constitutional right to a job in the public service was transformed into the "doctrine of privilege," which rests "on the premise that because there is no constitutional right to public employment, there are few or no constitutional rights which cannot be restricted while the citizen is in public employment."[4]

The privilege doctrine led to a series of extremely severe judicial rulings in state and federal courts, culminating in the notorious decision in *Bailey v. Richardson* (1950), wherein the U.S. Court of Appeals for the District of Columbia upheld the decision of the Loyalty Review Board to terminate the employment of Dorothy Bailey, a career civil servant, suspected of being a member of the Communist Party.[5] The Loyalty Review Board, established by an executive order from President Harry Truman in 1947, was intended to safeguard against "the infiltration of disloyal persons" into government service. The procedural safeguards to protect civil servants from false accusations were scandalously inadequate. The charges against Bailey came from faceless informers whom she was unable to confront. Indeed, referring to Bailey's accusers, the chairman of the Loyalty Board admitted he did not have "the slightest knowledge as to who they were." He further acknowledged that the only information the Loyalty Board had "about the informants is that unidentified members of the Federal Bureau of Investigation, who did not appear before the Board, believed them to be reliable."[6]

In upholding this travesty of justice, Judge Barrett Prettyman relied squarely on the doctrine of privilege. Over an eloquent dissent from Judge Henry Edgerton, Prettyman argued that "due process of law is not applicable unless one is deprived of something to which he has a right." Just as the New Bedford policeman had no right to his position in 1892, so Dorothy Bailey had no right to be a federal civil servant in 1950. Therefore she was not entitled to due process of law even though she was being terminated on the reputation-shattering grounds of disloyalty. Bailey's appeal to the Supreme Court failed because four justices supported the decision of the lower court and four others opposed it, thereby leaving that decision in force.

David Rosenbloom has aptly called *Bailey v. Richardson* "the transformational case" because its obviously unjust result led to careful scrutiny of the privilege doctrine on which it rested. Gradually, the courts began to chip away at its foundations, and in 1968 the Supreme Court rejected it with unmistakable clarity in *Pickering v. Board of Education.*[7]

Marvin L. Pickering was a teacher in a public high school in Will County, Illinois, who, in 1961, wrote a letter to a local newspaper critical of the way the local board of education and the district superintendent of schools managed the taxpayers' money. He was especially critical of what he saw as the board's over-emphasis on athletics. The board fired him, finding the letter to be "detrimental to the efficient operation and administration of the schools of the district."[8] Even though it appeared that some of Pickering's charges were inaccurate and even though he had been given a hearing before his dismissal, the Supreme Court found the school board's action had violated Pickering's First Amendment right to free speech. Writing for the Court, Justice Thurgood Marshall acknowledged that "the State has interests as an employer in regulating the speech of its employees that differ significantly from those it possesses in connection with regulation of the speech of the citizenry in general."[9] For Marshall, "the problem . . . is to arrive at a balance between the interests of the teacher, as a citizen, in commenting upon matters of public concern and the interests of the State, as an employer, in promoting the efficiency of the public services it performs through its employees."[10] Marshall's balancing test differs markedly from the doctrine of privilege, which would have offered Pickering the cold comfort of learning he had a constitutional right to criticize the school board but no constitutional right to be a teacher. Marshall ignored the question of whether Pickering had a right to the job he held, focusing instead on his rights within that job. Pickering's interest in exercising his right to free speech was to be weighed against the school board's interest in promoting efficient public service. In this particular case, the Court found the balance favored Pickering, but the fact that a *court* struck the balance presaged an increasingly active role for the judiciary in questions of public personnel management. Of particular significance was Marshall's reliance on Pickering's role "as a citizen, in commenting upon matters of public concern." In striking the balance in Pickering's favor, Marshall looked beyond whatever personal satisfaction Pickering might have derived from criticizing his employer and stressed instead his role as a teacher—persons who "are, as a class, the members of the community most likely to have informed and definite opinions as to how funds allotted to the operation of the schools should be spent."[11] Thus Pickering won his case not merely because the new balancing test favored individual rights but also because the Court weighed in the balance the likelihood that a public servant's freedom of speech would promote the public interest, precisely because he was a public servant.

The *Pickering* test announced by Justice Marshall continues to play a major role in constitutional adjudication of disciplinary actions taken against civil servants. Not surprisingly, the courts have not always applied the test consistently over the years because different judges will inevitably assign different weights to free speech claims of civil servants when they conflict with an agency's perception of its needs for efficiency and effectiveness.

Connick v. Myers[12] presents a good example of a case in which the Supreme Court put its thumb on the government's side of the scale. Sheila Myers, an assistant district attorney in New Orleans, was transferred from one section of the criminal court to another without her consent. She protested the decision to her boss, Harry Connick, the district attorney, and to Dennis Waldron, an intermediate superior. Her complaint went beyond her own transfer and cited other examples of general discontent among her fellow employees. When told that other employees did not share her negative view of the office, she decided to prepare a questionnaire to learn her colleagues' attitudes on such matters as office morale, transfer policy, and the need for a grievance committee. Particularly offensive to Connick were questions on whether the employees had confidence in the word of five named supervisors and whether they felt pressured to participate in political campaigns. Connick treated the questionnaire as insubordination and fired Myers, who served at his pleasure. She sued, alleging she was fired simply for exercising her First Amendment rights of free speech, which would be impermissible grounds for terminating even an employee serving at the pleasure of the person who had appointed her. Applying the *Pickering* test, the federal district court upheld her claim and ordered reinstatement, backpay, and attorney's fees. The court of appeals affirmed this decision.

Somewhat surprisingly, the Supreme Court reversed the lower courts and upheld Connick's dismissal of Myers. Justice Byron White, writing for the five judges who formed the narrow majority, maintained the lower courts had "misapplied our decision in *Pickering*."[13] Justice White stressed the "repeated emphasis in *Pickering* on the right of a public employee 'as a citizen, in commenting upon matters of public concern.'"[14] He then found that the grievances in Myers's questionnaire—with the sole exception of the complaint relating to political campaigns—could not "be fairly characterized as constituting speech on a matter of public concern" and that, therefore, it was unnecessary for the court to apply *Pickering*. He further asserted that where speech unrelated to public affairs was concerned, "government officials should enjoy wide latitude in managing their offices, without intrusive oversight by the judiciary in the name of the First Amendment."[15] He justified this deferential posture toward administrative agencies on the grounds that the Court's task was simply "to ensure that citizens are not deprived of fundamental rights by virtue of working for the government." This concern must not lead the Court "to require a grant of immunity for employee grievances not afforded by the First Amendment to those who do not work for the State."[16] Thus Justice White was trying to provide an even playing field for public and private employees where matters of public concern were not involved.

As far as the political campaign issue was concerned, Justice White applied the *Pickering* test and found District Attorney Connick's fear of a "mini-insurrection" in his office—speculative as it was— sufficiently important to justify his dismissal of Myers. He put particular emphasis on the fact that Myers's actions took place at the office, thereby threatening to disrupt the orderly management of the district attorney's responsibilities, whereas Pickering had written to a newspaper and therefore posed no threat to the management of his school. White's emphasis on the in-house character of Myers's complaint is quite instructive for public managers. He characterizes her complaints "as an employee grievance concerning internal office policy."[17]

Clearly, Sheila Myers was no whistle-blower, but had she gone public with her complaint and generated substantial news coverage, she might have won her case. If her grievances had won the attention of the media, Justice White would have been hard-pressed to claim they were of no public interest.[18]

From a management point of view, Sheila Myers acted far more responsibly by keeping her complaints in-house rather than airing them in public and thereby embarrassing her superiors. Ironically, this act of organizational loyalty on her part considerably weakened her case. It may have been a fatal error.

This ironic outcome underscores the tension between constitutional law and public management. In this case, the Constitution would have treated an irresponsible employee more kindly than it treated Sheila Myers. As a perverse corollary of this ironic conclusion, Justice White's analysis creates a strong incentive for agency heads to fire disgruntled employees at the first sign of their unhappiness and thereby preempt any risk of their going to the media with their story while they are still in the agency's employ. Such behavior would, of course, violate every standard of good management, to say nothing of common sense and decency. It serves to highlight, however, the clash of cultures between the worlds of public management and constitutional law.

Four years after *Connick v. Myers,* the Supreme Court revisited civil servants' freedom of speech with a strikingly different outcome, which suggests the difficulty the Court finds in defining its constitutional role in personnel matters. The case, *Rankin v. McPherson* (1987),[19] began on 30 March 1981, the day the world was shocked to learn that President Reagan had been wounded in an assassination attempt in Washington, D.C. When Ardith McPherson, a nineteen-year-old probationary clerical employee in the constable's office of Harris County, Texas, heard the news, she said to one of her coworkers, "If they go for him again, I hope they get him." A third employee overheard this ill-advised remark and reported it to Constable Walter H. Rankin, who fired McPherson after questioning her briefly. Shortly thereafter, she brought suit for reinstatement in the U.S. District Court for the Southern District of Texas, relying on a federal statute that prohibits state officials acting "under color of state law" from depriving any person of his or her rights under the Constitution or laws of the United States. McPherson maintained Rankin had deprived her of her constitutional right to freedom of speech. She argued that although her probationary status made her exceedingly vulnerable to termination, she could not be terminated simply because of her speech. This argument relied, of course, on the long-standing rejection of the privilege doctrine that had by then been firmly established in *Pickering* and other cases from the 1960s and the early 1970s. Under the privilege doctrine, she would have been told she had a constitutional right to wish President Reagan ill but that she had no constitutional right to work in the constable's office. Applying the *Pickering* balancing test, the district court rejected McPherson's argument; but the U.S. Court of Appeals for the Fifth Circuit reversed this ruling. Constable Rankin appealed this reversal to the Supreme Court of the United States. In a five to four decision, the Supreme Court upheld McPherson's claim.

Justice Marshall delivered the opinion of the Court, in which he first established McPherson's comment, despite its offensive character, "as constituting speech on a matter of public concern." Following *Pickering,* he set up a balancing test between McPherson's free speech interest and Rankin's managerial interest in firing her for what she had said. Justice Marshall then delved into the details of McPherson's employment. "She was not a commissioned peace officer, did not wear a uniform, and was not authorized to make arrests or to carry a gun." Her "duties were purely clerical," and she worked "in a room to which the public did not have ready access." Her offensive remark was heard by only two other persons, and there is "no evidence that it interfered with the functioning of the office."[20] At the end of this fact-driven analysis, Justice Marshall concluded,

"Given the function of the agency, McPherson's position in the office, and the nature of her statement, we are not persuaded that Rankin's interest in discharging her outweighed her rights under the First Amendment."[21]

Justice Antonin Scalia wrote a dissenting opinion, which three other justices joined. He got off to a good start by repeating a quip from Rankin's brief to the effect that "no law enforcement agency is required by the First Amendment to permit one of its employees to 'ride with the cops and cheer for the robbers.'" Relying on a rather strained definition of "public concern," Justice Scalia unconvincingly disputed Justice Marshall's finding that McPherson's remark satisfied this element of the *Pickering* test. Far more impressive was the second argument in his opinion, which began, "Even if I agreed that McPherson's statement was speech on a matter of 'public concern,' I would still find it unprotected. It is important to be clear on what the issue is in this part of the case."[22]

In drawing attention to what he considers "the issue in this part of the case," Scalia signals his displeasure with the Court's balancing test. He does not object to balancing tests as such but to what Justice Marshall wants to balance in this particular case. For Scalia, the issue "is not, as the Court suggests, whether Rankin's interest in *discharging* [McPherson] outweighs her rights under the First Amendment." Rankin's interest in this case, according to Scalia, must not be confined to discharging a wayward employee but must be expanded to include his "*interest in preventing the expression of such statements in his agency*" as those McPherson uttered. Scalia criticizes the opinion of the Court for what he sees as its misplaced emphasis on McPherson's termination. He acknowledges that the punishment Rankin imposed may, as a practical matter, have been excessive, but for Scalia, such an assessment is no part of the judicial function. As he puts it: "We are not sitting as a panel to develop sound principles of proportionality for adverse action in the state civil service."[23] That is, the suitability of the punishment visited upon McPherson is properly an administrative, not a judicial, question.

Scalia's reconstruction of the balance illuminates the true nature of balancing tests and reveals their problematic character as well. Scalia would balance McPherson's First Amendment interests not against Rankin's interest in firing her but against his interest in preventing expression of the sentiments McPherson announced. Having thus reset the balance, he would then find for Rankin. To do otherwise, that is, to find for McPherson once the balance had been reset to Scalia's liking, would mean she had a *right* to say what she said and therefore *no* disciplinary action could be taken against her. Indeed, she could repeat her outrageous comment day after day without fear of any disciplinary action at all. Scalia maintains that the Court's misplaced focus on the outcome of the incident—McPherson's dismissal—has obscured the true nature of the case. A court should confine itself to deciding whether or not the constable can punish McPherson for what she said. If he can, then the appropriateness of the punishment, for example, a letter of reprimand, a delayed promotion, or even dismissal should be determined by a civil service personnel board.

Scalia's dissent brings out the key problem in balancing tests. It is not to decide which side has the "weightier" claim; once the balance is set, this is often obvious. The real problem is to decide which weights should be placed on the scale. The answer to this question defines the difference between Marshall and Scalia in deciding this case. If Rankin's interest in *firing* McPherson goes in the scale, he loses because the punishment is too severe. If Rankin's broader interest in being able to take some (unspecified) sort of disciplinary action against an employee like McPherson is put on the scale, he wins because such intemperate speech in the workplace should not be allowed to pass without rebuke. If, as a matter of fact, the unspecified punishment turns out to be dismissal, Rankin still wins because, in Scalia's analysis, the precise nature of the punishment is not a judicial question.

Patronage

Political patronage in the United States is a practice as old as the Republic, but despite its longevity, the Supreme Court found most patronage practices unconstitutional in three important decisions during the fourteen-year period from 1976 to 1990. Like the decisions on free speech, the patronage decisions grew from the dual role of civil servants as employees and citizens.

The first case, *Elrod v. Burns* (1976),[24] involved three employees in the Sheriff's Office of Cook County, Illinois, who were fired by a newly elected sheriff, Richard Elrod, a Democrat. The three employees, all Republicans, had been appointed by Elrod's Republican predecessor and sued to maintain their positions on the grounds that their politically motivated terminations violated their rights under the First Amendment.

Cook County includes the city of Chicago, where patronage appointments and dismissals were well-established practices. Many observers of Chicago politics found the suit bizarre since the plaintiffs owed their jobs to their political affiliations in the first place. "If you live by the sword, you die by the sword" seemed to be the long and short of the matter. Unfortunately for Sheriff Elrod, five Supreme Court justices saw it quite otherwise.

Justice William Brennan, writing a plurality opinion joined by Justices Marshall and White,[25] found that the practice of patronage dismissals—however well established—imposed a severe burden on constitutionally protected beliefs and associations and therefore "must survive exacting scrutiny" if it was to be judged constitutionally acceptable. This "exacting scrutiny" included a showing by the state that its interest in encouraging patronage dismissals advanced an interest that was "paramount" and of "vital importance" and, furthermore, that the particular scheme of patronage at issue was the "least restrictive of freedom of belief and association" in securing the state's paramount interest.[26] Sheriff Elrod was unable to pass this demanding test, and therefore the Court found for the three employees. The decision was a stunning illustration of the marked tendency in

American constitutional law for individual rights to trump the claims of institutional interests—in this case the interests of political parties, which, as Justice Lewis Powell argued in dissent, had traditionally been regarded as vital components of democratic government.

Justice Brennan did not forbid all forms of patronage dismissals, allowing exceptions for persons in "policymaking positions," despite the problem of drawing a "clear line . . . between policymaking and nonpolicymaking positions."[27] Justice Potter Stewart, joined by Justice Harry Blackmun, wrote a concurring opinion that set aside much of Brennan's analysis—notably his language on "exacting scrutiny"—and stated "the single substantive question" to be "whether a nonpolicy making, nonconfidential employee can be discharged from a job that he is satisfactorily performing upon the sole ground of his political beliefs." He then added, "I agree with the Court that he cannot."[28] Thus Justice Stewart added a confidential employee exception to Brennan's exception for policy makers.

Although the thrust of Justice Brennan's opinion was clearly toward the individual rights of the employees fired by Sheriff Elrod, there was a faint echo of *Pickering*'s emphasis on the public interest served by upholding the rights of public servants. Brennan argued that patronage impeded "the free functioning of the electoral process" because "conditioning public employment on partisan support prevents support of competing political interests. . . . Patronage thus tips the electoral process in favor of the incumbent party, and where the practice's scope is substantial relative to the size of the electorate, the impact on the process can be significant."[29] Despite this bow to the integrity of the electoral process, *Elrod*'s perfunctory concern with the public interest is but a pale shadow of the bright hues we saw in *Pickering*. The latter defended the constitutional right of public servants to make robust contributions by their informed participation in the public argument; the former defended their right to be kept out of the political process by saving them from partisan dismissal. *Pickering*, therefore, presents a more positive view of the civil servant's role as citizen than *Elrod*.

The most interesting aspect of *Elrod* was the sharp contrast between Justice Brennan's argument based on legal precedents established, for the most part, in the decade or so preceding this decision and Justice Powell's dissenting opinion, which relied on the long history of patronage to support its importance for the stability of political parties as essential elements of a democratic regime. Starting with the administration of George Washington, Powell highlighted the ups and downs of patronage in American political life. He characterizes patronage as a "highly practical and rather fundamental element of our political system," which should not be subjected to "the theoretical abstractions of a political science seminar." He maintained that Justice Brennan's analysis "seriously underestimates the strength of the government interest—especially at the local level—in allowing some patronage hiring practices." These government interests include "encouraging stable political parties and avoiding excessive political fragmentation."[30] He concludes by quoting Justice Holmes to the effect that "if a thing has been practiced for two hundred years by common consent, it will need a strong case for the Fourteenth Amendment to affect it."[31]

In direct opposition to Justice Powell's historical approach, Justice Brennan asserts that "our inquiry does not begin with the judgment of history," even though history may shed some light on "the actual operation of a practice" like patronage. For Brennan, the paramount considerations are "constitutional limitations" revealed in Supreme Court decisions, many of which had been delivered during Brennan's tenure on the court. Brennan's reliance on legal precedent divorced from the actual workings of partisan politics gives credence to Justice Powell's complaint about "the theoretical abstractions of a political science seminar."

Just four years after *Elrod,* the constitutionality of a patronage dismissal was once again before the Supreme Court in *Branti v. Finkel* (1980).[32] The aggrieved parties were Aaron Finkel and Alan Tabakman, assistant public defenders in Rockland County, New York, who were threatened with dismissal by a newly appointed public defender, who, in turn, owed his position to a newly elected county legislature. Finkel and Tabakman were Republicans who had received their appointments in 1971 and in 1975, when their party controlled the county legislature. Control passed to the Democrats in 1977, and this led to the appointment of Peter Branti, a Democrat, as public defender. When he began to execute termination notices, Finkel and Tabakman sought and received an injunction from the Federal District Court for the Southern District of New York forbidding Branti from carrying out his planned terminations. The court of appeals upheld the injunction, and Branti appealed to the Supreme Court. Finkel had prevailed in the lower courts by relying squarely on *Elrod,* but Branti maintained the position of assistant public defender fell under the exceptions to *Elrod* that Justice Brennan had allowed for policy-making positions and Justice Stewart had recognized for confidential employees.

The precise meaning of *Elrod* was unclear because a majority of the justices had not agreed on one opinion to support the decision that the Republican employees in the Cook County Sheriff's Office should be reinstated. Whatever doubts *Elrod* had spawned were removed by Justice Stevens's opinion clearly upholding Finkel's position—an opinion in which five other justices joined, thereby creating a solid precedent for future patronage dismissal cases.

Stevens acknowledged that *Elrod*'s exceptions for policy-making and confidential employees had created considerable confusion. He noted, for example, that a football coach at a large state university might well be considered a policy maker, "but no one could seriously claim that Republicans make better coaches than Democrats or vice versa, no matter which party is in control of the state government."[33] Furthermore, election judges, who are neither policy makers nor confidential employees, are quite properly required to meet certain partisan conditions and could surely be dismissed if they changed their party registration. He then announced a new standard to be applied to patronage dismissals: "In sum, the ultimate inquiry is not whether the label 'policymaker' or 'confidential' fits a particular position; rather, the question is whether the hiring authority can demonstrate that party affiliation is an appropriate requirement for the effective performance of the public office involved."[34]

This new test may improve on *Elrod*, but it surely creates problems of its own. One might wonder if partisan affiliation is an "appropriate requirement" for some of the highest offices in the land. Recall the examples of Republicans Henry Stimson, Douglas Dillon, and William Cohen, who served with distinction in the cabinets of Democratic presidents Franklin Roosevelt, John Kennedy, and William Clinton. Could an incumbent secretary of defense challenge the right of an incoming president of the opposing party to remove him from office to make room for a defense secretary of the new president's party? It is settled constitutional law that the president has unfettered discretion to remove the heads of executive departments,[35] but can such discretion be squared with Justice Stevens's statement that before political officers can remove subordinates for their partisan affiliation, they must first "demonstrate that party affiliation is an appropriate requirement for the effective performance of the public office involved"?

Justice Powell dissented once again. Having made the historical case for patronage in his *Elrod* dissent, he offers in *Branti* a veritable paean to political parties, celebrating the many and varied ways in which they enrich American democracy. The need for patronage is then skillfully linked to the parties' well being to show that "patronage practices further sufficiently important interests to justify tangential burdening of First Amendment rights."[36] He supplements his defense of parties with an attack on the judicial activism he finds implicit in Stevens's opinion. "Government hiring practices long thought to be a matter of legislative and executive discretion will now be subjected to judicial oversight." This shift represents an "exercise of judicial lawmaking" and "a significant intrusion into the area of legislative and policy concerns."[37] This argument recalls the concern about judicial excesses in balancing tests wherein judges not only weigh the competing interests but also determine what goes on the scale. The judicialization of public personnel management has been a hallmark of constitutional law in the final third of the twentieth century.

In a third patronage case, a controversy arose over an executive order issued in 1980 by Illinois governor William Thompson, a Republican, establishing a hiring freeze that prohibited state officials from hiring any new employees or creating new positions without the "express permission" of the governor. As a matter of fact, hiring and other similar personnel actions continued apace, but they were all approved by a special agency in the governor's office. This office made the decisions on political grounds favoring Republicans and extended its sphere to promotions and transfers as well. Cynthia Rutan and her colleagues, the petitioners in *Rutan et al. v. Republican Party of Illinois*,[38] alleged that they suffered various forms of discrimination in personnel actions because they did not support the Illinois Republican Party. Two of them were denied promotions, two others were not recalled after layoffs, one was denied a transfer to an office near his home, and still another maintained he had been repeatedly denied employment by the state as a prison guard. They attributed their unhappy states to Republican partisanship.

Since *Elrod* and *Branti* had dealt only with patronage dismissals, the complaints alleged in this case required the Supreme Court to address the further question of whether the reasoning of the earlier cases "extends to promotion, transfer, recall or hiring decisions involving public employment positions for which party affiliation is not an appropriate qualification."[39] Writing for a closely divided Court, Justice Brennan answered the question in the affirmative, thereby finding "patronage an unconstitutional basis for almost all personnel actions, not just dismissals."[40]

Justice Powell had left the Supreme Court in 1987, and so it fell to Justice Scalia to pick up the dissenters' argument where his erstwhile colleague had left it in *Branti v. Finkel.* Building on Powell's historical argument, Justice Scalia offers a long and searching probe on the proper use of history in constitutional adjudication, thereby using this civil service case as the foundation for a serious, if necessarily incomplete, discussion of his jurisprudence of "original intent," a topic that merited a remarkable degree of attention from legal scholars during the 1990s.[41]

Following Powell's historical analysis, Scalia maintains that "patronage was, without any thought that it could be unconstitutional, a basis for government employment from the earliest days of the Republic until *Elrod*—and has continued unabated *since Elrod* to the extent permitted by that unfortunate decision."[42] Since the constitutional text is "ambiguous" in the sense that it says nothing explicit about patronage, judges should be guided more by historical practice than by "the latest 'rule,' or 'three part test,' or 'balancing test' devised by the court."[43] In view of the "unbroken tradition" in favor of patronage, Scalia maintains that there was "no basis for holding that patronage-based dismissals violated the First Amendment."[44] Hence, he concludes that *Elrod* and *Branti* should be overruled, or, failing that, at least not extended from dismissals to all forms of personnel actions.

Recognizing the far-reaching jurisprudential implications of Scalia's use of history, Justice Stevens took the unusual step of writing a concurring opinion for the sole purpose of refuting Scalia's position. Predictably, he argued that under Scalia's reasoning the Supreme Court's decision in *Brown v. Board of Education* was wrong because it declared unconstitutional the long-standing principle of separate-but-equal public schools for white and black children.

In a footnote to his opinion, obviously inserted after he had read Stevens's critique, Justice Scalia parries the thrust by arguing that history is his guide only when the constitutional text is ambiguous. He maintains that "the Fourteenth Amendment's requirement of 'equal protection of the laws,' combined with the Thirteenth Amendment's abolition of black slavery, leaves no room for doubt that laws treating people differently because of their race are invalid." For the benefit of those who do not find the constitutional text quite so clear, he adds that "a tradition of *unchallenged* validity did not exist with respect to the practice in *Brown.*" That is. there had always been serious criticism of the constitutional validity of separate but equal as the correct interpretation of the equal protection clause, regardless of Supreme Court rulings in this matter. Although there had always been partisan complaints about how patronage is used in specific instances, Scalia finds no challenge to its legitimacy as constitutional practice.

In light of the privilege doctrine, it is interesting to observe Stevens's charge that Scalia's reliance on history would reinstate the privilege doctrine because patronage rests on a sharp distinction between rights and privileges—a distinction that has met with "unequivocal repudiation" by the Supreme Court. Scalia's rejoinder is instructive:

> That will not do. If the right–privilege distinction was once used to explain the practice [of patronage,] and if that distinction is to be repudiated, then one must simply devise some other theory to explain it. The order of precedence is that a constitutional theory must be wrong if its application contradicts a clear constitutional tradition, not that a clear constitutional tradition must be wrong if it does not conform to the current constitutional theory. On Justice Stevens' view of the matter, this Court examines a historical practice, endows it with an intellectual foundation, and later, by simply undermining that foundation, relegates the constitutional tradition to the dustbin of history. That is not how constitutional adjudication works.[45]

Stevens's charge and Scalia's reply find the civil service at the heart of one of the most important constitutional issues of our time—the normative significance of constitutional practice. Scalia finds it unacceptable that the Court should endow a constitutional practice, like patronage, with an intellectual foundation, like the privilege doctrine, and then later reject that foundation (as the Court did in *Pickering*) and at the same time reject the constitutionality of the original practice. For Scalia, constitutional theories, like the privilege doctrine, are the handmaids, not the masters, of constitutional practice.

POWERS

In shifting from the rights of civil servants to the powers they exercise in governing the Republic, I examine first the development of the Post Office from the founding period to the eve of the Civil War, then some recent examples of how Supreme Court rulings have expanded the discretionary authority of civil servants to govern as their consciences prompt them, and finally, a series of administrative situations illustrating concretely how decisions taken by individual government employees have contributed to the development of the civil service as a great institution of the state.

The Post Office

When one thinks of the Post Office, the forerunner of today's semiprivatized Postal Service, one seldom thinks of the constitutional principle of freedom of the press—unless one has had the good fortune to have read Richard R. John's *Spreading the News: The American Postal System from Franklin to Morris.*[46] Beginning with the Post Office Act of 1792, John argues convincingly that the generous terms by which Congress encouraged the mailing of newspapers throughout the United States played a vital role in linking the eastern seaboard to the hinterland and thereby created not only a national market but also "a new kind of public sphere." Newspapers published in eastern cities provided extensive coverage of national and international affairs. They accounted in no small part for de Tocqueville's surprise to discover in 1831 that backwoodsmen in Michigan were remarkably conversant with the great affairs of the day. No longer was it "taken for granted that if a citizen wished to participate in public life he had no choice but to leave the countryside and move to the city." Thanks to the generous congressional subsidy for mailing newspapers, the "public sphere" leaped over the bounds of coastal cities and "became disembodied, that is, it became identified with a process that existed not in a particular place but rather in the imagination of millions of people, most of whom would never meet face-to-face."[47]

Blackstone's fiscal view of England's postal system as primarily a means of raising money for the state had yielded to Benjamin Rush's pedagogic vision of the American postal system as the best means of "conveying light and heat to every individual in the federal commonwealth." Indeed, the prominent political philosopher Francis Lieber could write in 1832 that the postal system "deserved to be ranked with the printing press and the mariner's compass as 'one of the most effective elements of civilization.'"[48]

The Post Office's contribution to the diffusion of knowledge of public affairs throughout the United States caught the attention of thoughtful observers from the 1790s to the 1830s, although they might draw different lessons from this startling phenomenon. For example, George Washington favored the elimination of all postage fees on newspapers because he hoped that their "faithful representation of public proceedings" would instruct the people in civic virtue; whereas James Madison saw the circulation of newspapers as a way of "encouraging the citizenry to participate in public affairs by consulting with its representatives with regard to the ongoing affairs of state."[49] Regardless of how prominent men might interpret the circulation of newspapers by the postal system, it brought a heightened awareness of public affairs that amply justifies John's thematic treatment of the Post Office as "an agent of change" in furthering the constitutional values of a free press.[50]

The Post Office's role as an agent of change inevitably drew it into controversy; and since the changes it effected were directly related to constitutional values, it is not surprising that the controversies themselves were often constitutional. One of the most interesting of these controversies began in 1808 at a postal distribution center in western Pennsylvania, where Hugh Wylie, an elder in the local Presbyterian Church, was postmaster. Postmaster General Gideon Granger required local postmasters to sort the incoming mail every day, including Sundays. Since he had to be at the post office on Sunday, Wylie decided to open it to the public as a courtesy to patrons coming into town to worship. Some of Wylie's coreligionists were offended at the sight of a church elder working on Sunday and scandalized at his opening the post office for secular affairs on the Lord's day. They complained to Postmaster General Granger about what they saw as Wylie's violation of the Sabbath, but to no avail. Granger dismissed their complaints with the bland assurance that he did not believe Wylie's activities were "immoral or will be offensive to Heaven."[51]

Wylie's situation was complicated by the fact that at that time Congress had not yet regulated the hours of postmasters by law. His duty to sort the mail daily was grounded in an administrative regulation; and his decision to open the post office on Sunday, though common practice in many parts of the United States, was taken on his own initiative. Consequently, Wylie's critics sought ecclesiastical sanctions against him for his Sabbath activities. Their complaint and Wylie's defense went through several levels of appeal before the Presbyterian General Assembly eventually decided against him and "expelled Wylie from the church" for his refusal to close the post office on Sunday.[52]

In 1810, Congress regulated by law the problems Wylie had encountered with his church, providing "that henceforth postmasters would be required to deliver on demand any item that they received at their office on every single day of the week, including the Sabbath, and to open their offices to the public on every day of the week that the mail arrived."[53] This legislation served only to nationalize the issue, thereby provoking the ire of many prominent Protestant clergymen. Opposition was particularly strong in New England, where general sentiment was running vigorously against the federal government as the nation prepared for what became known as the War of 1812, a war bitterly opposed in New England.

The Sunday mail controversy had to wait a full century for a final resolution in 1912 when the National Association of Letter Carriers added its considerable worldly weight to the concerns of pious clergymen to put an end once and for all to postal services on Sunday. Before its denouement in 1912, however, the Sunday mail issue had waxed and waned throughout the nineteenth century. Along the way, Sabbatarians argued that the Post Office Act of 1810 violated the free exercise of religion guaranteed in the First Amendment and was even "an *American test act,* that, by requiring postmasters to work on the Sabbath, was no different from English legislation that excluded from public office anyone who was not a member of the Church of England."[54]

The most intense debate over Sunday mail took place between 1826 and

1831. It was at that time that Americans began to grasp the potential role of the federal government in shaping their everyday lives. The postal system was a particularly powerful symbol of the presence of the federal government in their communities, especially in view of its capacity to "shape the pattern of everyday life" in a matter of local concern as important as observing the Sabbath. The growing awareness of the federal government's capacity to influence local communities was soon linked with the Calvinist theological principle "that Christians had an obligation to uphold a covenant with God that extended beyond the conduct of the individual and the local congregation to embrace the administration of the state." In the earliest days of the Republic, the spheres of the state and local governments were the areas in which this Christian duty could be discharged, but the Sunday mail issue led thoughtful religious leaders to subject this easy assumption to closer scrutiny. This, in turn, led them to wonder if the federal government "should be held morally accountable to God." This line of reasoning took on added importance when it shifted from the relatively tame issue of Sunday observance to the all-consuming issue of slavery. It was no coincidence that such leading Sabbatarians as William Lloyd Garrison, Lewis Tappan, and William Jay soon enlisted in the ranks of the abolitionists. The Sunday mail enabled the federal government to invade civil society and thereby made it morally accountable before God. "This was a momentous realization, and one that was destined to shape American public life for decades to come."[55]

It was a simple matter for Sabbatarians-turned-abolitionists to argue that if the mail could be used for the evil purpose of defiling the Lord's day, it could surely also be used for the salutary purpose of converting slaveholders from their sinful ways. As antislavery newspapers began to stream into southern states, local post offices became the targets of slaveholders' wrath. On the night of 29 July 1835, a small group of vigilantes broke into the post office in Charleston, South Carolina, and made off with a bundle of thousands of abolitionist newspapers, published by the American Anti-Slavery Society, that had arrived earlier in the day from New York. The next night the newspapers fueled a gaudy bonfire witnessed by some two thousand Charlestonians.

This spectacular event received immediate national attention and put Charleston's postmaster, Alfred Huger, in an extremely difficult position. Huger was a strong Union man, as one would expect the federal postmaster in a major city to be, but he was also a wealthy planter who owned some seventy slaves. He took personal offense at the abolitionists' denunciation of slavery as sinful, an affront to him and five generations of his ancestors. He also found himself in what he considered an impossible legal situation because as a federal officer he was obliged to "transmit promptly and without discrimination all mailable items that arrived at his office." South Carolina law, however, obliged him "to hand over to the appropriate state authorities any publication whose transmission might incite a slave rebellion." Huger's correspondence indicates his belief that the abolitionist papers might produce just that result.[56]

Before the arrival of the pilfered abolitionist papers, Huger had negotiated an understanding with his Charleston neighbors whereby he would execute his federal duties by delivering the papers that actually reached his office but would urge Postmaster General Amos Kendall to keep further shipments of abolitionist literature from reaching Charleston. Knowing Kendall's pronounced sympathy for the slaveholding states, Huger had every reason to think that his request would be granted. This arrangement did not survive the break-in because Huger now feared for the safety of the mail in transit on the streets of Charleston, for there was no assurance that the next group of thieves would be so single-minded as to steal only abolitionist publications. His fears for the rest of the mail were justified by the common practice at that time of sending cash by post. He made it known that henceforth he would not release any abolitionist literature from his office even in the unlikely event that Postmaster General Kendall should specifically order him to do so. He explained his position to his colleague, Samuel L. Gouverneur, the postmaster of New York, by sharing his belief "that the mail could not pass thro' the streets with those [abolitionist] pamphlets in it; I *therefore*, to *save the mail* took them out and told the citizens I had done so. . . . Where then has been the compromise? I have made none, and should think myself dishonored if I had."[57]

Huger had little to fear from his superiors for his violation of federal law. Secretary of State John Forsyth set the tone of the Jackson administration when he wrote to Vice-President Martin Van Buren in the immediate aftermath of the Charleston break-in that Postmaster Huger should be supported "in fixed resolve to prevent the circulation of those papers, the laws of the United States to the contrary notwithstanding." President Jackson, who despised the abolitionists, was proclaiming from the White House that the abolitionists "ought to be made to atone for this wicked attempt with their lives." As for Postmaster General Kendall, he wrote an "open letter" to Huger just one week after the break-in in which he allowed that ordinarily federal officials are obliged to obey federal laws, but that extraordinary situations may oblige one to honor a "higher" obligation to the "communities" where they reside. Although he did not explicitly authorize Huger's decision to suppress the abolitionist literature, his meaning was unmistakably clear. Two weeks later, he wrote another open letter, this time to Postmaster Gouverneur in New York, who had honored Huger's request to withhold shipment of abolitionist papers to Charleston. Once again, Kendall stopped just short of explicitly advocating lawlessness but assured his subordinate that the course he had followed was "best for the country" and added the comforting note "that if I were situated as you are, I would do as you have done."[58]

Public opinion in the North was outraged at Kendall's dereliction of duty. One did not have to be an abolitionist to see his abdication as a form of press censorship. Even seven years after the Charleston break-in, John Quincy Adams — himself no abolitionist — could still muster enough anger to denounce Kendall's open letters "as a violation of the freedom of the press, as a violation of the sacred character of the post office, and of the rights and liberties of all the free people of the United States."[59]

One of the most serious consequences of the crisis occasioned by the abolitionist literature was the rapid expansion of arguments in support of slavery as a positive good. If abolitionists were to denounce slavery as sin, slave owners inevitably responded in kind by celebrating it as an institution established by God and nothing less than the "cornerstone" of our "republican edifice." Such polarizing rhetoric is the enemy of serious public argument, as we have learned in our own time when unqualified denunciations of all abortions as murder have prompted the affirmative defense of abortion as simply a matter of choice—positions singularly ill-suited to guide a woman in need of help who knows only too well that she faces something that is far more than a choice but less than a murder.

The polarizing rhetoric unleashed by the abolitionists foreshadowed the ultimate polarization of civil war. Public administration through its postal service played a sorry but crucial role in this high constitutional drama of state. Richard John captures nicely the nub of the matter when he describes the crisis over abolitionist literature as "the tragic epilogue to the communications revolution that Congress had set in motion with the passage of the Post Office Act of 1792." For a while, "the expansion of the facilities of communication had worked to strengthen the bonds of the Union," but from 1835 to 1861, "the same facilities worked no less inexorably to drive the Union apart."[60]

Administrative Discretion

Political commentators have often remarked on the conservative bent of the Supreme Court over the past quarter century, especially when compared with its performance during the heady days of the Warren Court. This conservatism has often worked to the advantage of administrative agencies in suits brought against them by persons charging that certain individual rights have been illegally disregarded by a particular agency. I shall examine here several Supreme Court decisions favorable to administrative agencies that strike me—at least at first blush—as being exceedingly harsh and somewhat unfair to the persons challenging the agencies' action. I say "at first blush" because after careful reflection I found the Court's arguments in favor of the agencies to be at least plausible if not entirely convincing. The strength of the Court's arguments lay in their constitutional analysis, but they did little to allay my belief that the decisions were harsh and unfair even if they were constitutionally sound.

I select Supreme Court decisions that are constitutionally plausible and yet harsh and unfair to highlight the opportunity such decisions offer to conscientious civil servants to use their administrative discretion to bring about fairness in future cases with similar circumstances. My point is ethical rather than strictly legal. Supreme Court decisions upholding seemingly harsh and unfair treatment of persons *permit* agencies to continue to act in the same way in the future without *requiring* them to do so. Administrators have the discretion to take a gentle line even when the law permits a harsher one, if circumstances warrant such gentleness. Just when and where an administrator should be severe or gentle is a matter of prudence that is, of course, a crucial element in the responsible exercise of administrative discretion.

Lest my ethical argument become too abstract, I shall present some concrete cases to illustrate my point and then resume the ethical analysis. I shall first examine in some detail a child abuse case and then review more briefly cases involving law enforcement and federal pension benefits. The three cases, disparate as they are, point to the same conclusion—harsh principles of constitutional law open opportunities for the responsible use of administrative discretion.

The child abuse case, *DeShaney v. Winnebago County Department of Social Services,*[61] focused on the tragic plight of Joshua DeShaney, an abused child whose father had beaten him "so severely that he suffered permanent brain damage and was rendered profoundly retarded." The boy's mother sued the Department of Social Services (DSS) of Winnebago County, Wisconsin, claiming that its failure to intervene on Joshua's behalf deprived him of the liberty guaranteed by the due process clause of the Fourteenth Amendment.

Joshua arrived in Winnebago County in 1980 as a one-year-old infant. He was brought there by his father, Randy, who had won custody of the boy when he and Joshua's mother divorced while residing in Wyoming. Shortly after his arrival in Wisconsin, Randy married again, and this marriage also ended in divorce. Joshua's problems first came to the attention of the DSS in January 1982 during the divorce proceedings ending Randy's second marriage. His second wife told the police of his abusive treatment of Joshua, and the police advised the DSS of the allegation. The agency interviewed Randy, who denied the charge, and no further action was taken. In January 1983, Joshua was admitted to a local hospital "with multiple bruises and abrasions." Suspecting child abuse, the examining physician notified the DSS, and this time the agency persuaded a Wisconsin juvenile court to issue an order placing Joshua temporarily in the custody of the hospital. The county then appointed a Child Protection Team that included several DSS caseworkers to evaluate Joshua's situation. Finding insufficient evidence of child abuse, the team recommended to the juvenile court that Joshua be returned to his father's custody. The court accepted this recommendation. The team also urged Randy to enter into a "voluntary agreement" specifying that Joshua be enrolled in a preschool program, that Randy take advantage of certain counseling services, and that his girlfriend be encouraged to move out of his home. Randy agreed to these terms.

One month later, Joshua was again treated for suspicious injuries in an emergency room and the DSS was notified once again, but the caseworker found no basis for action. For the next six months, Joshua's caseworker noticed several suspicious injuries to the boy's head during her regular visits. She also noticed that Randy's girlfriend remained in his home and that Joshua was not in preschool. According to Chief Justice Rehnquist's opinion of the court: "The caseworker dutifully recorded these incidents in her files . . . but did nothing more."[62] In November 1983, the emergency room again alerted the DSS that Joshua had been treated for injuries that appeared to be the result of child abuse. On her next two house visits, the caseworker was told Joshua was too ill to receive her.

Finally, in March 1985, Joshua—now four years old—was beaten "so severely that he fell into a life-threatening coma. Emergency brain surgery revealed a series of hemorrhages caused by traumatic injuries to the head inflicted over a long period of time." Randy DeShaney was tried and convicted of child abuse, and Joshua was placed in an institution for the profoundly retarded where "he is expected to spend the rest of his life."[63]

Joshua's mother based her suit against the DSS on a federal statute authorizing suits against state officials who, acting in their official capacity, deprive persons of rights they have under federal law. The federal right in question was the liberty included in the Fourteenth Amendment's guarantee—"nor shall any State deprive any person of life, liberty or property without due process of law." In view of the DSS's disgraceful performance in handling Joshua's case, it comes as a surprise to learn that the Supreme Court dismissed his mother's claim and found for the agency.

Chief Justice Rehnquist based his argument primarily on the text of the due process clause, which says no *state* may deprive a person of liberty without due process of law. Relying on what Justice Blackmun's dissenting opinion called a "sterile formalism," the chief justice stressed the distinction between an "affirmative obligation" of the state to protect the life, liberty, and property of individuals against invasions by private actors and the right of persons to be protected from such invasions by the state itself without due process of law. The Constitution guarantees only the latter, not the former. The due process clause "is phrased as a limitation on the State's power to act, not as a guarantee of certain minimal levels of safety and security." The purpose of the clause "was to protect the people from the State, not to ensure that the State protected them from each other." Joshua DeShaney's tragedy was due to the crimes of his father.[64]

The chief justice acknowledged "that in certain limited circumstances the Constitution imposes upon the State affirmative duties of care and protection with respect to particular individuals," but these are limited to prisons, mental hospitals, and other institutions whose inmates are held against their will and therefore are deprived of the liberty to take proper measures to care for themselves. Joshua DeShaney's situation is quite different from that of a prisoner whom the state has an affirmative duty to protect. This duty "arises not from the State's knowledge of the individual's predicament or from its expression of intent to help him"—as was the case with Joshua—"but from the limitation which it has imposed on his freedom to act on his own behalf"—as is the case with a prisoner.[65]

The chief justice noted that it still might be possible for Joshua's mother to bring her suit in a Wisconsin court under the tort law of that state, but this would be a matter of state law with no bearing on the due process guarantee of the Fourteenth Amendment to the federal Constitution. Indeed, the Supreme Court must be vigilant in seeing to it that the "Due Process Clause . . . does not transform every tort committed by a state actor into a constitutional violation."[66]

In closing his argument, the chief justice emphasized once again that the harm suffered was "inflicted not by the State of Wisconsin, but by Joshua's father" and that the worst that can be said "of the state functionaries in this case is that they stood by and did nothing when suspicious circumstances dictated a more active role for them." Reprehensible as their inaction may have been, the chief justice adds the sober reminder "that had they moved too soon to take custody of the son away from the father, they would likely have been met with charges of improperly intruding into the parent-child relationship, charges based on the same Due Process Clause that forms the basis for the present charge of failure to provide adequate protection."[67] Such are the perils of administration under a Constitution dedicated to the preservation of individual rights.

In dissenting from the Court's opinion, Justice Brennan stressed the "action that Wisconsin *has* taken with respect to Joshua and children like him" simply by establishing the DSS. The very existence of this department means that complaints of possible child abuse are channeled to it instead of being handled by the community in an informal, neighborly manner. Thus, private citizens suspecting child abuse would correctly feel that they had discharged their duty once they had alerted the DSS to the problem. Any further action by a private citizen might well be considered meddling or snooping. The justice continued, "Through its child-welfare program, in other words, the State of Wisconsin has relieved ordinary citizens . . . of any sense of obligation to do anything more than report their suspicions of child abuse to DSS. If DSS ignores or dismisses these suspicions, no one will step in to fill the gap."[68]

Brennan concluded that Wisconsin's action in establishing the DSS created the additional obligation to take affirmative action to safeguard the Joshuas of this world once there is reason to believe that suspicions of child abuse were well founded. He criticized the chief justice for construing "the Due Process Clause to permit a State to displace private sources of protection and then, at the critical moment, to shrug its shoulders and turn away from the harm that it has promised to prevent."[69]

Brennan's point goes far beyond questions of child abuse. In effect, he is saying that the modern administrative state relieves citizens of the traditional bonds of civic friendship that impel us to look out for one another. We are no longer our brother's keeper once the state preempts this role by pledging to care for the well being of our children as well as our elderly, our disabled, our handicapped, our unemployed, and so forth. Public administration literature correctly stresses the need for administrators to encourage citizen participation in agency decision making, but it often fails to recognize that the heart of the problem is the preemptive character of the administrative state itself. It is all well and good that our friends on the Left tell us it takes a village to raise a child while our friends on the Right remind us of the importance of family values. These are sound and solid messages intended to reinforce the key role of civil society in fashioning the common good. In a constitutional order, however, driven by individual rights as strongly as ours is, we can hardly be surprised to discover the real welfare of the family relegated to a distant second place. Or to put it more precisely, we cannot be surprised to see the notion of family redefined to accommodate the self-centered pursuit of individual rights. The picture that Brennan draws is not a pretty one, but it correctly places administrative agencies front and center in our present constitutional order. Having preempted the traditional role of the citizen, the administrative state must follow the dynamic logic of its creation by taking affirmative actions to deliver the protection it promises.

It is important that civil servants learn the right lesson from the *DeShaney* case. It would be an ethical disaster if they were to rejoice in a frenzy of cost-cutting to celebrate *DeShaney* as giving a green light to those inclined to follow the bad example of the DSS officials who "stood by and did nothing when suspicious circumstances dictated a more active role for them." On the contrary, they should read *DeShaney* as giving them discretionary authority to fashion the best approach to handle situations like Joshua's in the future. The *DeShaney* decision did no more than exempt the DSS from liability under the due process clause. It put no limits whatsoever on what affirmative actions creative administrators might voluntarily take in the responsible exercise of their administrative discretion. *DeShaney* built a floor, not a ceiling.

Moran v. Burbine[70] reveals an argument similar in structure to *DeShaney* but dealing with a very different substantive matter—the *Miranda* rights of a criminal suspect. In 1979, Brian Burbine was arrested for a burglary committed in Cranston, Rhode Island. The police had reason to believe that he was the suspect sought for a murder in Providence several months earlier. The Cranston police advised their Providence colleagues of the arrest, and soon three officers from there were on their way to Cranston to interrogate the suspect. Meanwhile, Burbine's sister, knowing nothing about the possible link to the murder, called the Public Defender's Office in Cranston to seek legal counsel for her brother in connection with the burglary arrest. Allegra Munson, the public defender assigned to the case, notified the Cranston police that she was of counsel to Burbine in case they planned to question him that evening. An unidentified person in the Detectives' Division told her that her client was indeed in custody but that there would be no further questioning that night. The murder investigation was not mentioned.

Later that evening, contrary to the assurances given to Public Defender Munson, Burbine was interrogated by five officers from the two jurisdictions.

They read his *Miranda* rights to him, including the right to counsel, but no one told him he already had a lawyer who had been in touch with the police that very evening. During the course of the interrogation, he signed a statement waiving his right to have a lawyer present and eventually admitted committing the murder for which he was tried and convicted. He appealed his conviction on the grounds that the confession he signed was inadmissible evidence because the misinformation given to his lawyer deprived him of his *Miranda* rights.[71]

Writing for the Court, Justice Sandra Day O'Connor rejected Burbine's claim, citing precedents to the effect that a waiver of one's rights is valid, "provided the waiver is made voluntarily, knowingly, and intelligently." O'Connor found Burbine's waiver of his *Miranda* rights met these criteria. "Once it is determined that a suspect's decision not to rely on his rights was uncoerced, that he at all times knew he could stand mute and request a lawyer, and that he was aware of the State's intention to use his statements to secure a conviction, the analysis is complete and the waiver is valid as a matter of law."[72]

O'Connor dismissed the relevance of Burbine's complaint that the police action in misleading his lawyer rendered his confession inadmissible. Following the lead of the trial court, she noted that "the constitutional right to request the presence of an attorney belongs solely to the defendant and may not be asserted by his lawyer." She maintained that the purpose of the *Miranda* warnings is "to dissipate the compulsion inherent in custodial interrogation." Burbine's ignorance of his attorney's phone call had no bearing on the question of compulsion. The record was not entirely clear on whether the misinformation given to Public Defender Munson was simply a mistake or was deliberately intended to deceive her. O'Connor stated that in either case, "the state of mind of the police is irrelevant to the question of the intelligence and voluntariness of respondent's [Burbine's] election to abandon his rights."[73] Although the deliberate deception of an attorney would be "highly inappropriate," it could not possibly have any bearing on a suspect's decision to waive his *Miranda* rights because deception of the lawyer has no connection with the "compulsion inherent in custodial interrogation."

Particularly interesting for our purposes is O'Connor's comment that "'deliberate or reckless' withholding of information is objectionable as a matter of ethics," but it does not diminish "the constitutionality of a waiver otherwise valid." Here again we see, as in *DeShaney,* that the Constitution provides a floor, not a ceiling, for moral aspiration. The importance of this distinction is underscored by the Court's holding that Burbine's conviction will be upheld because "the challenged conduct falls short of the kind of misbehavior that so shocks the sensibilities of civilized society as to warrant a federal intrusion into the criminal processes of the States."[74] This is a rather robust view of police discretion and one that must be tempered by O'Connor's salutary reminder that the sharp dealing by the police officers in this case falls short of the ethical standards expected of men and women who follow their profession. Even though the Constitution permits the police to act in an unethical manner, individual departments may structure and confine their discretionary authority by issuing directives forbidding their personnel to take full advantage of abuses the law allows.[75]

The third case, *Office of Personnel Management v. Richmond,*[76] examines the sorry plight of Charles Richmond, a former welder at the Navy Public Works Center in San Diego, who took a disability annuity from the navy in 1981 after the Office of Personnel Management (OPM) had determined that his impaired eyesight kept him from doing his job. The terms of the annuity imposed statutory limits on the money he could earn without losing his benefits. From 1982 to 1985, Richmond took a part-time job driving a school bus, earning an average annual salary of $12,494, a sum within the limits of the earnings permitted without risk to his annuity. In 1986, he had an opportunity to supplement his income by working additional hours. Before doing so, he consulted an employee relations specialist at the site of his former employment, the Navy Public Works Center. The specialist assured Richmond that the additional income would present no problem and gave him an OPM document from the *Federal Personnel Manual* explaining the rules governing his situation. Unfortunately, the specialist's information and the document were out of date, reflecting rules in effect before 1982—four years prior to Richmond's query. Due to his additional working hours, Richmond earned $19,936 in 1986, a sum that, unbeknown to him, exceeded the permissible limits. Having discovered Richmond's newly found prosperity, the OPM discontinued his disability annuity on 30 June 1987 but reinstated it on 1 January 1988, because his earnings in 1987 were, once again, within the statutory limit. Because of the employment specialist's error, Richmond lost his disability annuity for a six-month period, which came to $3,993.

Richmond appealed the OPM's decision to the Merit System Protection Board (MSPB), arguing that the OPM should be "estopped," that is, prevented from withholding his annuity because he had relied in good faith on the erroneous information he had received from a navy personnel specialist. The MSPB rejected his argument, refusing to apply the principle of equitable estoppel against the OPM. (The principle of equitable estoppel means that "if A's statement or conduct reasonably induces B's detrimental reliance, A will not be permitted to act inconsistently with its statement or conduct."[77] In Richmond's argument, he is B and the federal government is A. To his detriment, he relied upon erroneous information given by A, and therefore A should be "estopped" from taking action against him for doing so.)

Richmond appealed the MSPB's decision to the Federal Court of Appeals for the District of Columbia, where he prevailed. The OPM then appealed to the Supreme Court. In a seven to two decision, the Court rejected Richmond's argument. Writing for the Court, Justice Anthony Kennedy relied primarily upon Article 1, section 9, of the Constitution, which provides, "No money shall be drawn from the Treasury, but in Consequence of Appropriations made by Law." The award Richmond seeks "would be in direct contravention of the federal statute upon which his ultimate claim to the funds must rest," and therefore it must be rejected.[78] In this case "there can be no estoppel, for the courts cannot estop the Constitution." Justice Kennedy supplemented his textual argument with policy considerations on the "endless litigation over both real and imagined claims of misinformation by disgruntled citizens, imposing an unpredictable drain on the public fisc."[79]

Justice Marshall's dissent lamented the rigidity and the undue harshness of the Court's decision, a point of view that derives considerable support from many state courts that have been far more willing to apply equitable estoppel against the executive authorities in their own jurisdictions than the *Richmond* Court. The Supreme Court of Arkansas, for example, applied estoppel against an Arkansas agency, and in doing so made light of a famous quotation from Justice Holmes that is often cited by those who oppose efforts to estop government entities. "Men must turn square corners when they deal with the Government," said Holmes in 1927.[80] Unintimidated by the great jurist's dictum, the Arkansas Supreme Court stated irreverently, "It is hard to see why the government should not be held to a like standard of rectangular rectitude when dealing with its citizens."[81]

Clearly, the lesson of *Richmond* is the importance for administrators to get it right. *DeShaney* teaches administrators to use their discretion to enhance their compassion. *Burbine* teaches them to use it to follow the ethical principles of their profession, even if the Constitution permits a lower standard. *Richmond* teaches them to use their discretion to enhance the training of their personnel who advise the public on the agency's rules, policies, and practices. In such matters, nothing less than "rectangular rectitude" will do.

Civil Servants as Constitutional Actors

The examples of how civil servants play their roles as constitutional actors are quite disparate, ranging from health care administration to passport regulation, but they all reinforce the point that civil servants "run the Constitution," i.e., they reduce its grand principles to practice by their actions both routine and extraordinary. I shall begin with two examples concerning law enforcement personnel. The first arose in Tennessee's South Central Correctional Center when inmate Ronnie Lee McKnight sued Daryll Richardson, a prison guard employed by a private corporation, for inflicting certain physical injuries upon him. The latter filed a motion to dismiss the suit on the grounds that, even though he worked for a private company, he enjoyed the same qualified immunity from such suits that covers prison guards employed by the state. He supported this claim by arguing that he performs the same functions as they.

The lower courts rejected this argument, and Justice Stephen Breyer, writing for a five-person majority of the Supreme Court, followed suit. He faulted Richardson's argument on the historical grounds that in both England and America there have been in centuries past many examples of private citizens serving as jailers with no indication of a pattern of immunity from suits for their torts.[82]

He also rejected the claim for immunity by arguing that the purpose of a grant of immunity is to ensure vigorous enforcement of the law and to safeguard against excessive timidity on the part of prison guards. For private employers, this can be ensured through market forces that will protect against excessive timidity by prompting the state agency involved not to renew the contract of a company burdened with timid guards. Conversely, the same market forces will ensure against abuse of prisoners' rights because the abused prisoners will sue the company for damages. In the present case, the contract is up for renewal every three years, and the private corporation awarded the contract must have insurance against suits for violations of prisoners' rights. Thus, Justice Breyer concludes, the market will achieve for private-sector employees the same goals a grant of qualified immunity will achieve for employees of the state.

In a dissenting opinion, Justice Scalia went out of his way to attack the principal reason given by the court of appeals for denying qualified immunity to privately employed guards. He summarizes the appellate court's position as holding "that officers of private prisons are more likely than officers of state prisons to violate prisoners' constitutional rights because they work for a profit motive, and hence an added degree of deterrence is needed to keep these officers in line." Scalia scolds the lower court for "offering no evidence to support its bald assertion that private prison guards operate with different incentives than state prison guards." For our purposes, a more interesting question than whether such a statement *is* true is whether it *should be* true. As a matter of professional standards, should officers of state prisons—precisely because they are state officers—be more alert to inmates' rights than their private-sector counterparts? An affirmative answer would presuppose that the professional training of state employees includes a solid grounding in the salience of individual rights in the American constitutional tradition.

The second law-enforcement case began on a Delaware highway when a policeman stopped a car driven by William Prouse to check his license and vehicle registration. As he approached the stopped car, the officer "smelled marihuana smoke" and moments later "he seized marihuana in plain view on the car floor."[83] Indicted for illegal possession of a controlled substance, Prouse entered a motion for a hearing to suppress the use of the marihuana as evidence against him. At the hearing, the police officer testified "that prior to stopping the vehicle he had observed neither traffic or equipment violations nor any suspicious activity, and that he made the stop only in order to check the driver's license and registration." He characterized the stop as "routine," stating, "I saw the car in the area and wasn't answering any complaints, so I decided to pull them off." The trial court granted Prouse's motion to suppress the evidence, "finding the stop and detention to have been wholly capricious" and therefore in violation of the

Fourth Amendment's prohibition against unreasonable searches and seizures.[84] The Delaware Supreme Court upheld the trial court's ruling, and the state appealed to the U.S. Supreme Court, where the trial court was again upheld.

In its appeal, Delaware had argued "that patrol officers be subject to no constraints in deciding which automobiles shall be stopped for a license and registration check because the State's interest in discretionary spot checks as a means of ensuring the safety of its roadways outweighs the resulting intrusion on the privacy and security of the persons detained." Justice White framed the central issue to be whether in pursuit of the admittedly important goal of safety on its highways, Delaware's "discretionary spot check is a sufficiently productive mechanism to justify the intrusion upon Fourth Amendment interests which such stops entail."[85] Since the spot check for the driver's license and vehicle registration could take place, as it did in this case, "where there is neither probable cause to believe nor reasonable suspicion that the car is being driven contrary to the laws governing the operation of motor vehicles," Prouse's Fourth Amendment rights had been violated.[86]

Although Justice White's argument was quite compelling, the interesting point for our purposes is that the police officer was *right*. Prouse was committing a crime when the officer pulled him over. It was a splendid example of professional intuition on the part of the officer, but it was also clearly unconstitutional. In other walks of life, the intuition of the professional is celebrated. Great artists, scientists, physicians, generals, linebackers, and so forth "just know" what to do without being able to explain why. The professional intuition of the policeman, however, is constitutionally suspect. Thus the Constitution singles out police officers and other law enforcement personnel for adverse treatment in comparison with professionals in other fields. On the other hand, the qualified immunity from suits in tort enjoyed by state-employed law enforcement personnel singles them out for constitutionally favorable treatment. In both cases, however, law enforcement personnel are a group apart from the rest of us because they are constitutional actors.

Administration is traditionally associated with the execution of law, but administrators often contribute to its interpretation as well. A particularly clear example of an agency influencing judicial interpretation of a statute appeared in the 1958 case *Kent v. Dulles*.[87] Rockwell Kent was denied a passport because he was a member of the Communist Party. The secretary of state took this action pursuant to a broadly worded statute passed in 1926 that seemed to give him virtually unfettered discretion to deny passports. In 1952, Congress passed another statute requiring every American citizen to have a passport before traveling abroad. Putting these two statutes together, it seemed that any citizen could be denied the fundamental right to travel for any reason at all—including one's membership in the Communist Party. Such an interpretation would raise serious First Amendment problems for the government.

Writing the opinion of the Court, Justice William Douglas sidestepped the constitutional issue by arguing that, despite the broad language of the 1926 statute, Congress had not intended to grant the secretary of state authority broad enough to deny passports on grounds of political affiliation. He reached this conclusion, which seemed to be at odds with the expressed language of the statute, by examining the administrative practice of the State Department prior to 1926 and found that there had ordinarily been but two reasons for denying passports: "questions pertinent to the citizenship of the applicant" and questions concerning "whether the applicant was participating in illegal conduct." Deriving the meaning of the statute from the administrative history that preceded it, Douglas held that "at the time the Act of July 3, 1926 was adopted, the administrative practice, so far as relevant here, had jelled only around the two categories mentioned" — viz., citizenship and illegal conduct. He therefore concluded that "in light of prior administrative practice," Congress did not intend to give the secretary of state "unbridled discretion" to grant or withhold passports. Administrative practice guided judicial interpretation.[88]

Administrative agencies interpret not only statutes but also court decisions. At the federal level, this practice applies especially to the Department of Justice (DOJ). When the Supreme Court decides a constitutional issue affecting a federal program, the DOJ often provides guidance to the appropriate agencies on how the decision is to be implemented in view of the policies of the administration of the day. Particularly instructive is the reaction of President Clinton's Justice Department to the bitter setback it received in *Adarand Constructors v. Peña*,[89] an extremely important case in which the Supreme Court subjected federal affirmative action programs based on race to "strict scrutiny." If one reads the Court's *Adarand* opinion without benefit of the DOJ's gloss, it is rather clear that the federal government suffered an absolutely stunning defeat. The application of "strict scrutiny" to all forms of affirmative action based on race seemed to sound the knell for such programs. A "Memorandum to General Counsels" from Assistant Attorney General Walter Dellinger, however, leaves a very different impression.[90] While stating accurately what the Court decided, Dellinger gives particular attention to what it did not decide. Thus he relies on the Court's rejection of the familiar legal aphorism that the strict scrutiny test is "strict in theory, [but] fatal in fact" as offering hope that some affirmative action programs might survive. Although it is true that Justice O'Connor, the author of the Court's opinion, did reject the idea that strict scrutiny is necessarily "fatal in fact," this was a minor theme in her rather vigorous argument that the scrutiny applied to affirmative action programs must be very strict indeed. The DOJ memorandum transforms the marginal rejection of the "fatal in fact" language into a central aspect of the opinion. Noting that only two justices, Scalia and Clarence Thomas, "advocated positions that approach a complete ban on affirmative action," Dellinger highlighted the dissenting justices' comment that a majority of the Court (all except Scalia and

Thomas) agreed that "'the unhappy persistence of both the practice and lingering effects of racial discrimination against minority groups in this country' may justify the use of race-based remedial measures in certain circumstances."[91]

The DOJ memorandum, though faithful to the letter of *Adarand,* took considerable liberties with its spirit, serving primarily as a thinly veiled effort to rally the troops to fight the good fight for whatever remained of the administration's affirmative action efforts by minimizing the impact of the decision. It was a lawyerly version of damage control. The political aspect of the memorandum is plain for all to see, but no less important is its legal dimension as a statement on behalf of the DOJ's client, the United States of America. Presumably, the United States wants its affirmative action policies to be saved to the extent the law allows, and the DOJ memorandum is an advocate's statement intended to do just that. The fact that many federal affirmative action programs are still in place six years after *Adarand* underscores the importance of the DOJ's Office of Legal Counsel as a significant constitutional actor.[92]

Rosemary O'Leary's thorough study of the vicissitudes of the Environmental Protection Agency in the federal courts reports the curious remark, "I pray for lawsuits," from a career civil servant frustrated by the way the Office of Management and Budget subjected proposed EPA regulations to interminable delays. He felt that lawsuits initiated against his agency by environmental groups might be the only way to dislodge the regulations from the OMB so that the EPA could meet its legally mandated deadlines.[93] Other administrators have supplemented their prayers for lawsuits with good works. A case in point is the suit brought by discharged mental hospital employees in Alabama who joined forces with their former patients to sue over the inadequate treatment the inmates were receiving after cost-cutting initiatives had led to a severe reduction in force.[94]

The most dramatic example, however, of civil servants using the legal process against their political masters occurred in the first year of the Nixon administration, when sixty-five lawyers in the Civil Rights Division of the Justice Department drafted a memorandum opposing Attorney General John Mitchell's efforts to delay the integration of public schools in Mississippi. They based their protest on their oath to uphold the Constitution, stating that "we could find, as lawyers, no grounds for these actions that did not run cross-grain to the Constitution" and that therefore "the request for delay in Mississippi was . . . insupportable under the law we were sworn to uphold."[95] Some of the protesting lawyers took the additional step of refusing to defend the government's position in court; others resigned for reasons of conscience. Still others took the extreme action of passing crucial information to the NAACP Legal Defense Fund, the adversaries of these lawyers' client, the government of the United States, in the Mississippi litigation—an action that almost certainly violated the canons of legal ethics. The Supreme Court eventually upheld the position taken by the Civil Rights Division lawyers.[96]

The curious role certain New Jersey legislators envisioned for civil servants during an interesting debate over legalizing Laetrile in that state in 1977 provides a final example of administrators as constitutional actors. Since 1962, the federal Food and Drug Administration (FDA) has banned the sale of Laetrile because it fails to meet the statutory requirement that drugs be safe and effective. Throughout the 1970s, New Jersey law required that drugs manufactured and sold within the state be safe but was silent on the question of effectiveness. Taking advantage of this relaxed standard, a New Jersey company announced plans to manufacture Laetrile for the intrastate market. The announcement triggered a heated debate featuring opposition to Laetrile from scientists and physicians, including New Jersey's commissioner of health, and support from articulate cancer victims, prominent state legislators, and the Committee for Freedom of Choice and Options. The scientists were no match for the powerful rhetoric of "the right to hope" and the confident assertion that "only the individual can know what is good for himself."[97] The legislature passed a bill explicitly authorizing the manufacture and sale of Laetrile subject, of course, to an administrative finding for its safety, regardless of its effectiveness. The governor signed it into law even as he candidly acknowledged that "it is no more than a source of psychic comfort to cancer patients." Interviews with legislators known to believe that Laetrile was useless revealed that some of them voted for the bill because they knew that "Laetrile almost certainly could not be manufactured in New Jersey for at least seven or eight years." They were well aware "that the New Jersey Department of Health had the intention and authority to prolong the procedure for testing the safety of Laetrile." The seven- or eight-year estimated delay came from Donald Foley, the deputy commissioner of health, who voiced the hope that this "may be enough time for people to come to their senses. . . . Hopefully by then they will have taken it upon themselves to vote down Laetrile."[98] Here we have a remarkably unorthodox view of separation of powers, whereby legislators count on bureaucratic red tape and foot-dragging to provide political cover for a popular but useless bill they voted into law.

By focusing on individual civil servants, in this chapter I have departed from the emphasis in those that immediately precede and follow it, both of which address questions of constitutional structures, i.e., separation of powers and federalism. The focus on individual civil servants has revealed their salient roles in such great constitutional issues as freedom of speech, abolitionist tracts, remedies for abused children, *Miranda* rights, and affirmative action as well as in such middling matters as prison discipline, bureaucratic error, passport management, and the legalization of Laetrile. In a word, their presence in constitutional issues great and small is pervasive. The key supporting role assigned to civil servants in the great American constitutional drama has not always been a noble and uplifting one. Indeed, at times it has been just the opposite. It has been an important one, however, even when they were on the wrong side of history. For weal and for woe, civil servants are part of the story.

6

Federalism

In a passage one might find in a memo from a political campaign consultant today, the ever-contemporary Alexis de Tocqueville wrote in the 1830s that "in America centralization is by no means popular, and there is no surer means of courting the majority than by inveighing against the encroachments of the central power."[1] This sage observation sets the stage for a discussion of federalism, an absolutely indispensable element of the American constitutional order whereby the sovereign power of the people is divided in a dynamic and unstable manner between the federal government and the states. In this chapter I shall examine three aspects of federalism: the Anti-Federalist criticism of the federal taxing power, a recent major Supreme Court decision on unfunded mandates, and the deference federal courts owe to Congress on the one hand and to state legislatures on the other. These three topics are intimately connected to public administration.

THE ANTI-FEDERALISTS ON TAXATION

The most forceful arguments against what the Anti-Federalists saw as the excessive taxing powers of the federal government came from the pen of a brilliant New Yorker writing under the pseudonym of Brutus. To this day his identity is uncertain.[2] Writing between October 1787 and April 1788, Brutus found a worthy opponent in his fellow New Yorker, Alexander Hamilton, who joined James Madison and John Jay as Publius, the celebrated pseudonymous author of *The Federalist.*

    The argument over taxation was part of a larger argument over the powers of the federal government in general, the gist of which is captured in the very different conclusions that each author draws from their shared recognition that the objects of the proposed government are great indeed. Brutus concludes that a government with goals that are "very extensive" stands in need of "special guards against abuse"; but Publius maintains that such a government must be given "an unconfined authority as to all those objects which are intrusted to its management," for "the *means* ought to be proportional to the *end*." Thus Publius takes a managerial view of the Constitution, arguing that "the persons, from whose agency the attainment of any *end* is expected, ought to possess the *means* by which it is to be attained." Brutus agrees that "the means should be suited to the end" but has very different ends in mind when he sees the central problem as one of determining "whether the legislature is so constituted, as to provide proper checks and restrictions for the security of our rights, and to guard against the abuse of power." For Brutus, the task at hand is to provide adequate constitutional limitations on the powers of those who govern.[3]

Developing the theme of ends and means, Brutus claims that the proposed constitution should "secure and guarantee to the separate states the exercise of certain powers of government" to implement that document's preamble, which states that the formation of "a more perfect union" is the very first of the ends for which the constitution is ordained and established. Given this lofty goal, Brutus maintains that the proposed constitution "certainly ought to have left in [the states'] hands some source of revenue." He then turns to a close examination of the constitutional text to show that the taxing powers of the federal government are so extensive that "no source of revenue is therefore left in the hands of any state."[4]

Brutus's textual analysis begins with the provision in the eighth section of Article 1 that "Congress shall have Power To lay and collect Taxes, Duties, Imposts and Excises to pay the Debts and provide for the common Defence and general Welfare of the United States." Setting aside a certain ambiguity in the text that might mean that Congress has an unqualified power to provide for the general welfare, Brutus concedes for the sake of argument that the text should be read more narrowly as conferring the taxing power on Congress and that the general welfare along with the common defense and the payment of debts are the sole purposes for which Congress may vote taxes. Therefore he develops his argument as though the text had conferred on Congress "the power to lay and collect taxes etc. *in order to* provide for the common defence and general welfare."[5]

He then examines the sorts of fiscal measures included in the terms "taxes, duties, imposts and excises" that might be levied to achieve the broad and vague goal of the general welfare. Warming to his topic, he finds lurking in the recesses of this language "a poll-tax, a land-tax, a tax on houses and buildings, on windows and fire places, on cattle and all kinds of personal property; . . . duties on all kinds of goods to any amount, to tonnage and poundage on vessels, to duties on written instruments, newspapers, almanacks, and books; . . . an excise on all kinds of liquors, spirits, wines, cyder, beer, etc. . . . and indeed on every necessary and conveniency of life whether of foreign or home growth or manufacturing."[6]

Having established the comprehensive nature of Congress's dangerous taxing power, Brutus trains his sights on public administration to interpret the words "lay and collect," an expression of "great latitude" that "opens a door to the appointment of a swarm of revenue and excise officers to pray (*sic*) upon the honest and industrious part of the community, eat up their substance, and riot on the spoils of the country."[7] No mean rhetorician, Brutus chooses his words carefully. The reference to a "swarm" of officers who "eat up [the people's] substance" was clearly intended to echo the complaint in the Declaration of Independence against King George III for having "sent hither Swarms of Officers to harass our People, and eat out their Substance." Thus Brutus cleverly links the government envisioned in the Constitution of 1787 to the oppressive government Americans had overthrown in the previous decade.

Brutus reinforces the image of an unlimited federal taxing power by directing the reader's attention to the constitutional text conferring upon Congress the power "to make all Laws which shall be necessary and proper for carrying into Execution the foregoing Powers." Prominent among these is the dread power to lay and collect taxes, duties, imposts, and excises. The upshot of these congressional powers is that there will be nothing left for the states to tax once Congress has exercised its plenary taxing power. Brutus supports this conclusion by citing the "supremacy clause" of Article 6 providing that "this Constitution, and the Laws of the United States which shall be made in Pursuance thereof; and all Treaties made, or which shall be made, under the authority of the United States, shall be the supreme Law of the Land; and the Judges in every State shall be bound thereby, any Thing in the Constitution or Laws of any State to the Contrary notwithstanding." From this unequivocal statement of national supremacy, Brutus argues that "should any state attempt to raise money by law, the general government may repeal it or arrest it in execution, for all their laws will be the supreme law of the land."[8]

The concentration of the taxing power in the hands of Congress will inevitably lead to the demise of the states, for "the legislature of the United States will have a right to exhaust every source of revenue in every state, and to annul all laws of the states which may stand in the way of effecting it."[9] Instead of achieving its stated goal of perfecting the Union, the proposed constitution will destroy it by putting an end to state governments because "the idea of any government existing, in any respect, as an independent one, without any means of support in their own hands, is an absurdity." Brutus goes on to argue that if Americans are to have a new constitution, clear limitations must be placed on the taxing powers of the central government to protect the revenue base of state governments, "for a government without the power to raise money is one in name only."[10] Since there is no such limitation in the proposed constitution, he concludes it should be rejected.

Brutus captures nicely the Anti-Federalists' horror of unlimited taxing authority at the federal level in a lengthy, but memorable, diatribe that would surely appeal to many taxpayers in any period of American history:

> This power [of taxation], exercised without limitation, will introduce itself into every corner of the city, and country. It will wait upon the ladies at their

toilett, and will not leave them in any of their domestic concerns; it will accompany them to the ball, the play and the assembly; it will go with them when they visit, and will, on all occasions, sit beside them in their carriages, nor will it desert them even at church; it will enter the house of every gentleman, watch over his cellar, wait upon his cook in the kitchen, follow the servants into the parlour, preside over the table, and note down all he eats or drinks; it will attend him to his bed-chamber, and watch him while he sleeps; it will take cognizance of the professional man in his office, or his study; it will watch the merchant in the counting-house, or in his store; it will follow the mechanic to his shop, and in his work, and will haunt him in his family, and in his bed; it will be a constant companion of the industrious farmer in all his labour, it will be with him in the house, and in the field, observe the toil of his hands, and the sweat of his brow; it will penetrate into the most obscure cottage; and finally, it will light upon the head of every person in the United States. To all these different classes of people, and in all these circumstances, in which it will attend them, the language in which it will address them will be GIVE! GIVE![11]

In perusing this amusing text, the reader could easily misinterpret Brutus's position to be one of opposition to taxation as such. This would be a serious error, for in the paragraph immediately following this polemic he draws the moral of his story—that unlimited taxing power by the federal government "must necessarily, from its very nature, swallow up all the power of the state governments."[12] He never tires of grounding his attack on the federal taxing power in the needs of state governments for adequate revenue. "It is as necessary that the state governments should possess the means to attain the ends expected from them, as for the general government." The basis of Brutus's argument is *federalism,* not laissez-faire economics.

Fortunately, Brutus's worst fears have never come to pass even though his sentiments surely resonate with taxpayers of every era. Ironically, his argument supports those who favor aggressive taxation by the federal government today, because it shows that the opponents of the Constitution clearly understood the extremely broad—indeed virtually unlimited—taxing power of the federal government. The text they opposed was approved by their fellow citizens and for the past two centuries has provided the constitutional basis for any taxes Congress may have voted.

UNFUNDED MANDATES

In 1995, the 104th Congress enacted the Unfunded Mandates Reform Act (UMRA) as part of the "Contract with America," which had delivered the House of Representatives to the Republican Party for the first time in forty years. The statute defined an unfunded mandate as any provision in federal legislation, statute, or regulation that would impose an enforceable duty on state, local, or tribal governments without providing funds to carry out the duties in question. Statutory conditions for receiving federal assistance and participation in voluntary federal programs were not considered unfunded mandates. In passing UMRA, Congress imposed upon itself high procedural hurdles before it could enact future unfunded mandates but softened the blow with many exemptions, including "legislation that enforces the constitutional rights of individuals, prohibits discrimination, requires compliance with accounting and auditing systems with respect to grants," and so on.[13] The statute seems to have gone a long way toward quieting the most vociferous complaints against unfunded mandates.

Meanwhile, the Supreme Court entered the unfunded mandate fray at the constitutional level in *Printz v. U.S.*[14] when it examined the mandatory background check imposed on persons purchasing handguns in the Brady Handgun Violence Prevention Act of 1993. The Brady Act imposed on "chief local enforcement officers" (CLEOs) certain duties for which they received no compensation. These duties were "interim" in that the act required the attorney general to have a fully automated system for checking the backgrounds of handgun purchasers in place by November 1998. In the meantime, CLEOs were required to conduct background checks on prospective buyers upon receipt from gun dealers of duly executed Brady Act forms. The act did not apply to states with their own systems of background checks already in place. The forms were to be verified by the CLEO to ensure that the prospective buyer did not fall into a category of persons forbidden to purchase guns—e.g., convicted felons, fugitives from justice, illegal aliens, and so on. The background checks were to be completed within five days, and if the prospective buyer should fall into one of the prohibited categories and the dealer is so notified, the CLEO must, upon request, provide the prospective buyer with the reasons why he cannot buy the gun. If the prospective buyer does not fall into one of the prohibited categories, the CLEO must destroy all records from the Brady search.

Sheriff Jan Printz of Ravalli County, Montana, and Sheriff Richard Mack of Graham County, Arizona, sought to enjoin enforcement of the Brady Act on the grounds that it was unconstitutional for Congress to compel local law enforcement officials to administer a federal program. Their complaint included both funded and unfunded mandates. Federal district judges in Montana and Arizona agreed with the sheriffs but the U.S. Court of Appeals for the Ninth Circuit reversed, and the sheriffs appealed to the Supreme Court. In a five to four decision, the Supreme Court found the mandates imposed on the sheriffs unconstitutional. Their unfunded character served only to strengthen this conclusion, which also reached funded mandates imposed on state officials against their will.

This case is particularly interesting for our purposes because it presents a full-dress review of the fundamental principles of federalism in a context focused directly on public administration. Lest readers miss the forest for the trees, I must note at the outset that the details of the constitutional arguments in *Printz* must be examined to establish the far-reaching ramifications of a rather simple, though controversial, administrative process—running a background check on a prospective gun buyer. The theme of this book is thus highlighted by linking mundane administration to grand principles of constitutional law and history. Furthermore, the arguments in *Printz* give exceptionally close attention to *The Federalist,* thereby relating a contemporary administrative problem to the founding of the Republic.

One of the most remarkable aspects of the decision is that Justice Scalia, writing for the Court, and Justice John Stevens, in dissent, cover exactly the same points and in the same order, disagreeing on all of them. For both justices, the Court's task was to measure the constitutionality of the Brady Act's mandate against the text of the Constitution, the history of constitutional practice, the structure of the Constitution, and the jurisprudence of the Supreme Court.[15] I shall examine each of these points and then conclude with a further examination of Justice David Souter's reliance on *The Federalist* to support his dissent and of Justice Scalia's reply.

Constitutional Text

At the outset of his opinion for the Court, Justice Scalia dismisses the textual argument "because there is no constitutional text speaking to the precise question."[16] Shortly thereafter he revisits it because Justice Stevens, in dissent, finds that the unadorned "text of the Constitution provides a sufficient basis for a correct disposition of this case."[17] For Stevens, it is all quite simple. The regulation of handgun purchases clearly falls within the scope of Congress's power to regulate commerce among the states, and the duties imposed upon the sheriffs can be justified by the constitutional provision empowering Congress "to make all Laws which shall be necessary and proper" for carrying into effect the power to regulate commerce and all other powers granted by the Constitution. Scalia rejects Stevens's reliance on the necessary and proper clause as simply "the last, best hope of those who defend *ultra vires* congressional action."[18] He maintains that the imposition of a mandate, especially an unfunded one, on a CLEO is not "proper" because it "violates the principle of state sovereignty."[19] Stevens counters by appealing to the authority of Chief Justice John Marshall, who held that the word "proper" was to be interpreted broadly "to enlarge, not to diminish the power vested in the government."[20]

Constitutional Practice

In preceding cases we have seen Justice Scalia's reliance on constitutional practice, especially in the early years of the Republic, as an important aid in interpreting constitutional silences and unclear constitutional texts. He agrees entirely with the federal government's assertion that "early congressional enactments provide 'contemporaneous and weighty' evidence of the Constitution's meaning," and therefore he embarks on a careful examination of what the historical record shows about the "enlistment of state executive officers for the administration of federal programs."[21]

The government's brief reveals ample evidence of early Congresses imposing on state courts a broad range of duties concerning applications for citizenship and other naturalization matters as well as a duty to resolve "controversies between a captain and the crew of his ship concerning the seaworthiness of a vessel."[22] Scalia maintains, however, that these examples are irrelevant to the government's position in this case because they deal only with state *courts,* whereas Sheriff Printz is an *executive* officer.

Scalia argues that the Constitution itself explains why the early Congresses turned to state courts to enforce federal law. Article 3 provides for only one Supreme Court, leaving to Congress the decision as to whether there would be a system of "inferior courts." As a matter of fact, the first Congress created such a system, but if it had chosen otherwise—and the Constitution clearly would have permitted it to have done so—state courts would have been the courts of first instance for nearly all federal litigation. This point is reinforced in Article 6, which singles out "the Judges in every State" as having a special obligation to follow the Constitution and laws of the United States, "any Thing in the Constitution or Laws of any State to the Contrary notwithstanding." This directive would have been an absolute imperative if there had been no federal courts other than the Supreme Court. Scalia therefore argues that the special ties between state judges and the text of the federal Constitution explain the reliance of the early Congresses on state courts to implement federal laws. He refuses to extend these precedents to executive officers in state government today to support unfunded mandates. He concludes that the failure of the early Congresses to impose the enforcement of federal laws on state executives, despite their willingness to impose such enforcement on state courts, "suggests an assumed *absence* of such power."[23] Congress's failure to use a power to compel state executives to administer federal law creates the presumption that such power does not exist.

Justice Stevens eagerly accepts Scalia's historical challenge, noting that under the Articles of Confederation, "the National Government had power to issue commands to the several sovereign states, but it had no authority to govern individuals directly." For example, it raised and supported the Revolutionary Army by issuing requisitions to the states "rather than by creating federal agencies to draft soldiers or to impose taxes." Therefore, Stevens argues, it would be strange indeed if the Constitution, which was clearly "designed to enhance the power of the National Government," would reduce the powers of that government by providing "some new, unmentioned immunity for state officers." This, however, is the inexorable conclusion of Scalia's argument when he says that

Congress has no authority to require state executive officers to implement federal laws.[24]

Stevens takes particular exception to Scalia's argument that the failure of Congress to exercise the power to enlist state executives for federal purposes "suggests an assumed *absence* of such power." Although he agrees with Scalia on the importance of examining the early years of the Republic for enlightenment on the practical meaning of the Constitution, "we have never suggested that the failure of the earlier Congresses to address the scope of federal power in a particular area or to exercise a particular authority was an argument against its existence."[25] Stevens also rejects Scalia's rigid distinction between the tasks of judicial and executive officers, noting that in the early years of the Republic "state and local judges and associated judicial personnel performed many of the functions today performed by executive officers, including such varied tasks as laying city streets and ensuring the seaworthiness of vessels."[26]

Pursuing the question of the seaworthiness of vessels, Stevens shows that state judges were expected to appoint an investigative committee of three persons "most skilled in maritime affairs" to report back to them. On the basis of the committee's findings, the judge would determine whether the ship was fit for its intended voyage. Thus the federal statute tasking state judges with settling disputes over seaworthiness "set forth, in essence, procedures for an expert inquisitorial proceeding, supervised by a judge but otherwise more characteristic of executive activity."[27] Stevens, therefore, rejects Scalia's sharp distinction between judges and executive officers as "empty formalistic reasoning of the highest order." If Scalia had taken "a functional approach in assessing the role played by these early state officials," he would have seen that it was quite common for "state judges and their clerks to perform executive functions."[28]

Not content with confining their historical analysis to the early years of the Republic, Scalia and Stevens advance their juridical jousting to President Woodrow Wilson's effort to rally the states to support the military draft during World War I. Responding to the president's request, Congress in 1917 gave him authority to use state officials to administer the conscription program. Scalia finds this example irrelevant because in the Presidential Proclamation issued pursuant to the statute, the governors of the several states were "requested," not commanded, to implement the draft. The absence of compulsion leads Scalia to find it "impressive that even with respect to a wartime measure the President should have been so solicitous of state independence." Stevens counters that President Wilson's decision respectfully to request state action rather than to "bluntly command it is evidence that he was an effective statesman but surely does not indicate that he doubted either his or Congress' power to use mandatory language if necessary."[29]

Summing up his own argument from constitutional practice, Justice Scalia finds that it "tends to negate the existence of the congressional power asserted here [i.e., the power to issue mandates to state officials], but is not conclusive."

It is therefore necessary to "turn next to consideration of the structure of the Constitution" for further enlightenment on the constitutionality of the mandates. Justice Stevens follows him to the new arena.[30]

Constitutional Structure

Justice Scalia begins his examination of the structure of the Constitution by stating that the purpose of the quest is "to see if we can discern among its 'essential postulates' a principle that controls the present case."[31] It did not take him long to find one. In his very next sentence, he asserts, "It is incontestable that the Constitution establishes a system of 'dual sovereignty.'" There follows a lengthy argument to support the proposition that the "residual and inviolable sovereignty of the states is violated when Congress imposes upon state officers the duty to enforce federal laws without the prior consent of the states." This is especially true when, as with the Brady Act, the federal government does this "at no cost to itself"—that is, without providing funds to cover the administrative costs incurred by the states in implementing federal law.

"Dual sovereignty" is the central concept in Scalia's analysis of the structure of the Constitution. Its salience in his opinion may provide the key to understanding the profound changes in federalism now under way in American constitutional law. Throughout the 1990s, the Supreme Court handed down several major opinions that have already signaled a shift in the constitutional balance of power away from the federal government to the states.[32] The frequent reliance on the unusually strong expression "dual sovereignty" at key points in *Printz* suggests that the present Supreme Court may be willing to go a long way toward reversing the nationalistic jurisprudence that has dominated American constitutional law for the past sixty years.

"Dual federalism" rather than "dual sovereignty" has been the traditional expression to describe the states' rights position in American constitutional law. A cursory review of leading constitutional treatises reveals that "dual federalism" is nearly always mentioned, but "dual sovereignty" hardly ever appears.[33] The reason for this is that the states cannot be called sovereign in any real sense of that term. Recall the traditional definition of sovereignty: "The supreme, absolute and uncontrollable power by which any independent state is governed."[34] Recall further that the Constitution of the United States explicitly prohibits the states from adhering to treaties, coining money, taxing imports and exports, granting titles of nobility, and taking military action without the consent of Congress. Moreover, the same Constitution asserts its own supremacy and the supremacy of federal laws passed pursuant to it to the constitutions and laws of the states and even requires the principal officers of the several states to take an oath to uphold it. Clearly, when Americans—including Supreme Court justices—speak of the "sovereign states," they have a very relaxed understanding of the term in mind. It has more meaning as a political, and rather nostalgic, expression

than as an instrument of careful legal analysis, hence, the curious character of
Justice Scalia's opinion, which relies so heavily on "dual sovereignty" as the crucial principle in a major constitutional decision. For Scalia, state sovereignty is a
fundamental principle of the very structure of the Constitution.[35]

Justice Stevens does not directly challenge Scalia's use of the word "sovereignty" but asserts instead that it "simply does not speak to the question whether
individual state employees may be required to perform federal obligations." He
then tries to show that Scalia's interpretation proves too much, for, if taken at
face value, it would prohibit the federal government from requiring the states to
perform such obviously useful services as "creating state emergency response
commissions designed to manage the release of hazardous substances . . . , col-
lecting and reporting data on underground storage tanks that may pose an environmental hazard . . . , and reporting traffic fatalities . . . ; and missing children
to a federal agency."[36]

Scalia replies rather lamely that Stevens's examples "require only the provision of information to the Federal Government" rather than "the actual administration of a federal program."[37] He gives no reason to explain why mandating
compliance with a federal law requiring the states to provide certain information to
the federal government is not "actual administration of a federal program," but the
role of Sheriff Printz in running a background check on a would-be gun buyer is.

Stevens's reference to reporting missing children touched a raw nerve. Justice O'Connor joined Justice Scalia's opinion of the Court but felt obliged to
write a brief concurring opinion stating that the case at hand did not affect the
federally imposed duty of local law enforcement agencies to report cases of
missing children to the Department of Justice. Like Justice Scalia, she failed to
give a convincing reason for the constitutional difference she finds between
reporting missing children and checking the background of gun buyers.

The administrative aspects of Justice Scalia's interpretation of sovereignty
are not confined to the tasks Sheriff Printz found so burdensome. Scalia introduces an interesting managerial consideration when he argues that in imposing
duties on state officers, Congress ignores the constitutional provision that the
president is to "take Care that the Laws be faithfully executed." Instead of following the constitutional path of a unified federal executive enforcing federal
law, the Brady Act effectively hands this responsibility to thousands of law
enforcement officers "in the fifty States, who are left to implement the program
without meaningful Presidential control."[38] Thus, Justice Scalia faults the Brady
Act not only on grounds of federalism but also on separation-of-powers grounds.
Although the argument raises interesting questions on the relationship between
constitutionalism and administration, it seems to prove too much. Justice Scalia
concedes that Congress may impose duties on state officers that they willingly
accept, but the president still loses control over the execution of federal law carried out by state officers, regardless of the willingness they bring to their task. If
a constitutional problem arises whenever the president loses control over officers

executing federal law, what difference does it make if they execute these laws willingly or unwillingly?[39]

In his dissenting opinion, Justice Stevens resumes his attack on Scalia's position when he states that by "limiting the ability of the Federal Government to enlist state officials in the implementation of its program, the Court creates incentives for the National Government to aggrandize itself." Purporting to defend the rights of the states, Justice Scalia's opinion would encourage the federal government to "create vast national bureaucracies to implement its policies."[40] Although the present political climate in the United States is profoundly opposed to the creation of "vast national bureaucracies," such moods are short-lived when compared to the abiding principles of constitutional law. Justice Robert Jackson once remarked that a Supreme Court decision "lies about like a loaded weapon ready for the hand of any authority that can bring forth a plausible claim of an urgent need."[41] It would be ironic indeed if the Supreme Court's opinion in *Printz,* so dogged in its defense of state sovereignty, should someday in circumstances now hidden from our eyes provide the constitutional foundations for erecting a new system of "vast national bureaucracies."

Jurisprudence

Having concluded his structural argument with the finding that the power of the federal government would be "augmented immeasurably" by a federal mandate—especially one unaccompanied by federal funding—to an executive state official, Justice Scalia turns "finally and most conclusively" to the "prior jurisprudence of this Court."[42] Here he focuses on the Supreme Court's 1992 decision in *New York v. U.S.,* in which it found unconstitutional a key provision in the Low-Level Radioactive Waste Policy Amendments Act of 1985.[43] The statute provided an elaborate regimen of incentives to state governments to dispose of radioactive waste generated within their borders. The offending provision "gave the States the option either of adopting regulations dictated by Congress or of taking title to and possession of the low level radioactive waste." The Supreme Court struck down this provision because it required "the States either to legislate pursuant to Congress's directions or to implement an administrative solution." The Court held that even though Congress had plenary power to regulate radioactive waste, it "may not compel the States to enact or administer a federal regulatory program." To do so would be to "commandeer" the machinery of state government, and this the Constitution will not allow. In a word, the federal government's extensive power to regulate commerce does not include the power to make the states do the regulating.[44]

The brief submitted by the federal government distinguished the *New York* precedent from *Printz* on the grounds that formulating a regulatory scheme for radioactive waste would involve policy making by the states, whereas the Brady Act imposes on CLEOs, like Sheriff Printz, the merely ministerial duty of implementing a federal law. Justice Scalia rejected the distinction between policy making and mere implementation in language that would earn him high marks from the public administration community: "Executive action that has utterly no policymaking component is rare, particularly at an executive level as high as a jurisdiction's chief law enforcement officer." He stressed the statutory language requiring CLEOs to make "reasonable efforts" to complete their background checks in a timely manner as a clear incentive to make policy because some CLEOs will decide to expend "maximum 'reasonable efforts'" while others will rest content with "minimum 'reasonable efforts.'"45

Shifting the grounds of his argument, Scalia asserts that if the CLEOs' efforts are not considered as policy making, another set of problems arises. It would be utterly incompatible with the dignity of the states as independent and autonomous political entities to have their officers "dragooned" into executing federal law, thereby treating them as mere "puppets of a ventriloquist Congress."46 Thus, regardless of whether the duties of the CLEOs do or do not involve policy making, they surely present an affront to the dignity of the states.

Justice Stevens distinguished *New York* from *Printz* on the grounds that the earlier case involved Congress giving directives to state legislatures, whereas the Brady Act's directives are issued to state executive officers. This argument exposes Stevens to the rejoinder that he indulges in the same "empty formalistic reasoning" he found in Scalia's opinion. Furthermore, he fails to deal adequately with the explicit wording in *New York,* which states quite clearly that "the Federal Government may not compel the States to enact or *administer* a federal regulatory program."47 The inclusion of the word "administer" renders questionable Stevens's effort to confine *New York* to its legislative quarters. Wisely, Stevens closes his dissent by retreating to the high ground of the federal mandate to state officials to report cases of missing children to the Department of Justice. No one wants to be in the politically embarrassing position of declaring this sound legislation unconstitutional—as Justice O'Conner's concurring opinion eloquently attests.

The Federalist Papers

Justice David Souter agreed with the broad outlines of Justice Stevens's dissent but added a dissenting opinion of his own based exclusively on *The Federalist Papers*. Although references to *The Federalist* are quite common in Supreme Court opinions—some would say almost de rigueur—it is most extraordinary to find an opinion based exclusively thereon. Souter's opinion and Justice Scalia's spirited response are grist for our mill, for together they provide a fine example of two learned justices trying to settle the constitutionality of an administrative process by appealing to the first, the most venerable, and the most authoritative commentary on the Constitution. One cannot hope for a better example of grounding administration in the most fundamental principles of our constitutional tradition.

Justice Souter's dissent targets only the broader point in Scalia's opinion, wherein the latter finds funded as well as unfunded mandates unconstitutional. Souter acknowledges that he does not "read any of The Federalist material as requiring the conclusion that Congress could require administrative support without an obligation to pay fair value for it."[48] Thus, the debate over *The Federalist* concerns only funded mandates, with Souter upholding this practice and Scalia rejecting it.

Souter relies primarily on *Federalist* no. 27, in which Alexander Hamilton states that the federal government could "employ the ordinary magistracy of each [state] in the execution of its laws." Conceding this might mean nothing more than "cooperative arrangements by agreement"—the sort of voluntary arrangements Scalia acknowledges—Souter finds support for the notion of a congressional mandate when Hamilton goes on to affirm that "the Legislatures, Courts, and Magistrates of the respective members will be incorporated into the operations of the national government, *as far as its just and constitutional authority extends;* and will be rendered auxiliary to the enforcement of its laws." Linking this strong language to Hamilton's further comment on how state officials will be "bound by the sanctity of an oath," Souter concludes that "the natural reading" of this text means these auxiliary functions of the state officers will be "the products of their obligations thus undertaken to support federal law, not of their own, or the States', unfettered choices."[49]

This interpretation is supported by James Madison's explanation in *Federalist* no. 44 as to "why state magistrates should have to swear to support the National Constitution, when national officials will not be required to support the state counterparts." Madison answers his own question by stating that "national officials will have no agency in carrying the State Constitutions into effect. The members and officers of the State Governments, on the contrary, will have an essential agency in giving effect to the Federal Constitution." Madison then cites the crucial role to be played by the states in selecting the president and the senators.[50]

For additional support, Souter turns to Hamilton's discussion of how the states will assist in the collection of federal revenue to counter Anti-Federalist fears "of a proliferation of tax collectors." (Recall Brutus's skillful manipulation of "a swarm of revenue and excise officers.") In *Federalist* no. 45, Hamilton envisions that the "eventual collection [of federal taxes] under the immediate authority of the Union, will generally be made by the officers, and according to the rules, appointed by the several States." Further, in *Federalist* no. 36, Hamilton predicts that rather than appoint federal revenue collectors, the national government will be more likely to "employ the State officers as much as possible, and to attach them to the Union by an accumulation of their emoluments."[51]

Scalia brushes aside Souter's references to the revenue officers by arguing that the context suggests that the cooperation Hamilton foresees from these state officers would be voluntary rather than mandated. He questions the relevance of Madison's statements in *Federalist* no. 44 by confining these remarks to state support for federal elections mandated by the Constitution itself, whereas the Brady Act involves a *statutory* mandate from Congress. Scalia stumbles badly, however, when he tries to explain the statement in *Federalist* no. 27 on state officials being "incorporated into the operation of the national government" and being "rendered auxiliary to the enforcement of its laws." This language provides powerful evidence to support the proposition that Alexander Hamilton, writing as Publius, thought the federal government would have the power to impose mandates upon the institutions of state governments. The best Scalia can do is to maintain that these words mean only that state officials have the duty to enforce state laws "in such fashion as not to obstruct the operation of federal law." Souter's rejoinder is right on target: "I doubt that Hamilton's English was quite as bad as all that." An official whose duty consists in "not obstructing administration of the law is not described as 'incorporated into the operations' of a government or as an 'auxiliary' to its law enforcement." He concludes that "one simply cannot escape from Hamilton by reducing his prose to inapposite figures of speech."[52]

Scalia tries another avenue to escape from Hamilton by dismissing him as "the most expansive expositor of federal power." He then cites scholarly opinions to support the theory that "'The Federalist reads with a split personality' on matters of federalism" and that, in any event, it was Madison's viewpoint, not that of the nationalistic Hamilton, that eventually prevailed.[53] Undaunted, Souter finds scholarly opinions unsympathetic to the "split personality" theory of *The Federalist,* concluding with a statement from Clinton Rossiter that whatever tensions one might find in this great book "are in fact an honest reflection of those built into the Constitution it expounds and the polity it celebrates."[54]

Scalia recoups some of his losses from the troublesome *Federalist* no. 27 by noting correctly that it mentions state legislatures alongside judges and executives as the "auxiliaries" to federal power and, therefore, is at odds with the Supreme Court's holding in *New York v. U.S.,* where the Court had held that Congress could not mandate legislative action. Souter supported the *New York* ruling and answers Scalia rather unconvincingly by simply repeating the Court's argument in that case without trying to reconcile it with his prized *Federalist* no. 27.

And so it goes, point and counterpoint. Two first-rate legal minds pore over the subtle nuances of a two-hundred-year-old text expounding the Constitution in order to solve a contemporary problem in public administration. What better evidence can there be of the profoundly constitutional character of American public administration?

JUDICIAL DEFERENCE

A brief examination is in order of the implications for federalism in the constitutional question of the degree of deference federal courts owe to state governments on the one hand and to the federal government on the other. Thus I revisit *Adarand Constructors v. Peña,* a case analyzed previously for different purposes. Readers will recall that the *Adarand* Court held that "all racial classifications imposed by whatever federal, state, or local governmental actor, must be analyzed by a reviewing court under strict scrutiny." Strict scrutiny is a technical term meaning that classifications submitted to it "are constitutional only if they are narrowly tailored measures that further compelling governmental interests."[55] So strict are the demands of this test that government programs hardly ever prevail against it, and consequently, one finds in legal circles the aphorism that the test is "strict in theory, but fatal in fact." In writing the opinion of the Court in *Adarand,* Justice O'Connor went out of her way to emphasize the aphorism's exaggeration; neither state nor federal governments always fail, but they fail frequently enough to make it abundantly clear that government officials ignore the aphorism at their peril.

The administrative problem that led to the *Adarand* decision arose from what Justice O'Connor, with considerable understatement, called "a complex scheme of federal statutes and regulations."[56] The statutes in question were the Small Business Act and the inelegantly named Surface Transportation and Uniform Relocation Assistance Act, each of which was generously supplemented with a maze of administrative regulations emanating from the Small Business Administration and the Department of Transportation. For our purposes, it will suffice to note that prime contractors for highway construction projects received a considerable financial advantage for hiring subcontractors from firms owned by racial minorities. The Adarand Company was not such a firm. It complained that Mountain Gravel and Construction Company, the prime contractor on a federally funded highway project, had awarded a subcontract for guardrails to the minority-owned Gonzalez Construction Company, even though Adarand had submitted a lower bid. Mountain Gravel signed an affidavit affirming that it "would have accepted Adarand's bid, had it not been for the additional payment it received by hiring Gonzalez instead."[57]

Justice O'Connor based her ruling on three salient principles that she culled from the Supreme Court's previous decisions on racial classifications. The first is "skepticism," which she found in earlier rulings stating that race-based decisions are "inherently suspect" and "must necessarily receive a most searching examination." The second is "consistency," meaning that the standard of review is not dependent on the race of those burdened or benefited by a particular classification. "Congruence" is the third principle, which means that "equal protection analysis in the Fifth Amendment area is the same as that under the Fourteenth Amendment." This third principle, congruence, is the most pertinent to federalism, but the references to the Fifth and Fourteenth Amendments require a word of explanation.

The most important decision rendered by the Supreme Court in the twentieth century is *Brown v. Board of Education* (1954), wherein the Supreme Court found unconstitutional the practice of racial segregation in public schools.[58] The decision rested on the Court's interpretation of the equal protection clause, which provides that "no State shall . . . deny to any person within its jurisdiction the equal protection of the laws." Prior to *Brown,* the rule had been that "separate but equal" schools were constitutionally permissible, but Chief Justice Earl Warren put an end to this pernicious doctrine with his ringing affirmation that separate educational facilities were "inherently unequal."

The *Brown* case came to the Supreme Court from Kansas along with companion cases from South Carolina, Delaware, and Virginia raising the same question. A fourth companion case, *Bolling v. Sharpe,* came from the District of Columbia and presented a different issue. Since the District of Columbia is not a state, its actions do not fall under the equal protection clause. Hence, a literal reading of the Constitution would lead to the politically egregious conclusion that state legislatures must stop segregating students in the schools under their jurisdiction but that Congress could continue to do so. Chief Justice Warren circumvented this embarrassing problem by discovering what has come to be called an equal protection component within the due process clause of the Fifth Amendment that does apply to Congress. Whatever the technical problems with this creative jurisprudence, the chief justice surely had it right when he stated, "In view of our decision that the Constitution prohibits the states from maintaining racially segregated public schools, it would be unthinkable that the same Constitution would impose a lesser duty on the Federal Government."[59]

Since *Bolling,* the federal government has been held to the same equal protection standard as state governments, with only a few exceptions. One of the exceptions—until *Adarand*—was affirmative action. While *Brown* and *Bolling* set in motion the principles that eventually led to the current doctrine subjecting *invidious* discrimination to strict scrutiny at all levels of government, the standard governing the *benign* discrimination in affirmative action was less clear. For Justice O'Connor, it was perfectly obvious that the only way to tell the difference between invidious and benign discrimination is to subject the particular discrimination in question to the rigors of strict scrutiny. The judicial precedents, however, were not at all clear in this matter. Since the Court first waded into the affirmative action morass in 1978, its decisions had been quite inconsistent. As Justice O'Connor correctly notes, it was not until *Richmond v. Croson* (1989), a Virginia construction case, that "the Court finally agreed that the Fourteenth Amendment requires strict scrutiny of all race-based action by state and local governments."[60] In *Adarand,* Justice O'Connor, relying primarily on *Bolling* and its progeny, extended the *Croson* ruling to the federal government's affirmative action programs.

This conclusion prompted a long and vigorous dissent from Justice Stevens, who began by criticizing O'Connor's opinion of the Court for "ignoring practical and legal differences between federal and state or local decisionmakers." Chief among these differences is that Congress, unlike state legislatures, is "a co-equal branch charged by the Constitution with the power to 'enforce by appropriate legislation,' the equal protection guarantees of the Fourteenth Amendment." He also justified the Court's traditional practice of "giving greater deference to the National Legislature than to a local law-making body" on the grounds that "federal affirmative-action programs represent the will of our entire Nation's elected representatives, whereas a state or local program may have an impact on nonresident entities who played no part in the decision to enact it." This Stevens finds unfair because it is quite possible that persons unable to vote for representatives who create a state or local affirmative-action program may nonetheless feel its adverse effects when they try to do business in these areas. Hence, Stevens concludes, it is altogether fitting that the federal courts should impose strict scrutiny on state and local affirmative-action initiatives but not on those emanating from Congress and implemented by regulations from federal agencies.[61]

As for the evenhanded notion of equal protection upheld in *Bolling v. Sharpe*, Stevens notes that such a standard is quite appropriate "when a federal rule is applicable to only a limited territory, such as the District of Columbia, or an insular possession." This is a good point because, in effect, it holds the federal government to the same equal protection standard as a local government when it functions as a local government, which it most assuredly does in the District of Columbia.

As a parting shot, Justice Stevens reminds Justice O'Connor of comments she had made in *Croson* quite different in tone and substance from her views in *Adarand*. When the issue was whether the Court should apply strict scrutiny to state and local affirmative-action programs—as it was in *Croson*—O'Connor seized upon section 5 of the Fourteenth Amendment, which gives Congress the power to enforce the equal protection clause. She noted that "unlike any State or political subdivision," Congress has an impressive array of power "to define situations which *Congress* determines threaten the principles of equality and to adopt prophylactic rules to deal with those situations." She used this argument in 1989 to justify strict scrutiny against state and local governments in *Croson* and then reversed her field by using *Croson* as a precedent to justify strict scrutiny against the federal government.[62]

When confronted with this critique, Justice O'Connor was not amused. Rather lamely, she replied, "For now, it is enough to observe that Justice Stevens' suggestion that any Member of this Court has repudiated in this case his or her previously expressed views on the subject . . . is incorrect."[63] Despite this weak rejoinder, *Adarand* is the law of the land, thereby confirming the old adage that judges can decide what they cannot prove.

In this chapter I have shown the relevance of the great debate over federalism between the Federalists and the Anti-Federalists two centuries ago to such contemporary issues as the administration by state governments of federal mandates and state and federal efforts at affirmative action. These contemporary administrative problems set the stage for a full-dress review by the Supreme Court of the basic principles of American federalism.

Conclusion

Throughout this book I have tried to link the public administration to constitutions in several countries as a "gentle corrective" to the New Public Management so that American civil servants might see themselves and be seen by others as men and women ready to assume their rightful place as constitutional actors. As the great constitutional drama of the American Republic has unfolded over the centuries, leading roles have been assigned to state governments, newspapers, churches, corporations, and racial minorities. I hope I have convinced readers that civil servants are part of that story as well. In the chapters on the Constitution of the United States I have addressed this issue directly. In those on constitutions abroad I have done so indirectly by culling examples from different times and places to suggest that the constitutional role of American civil servants comes not only from specific American experiences but from the *nature of the civil service.*

Connections between the public administration and the U.S. Constitution are not without precedent. Political figures as different as Arthur Burns, Jimmy Carter, and George Will have, independently of one another, made telling comparisons between the Federal Reserve Board and the Supreme Court of the United States.[1] These comparisons clearly were due to the high regard in which the Federal Reserve is currently held—although it has not always been so. There is no danger, however, that anyone will ever mistake the Immigration and Naturalization Service, or the Bureau of Indian Affairs, or the Army Corps of Engineers for the Supreme Court. To make my argument, I had to get beyond glittering generalities applicable only to the best and the brightest of government agencies, like the Federal Reserve, that position themselves happily on the bridge of the ship of state. I had to descend to the engine room where cursing, sweat, and toil replace high-minded projections on the direction of the nation's economy. There we find the public administration with all its warts and wrinkles tend-ing to the mundane details of translating great constitutional principles into everyday actions.

My approach has been highly anecdotal—no small failing in academic circles where a premium is set on grand theory, which I have neither the wit nor the inclination to develop. Although I do plead guilty to the charge of relying on anecdotes, I offer the old saw that data is but the plural of anecdote. By relying so heavily on specific cases, I hope I have at least made clear in a concrete way the intimate connection between the public administration and constitutions.

Some readers may find a certain paradox in linking the public administration, which is usually associated with the state and its powers, to constitutions, which usually imply limitations on such powers. The American Constitution has a way of generating many paradoxes. When one is defending freedom of speech, the metaphor of the free market of ideas comes readily to mind, but few indeed are the advocates of free speech who would oppose the regulations routinely placed on the real markets that drive the nation's economy. The paradox vanishes as soon as one takes care not to be imprisoned by one's metaphors. Similarly, the paradox of linking administration to constitutions disappears when we recall the etymology of the word *constitution.* It comes from the Latin verb *constituere,* meaning to set up or to establish. The primary purpose of a constitution is to create a government, a task quite congruent with administration, and only then to limit the powers of its creation.

A more serious paradox arises from the obligation of all federal officers and employees and many state and local officials to take an oath to uphold the Constitution of the United States. Over the years many people have raised many objections to my comments on the Constitution—many of them, alas, distressingly on target. I find it remarkable, however, that in teaching, writing, and lecturing in the United States for over thirty years, I have never been questioned as to why the federal government has the authority to demand an oath to uphold the Constitution from even the humblest clerk-typist. The careful reader will notice that I hedged my comment by saying that I have never encountered this objection "in the United States." Rest assured that I most certainly did encounter it when, as a Fulbright scholar in France, I studied the ways in which ethical issues for civil servants were handled in that country. I was surprised to discover that thoughtful French colleagues were simply appalled at the notion of an oath to uphold a constitution. This reminded them of the authoritarian Vichy regime of Maréchal Pétain, which did require an oath from its civil servants. French jurists assured me that an oath to uphold a constitution was utterly at odds with the French republican tradition.

Discussions along these lines in France alerted me to how remarkable it is that so little fuss is made over the obligation to swear to uphold the Constitution as a condition of federal employment. Federal employees must swear that they "bear true faith and allegiance" to the Constitution. Thus the oath is not confined to on-the-job behavior but to what the civil servant *believes.* Civil servants cannot leave their "true faith and allegiance" at the office at five o'clock and pick them up the next morning at nine. Further, in taking this oath, civil servants surrender their natural right to revolution as long as they remain civil servants. No small matter this for the spiritual heirs of John Locke!

Furthermore, I have heard many state and local government employees complain that they are not required to take an oath to uphold the Constitution—as though they had been somehow diminished or slighted by being deemed unworthy of the privilege of taking such an oath. I believe this attitude underscores the profound respect for our Constitution throughout our society—a respect that does not require an oath. Civil libertarians despise loyalty oaths, but the oath to uphold the Constitution, presumably because of its prospective character, escapes their ire.

My focus in this book has been on the Constitution as a standard for civil servants, but it plays a larger role as a standard in civil society as well. A clear example of this larger role appeared, of all places, in the flap over the offensive remarks of pitcher John Rocker, then with the Atlanta Braves, near the end of the 1999 baseball season. After a game with the New York Mets, the archrivals of the Atlanta Braves, Rocker delivered himself of some singularly ill-considered remarks about members of racial minorities, homosexuals, and other New Yorkers who failed to meet his crabbed view of "normality." The offensive remarks ignited a firestorm of entirely justified outrage. Many baseball fans joined sportswriters and television commentators in calling upon the Atlanta Braves and the commissioner of baseball to discipline Rocker for his remarks. Many other fans and commentators, although deploring Rocker's comments, argued that to punish him for his speech would violate his First Amendment rights. Strictly speaking, this argument is sheer nonsense because the First Amendment applies only to efforts by a government—local, state, or federal—to suppress or punish speech. If the commissioner of baseball or the ownership of the Atlanta Braves thought it was in the best interest of the game or the team to punish Rocker, the First Amendment would raise no problem. For our purposes, the significant point is that a constitutional principle can slip its rather narrow legal bonds and enter the broad arena of civil society on a matter having absolutely nothing to do with state action. It suggests the pervasive character of constitutional values as opposed to constitutional law.[2]

I am sure the reasons for this nascent panconstitutionalism are many and varied, but as I have argued at some length elsewhere, it may be due to the increasingly secular spirit of our times.[3] The weakness and, at times, the absence of religious beliefs prompt us to look to the Constitution as some kind of higher authority or even higher truth—not necessarily a wholesome development for either the Constitution or religion. As straws in the wind, consider the semi-sacral language one finds in the titles of relatively recent, serious books on the Constitution of the United States: *Constitutional Fate: A Theory of the Constitution; Constitutional Dialogues: Interpretation as Constitutional Process; Con-*

stitutional Faith; and *Moral Foundations of Constitutional Thought: Current Problems, Augustinian Prospects.*[4]

The interrelationships we find among religion, morality, and the Constitution are not without precedent. The two greatest moral crises in American history—slavery and abortion—bristle with moral-religious-constitutional arguments. The abolitionists attacked the Constitution itself as a "pact with Satan" because of its permissive posture on slavery, whereas pro-life advocates concentrate their argument on one Supreme Court decision, *Roe v. Wade,* which they denounce as a moral abomination because it has led to well over a million abortions annually for over a quarter of a century. Their strategy follows the example of Thurgood Marshall and the NAACP in chipping away at the edges of the "separate but equal" doctrine of *Plessy v. Ferguson,* in the hope of eventually laying bare the moral rot at its core. Where pro-life advocates see moral rot, their pro-choice adversaries see the fundamental right of a woman's autonomy over her own person. Despite all the slogans, marches, and placards, the underlying argument is serious, profound, and worthy of a great deliberative democracy. It is no surprise to find the Constitution of the United States front and center in the great religious and moral debate that so painfully divides civil society.

A sound academic tradition counsels authors to conclude their books with a few words on further research. This serves the wholesome purpose of reminding readers—and, perhaps, more important, authors themselves—that they have not exhausted the topic they have addressed. (This is true even if they have exhausted their readers and themselves.) To honor this custom, I shall mention three countries that have impressed me as raising particularly interesting questions on the connection between constitutions and administration: Austria, Thailand, and the Czech Republic.

Austria is of interest because of the exceedingly detailed attention its Constitution bestows on administrative matters. As a federal republic, it suggests lines of inquiry for those interested in administrative federalism. For example, various articles of the Constitution distribute powers between the Federal Government *(das Bund)* and the states *(die Länder),* according to the subject at hand. Thus the *Bund* has the responsibility for legislation and execution of matters concerning external affairs, the banking system, criminal law, and so forth.[5] The Constitution gives legislative authority to the *Bund* and executive authority to the *Länder* for highway police, sanitation, and "professional associations . . . in the field of agriculture and forestry as well as in the field of alpine guidance and skiing instruction."[6] Refining the notion of administration, another article distinguishes between legislation "as regards principles," which goes to the *Bund,* and "implementing laws and execution," which falls to the *Länder.* This distinction applies to such matters as "hospitals and nursing homes," "land reform," and "the protection of plants against diseases and pets."[7] Finally, legislative and executive powers go to the *Länder* in many areas concerning public education.[8]

One wonders how the extremely detailed provisions of the Austrian Constitution influence administrative behavior in that country. It suggests an interesting comparison with the laconic Constitution of the United States.

Thailand is a promising field for constitutional-administrative studies because a new Constitution adopted in 1997 "places stiff checks on Thai politicians by vesting real power in independent institutions and encouraging the new bodies to get tough on money politics."[9] This reliance on independent administrative bodies is attributed to the widespread disgust with the corruption of certain elected officials who were blamed for Thailand's economic collapse in 1997. The parliamentary election of 6 January 2001 put the spotlight on one of these independent institutions, the National Counter-Corruption Commission (NCCC), an agency described in great detail in the 1997 Constitution. Its nine members serve for nine years and are appointed "by the King with the advice of the Senate."[10] Its duties include nothing less than "to inquire and decide whether a State official has become unusually wealthy or has committed an offence of corruption [or] malfeasance in office."[11]

On 26 December 2000, less than two weeks before the parliamentary election, the NCCC found that Thaksin Shinawatra, the leader of the *Thai Rak Thai* (Thais Love Thais) Party, had illegally failed to disclose personal assets over $232 million and was therefore ineligible for public office for a period of five years. Thaksin Shinawatra appealed this ruling to the Constitutional Court, which has the final say in such matters.

Meanwhile, on 6 January 2001, the *Thai Rak Thai* Party won by far the largest parliamentary majority in Thailand's rather brief democratic history, thereby making Thaksin Shinawatra prime minister and setting the stage for a classic confrontation before the Constitutional Court between the rule of law as interpreted by a constitutionally created anticorruption commission and the overwhelmingly popular choice of Thailand's citizens.[12] In early August 2001, the Constitutional Court decided in favor of the prime minister by a vote of eight to seven.

The Czech Republic is of considerable interest for our purposes because of the smooth ways it has both effected and undergone massive political changes in recent years. The rapid transition from a Soviet satellite as of 17 November 1989 to a free democratic society in less than six weeks has been aptly called the "velvet revolution." The "velvet divorce" is the term that captures best the peaceful dissolution of the Czech and Slovak Federative Republic—the technical name for Czechoslovakia since 1968—into two independent states, the Czech Republic and Slovakia.[13] The victory of the Czech Social Democratic Party in the parliamentary elections of June 1998 brought the Czech Republic its first left-of-center government in the post–Communist era and has been fittingly dubbed the "velvet restoration."[14] To bring about changes of this magnitude smoothly and peacefully requires considerable administrative competence to complement the heroic statesmanship of Vaclav Havel, the erstwhile dissident playwright and poet turned president, first of the Federative Republic and then of the Czech Republic. Havel's epic role is a familiar tale, but the administrative story remains to be told.

The collapse of the Communist regime brought predictable demands to settle old scores from Czechs who had suffered great injustices at the hands of their former masters. This led to a policy of "lustration," a word whose "etymological roots lie, ominously, in the Latin term *lustrum,* meaning a purifying sacrifice."[15] The program targeted those who had served as secret informers on their countrymen during the Communist era, many of whom had been civil servants. Not surprisingly, the lustration program led to excesses that have been compared to American-style McCarthyism.[16] At the same time, those who administered the program were bringing wrongdoers to justice when they exposed and, in some cases, punished contemptible collaborators in league with the Communist oppressors. For better and for worse, civil servants were essential actors in executing this unsettling, but probably inevitable, policy.

The velvet divorce caused many administrative headaches. Vaclav Havel, as president of the Czech and Slovak Federative Republic, opposed the dissolution and resigned his office on 13 July 1992 when its inevitability became obvious. Although he announced that he would be a candidate for the soon-to-be-created Czech Republic, he refused to complete the two remaining months of his term at the head of the moribund federal regime. In the grand style, he declined to serve as "liquidating clerk" of the Czech and Slovak Federative Republic.

Now it is all well and good for the Vaclav Havels of this world to disdain the work of a "liquidating clerk," but somebody had to take on this painstaking service. Enter the civil servants of the two new countries. Amicable settlements had to be negotiated on how to allocate assets and properties, both movable and immovable, between these emerging nations. Should the same allocation ratio be applied to debts? What about property in embassies and consulates abroad? Or military assets and equipment? Should special arrangements be made for Slovak army officers who want to join the army of the Czech Republic? Should they be required to change their citizenship? What kind of severance bonus should be given to the civil servants who had worked for the defunct federal republic? How should border disputes be resolved? What joint management arrangements would be appropriate for the pipeline bringing gas from Russia?

Further problems concerned "the establishment of a joint customs union to monitor tariff-free exchange of goods and services between the two countries, common external tariff and trade policies, and a joint coordinating council and Secretariat."[17] Moreover, the currency arrangements proved particularly nettlesome. An agreement to retain a common currency for six months after dissolution fell apart when the national banks in the two new countries began circulating separate currencies some four months ahead of the agreed timetable. The velvet divorce that made two countries out of one would have been impossible without a host of liquidating clerks who mastered its administrative details.

Reflecting on the vagaries of the Czech Republic recalls the story of the American legal scholar who was approached for advice to an Eastern European country drafting its first post–Communist constitution. Promptly, he produced an elaborate text entitled "Constitution of the Republic of ——."[18] One can only hope that the story is apocryphal, but it comes uncomfortably close to the caricature of American jurists of the early 1990s preaching the gospel of free markets and individual rights throughout the former Communist world with a "one size fits all" approach to constitution making. I hope this book has convinced its readers, especially readers of the NPM persuasion, of the need to see in constitutions far more than a blend of formal rights and powers. I hope they will look upon them as texts and traditions capable of providing justice and ordered liberty when wisely administered. Perhaps someday NPM scholars will grace their innovative proposals with a constitutional impact statement.

Notes

PREFACE

1. Curtiss Ventriss, "New Public Management: An Examination of Its Influence on Contemporary Affairs and its Impact on Shaping the Intellectual Agenda of the Field," *Administrative Theory and Praxis* 22 (September 2000): 505.

2. Laurence E. Lynn, "The New Public Management Theme: How to Transform a Theme into a Legacy," *Public Administration Review* 58 (1998): 231.

3. David Osborne and Ted Gaebler, *Reinventing Government: How the Entrepreneurial Spirit Is Transforming the Public Sector* (Reading, Mass.: Addison-Wesley, 1992); Albert Gore, *Creating a Government That Works Better and Costs Less: Report of the National Performance Review* (Washington, D.C.: U.S. Government Printing Office, 1993).

4. Phillip J. Cooper, *Public Law and Public Administration,* 3d ed. (Itasca, Ill.: Peacock, 2000), 116.

5. Anne Khademian, "What Do We Want Managers to Be? Comparing Reforms," *Public Administration Review* 58 (1998): 270.

6. Andrew Dunsire, "Administrative Theory in the 1980s: A Viewpoint," *Public Administration* 73 (1995): 29, citing J. Stewart and K. Walsh, "Change in the Management of Public Services," *Public Administration* 70 (1992): 499–518.

7. Barry Bozeman, ed., *Public Management: The State of the Art* (San Francisco: Jossey-Bass, 1993), 2–3.

8. James Q. Wilson, *Bureaucracy: What Government Agencies Do and Why They Do It* (New York: Basic Books, 1989), 28.

9. Ibid.

10. Robert Behn, "Public Management: Should It Strive to Be Art, Science, or Engineering?" *Journal of Public Administration Research and Theory* 6 (1996): 91–123.

11. David H. Rosenbloom and Rosemary O'Leary, *Public Administration and Law,* 2d ed. (New York: Marcel Dekker, 1997), 4.

12. Jacob E. Cooke, ed., *The Federalist* (1961; reprint, Middletown, Conn.: Wesleyan University Press, 1977), no. 72.

13. Ibid.

14. Woodrow Wilson, "The Study of Administration," in *Classics of Public Administration,* ed. Jay M. Schafritz and Albert C. Hyde (Oak Park, Ill.: Moore, 1978), 11. Wilson's article originally appeared in *Political Science Quarterly* 2 (June 1887).

15. Among the best of the articles criticizing the NPM on grounds of the rule of law are Chester A. Newland, "A Field of Strangers in Search of a Discipline: Separation of Public Management Research from Public Administration," *Public Administration Review* 54 (May–June 1994): 486–488; James D. Carroll, "The Rhetoric of Reform and Political Reality in the National Performance Review," *Public Administration Review* 55 (May–June 1995): 302–312; and Ronald C. Moe and Robert S. Gilmore, "Rediscovering Principles of Public Administration: The Neglected Foundation of Public Law," *Public Administration Review* 55 (March–April 1995): 135–146.

16. Laurence Lynn, "A Critical Analysis of the New Public Management," *International Public Management Journal* 1 (1998): 120–121.

17. Ibid., 121.

18. H. George Frederickson, "The Repositioning of American Public Administration," *PS: Political Science and Politics* 32 (December 1998): 706.

1. FRANCE

1. *Documents pour servir à l'histoire de la constitution du 4 octobre 1958,* 3 vols. (Paris: La Documentation française, 1987, 1988, 1991), 2:104.

2. John A. Rohr, *Founding Republics in France and America: A Study in Constitutional Governance* (Lawrence: University Press of Kansas, 1995), 156–158.

3. Alexis de Tocqueville, *The Old Regime and the French Revolution,* trans. Stuart Gilbert (1955; reprint, New York: Doubleday, 1983), vii.

4. Ibid.
5. Ibid.
6. Ibid., viii.
7. Ibid., x.
8. Ibid., 32.
9. Ibid., 60.
10. Ibid., 34.
11. Ibid., 35.
12. Ibid., 33.
13. Ibid., 52.
14. Ibid., 53.
15. Ibid.
16. Ibid., 91.
17. Ibid., 262.
18. Ibid., 109.
19. Ibid., 105.
20. Ibid., 201–202.

21. Ernest Barker, ed. and trans., *The Politics of Aristotle* (New York: Oxford University Press, 1962). See especially Book 3, chapters 1–4.

22. David P. Jordan, *Transforming Paris: The Life and Labors of Baron Haussmann* (Chicago: University of Chicago Press, 1995), 49.

23. Ibid., 180.

24. Ibid., 157, 228.

25. Ibid., 223.

26. Ibid., 5.

27. Ibid., 335.

28. Ibid., 5, 334, 367.

29. Ibid., 5 (emphasis added).

30. Jean Des Cars, *Haussmann, la gloire du Second Empire* (1957; reprint, Paris: Librairie Académique Perrin, 1978), 242; J. M. Chapman and Brian Chapman, *The Life and Times of Baron Haussmann: Paris in the Second Empire* (London: Wiedenfeld and Nicolson, 1957), 150.

31. Chapman and Chapman, *Life,* 33.

32. Des Cars, *Haussmann,* 242.

33. Jordan, *Transforming Paris,* 151.

34. Chapman and Chapman, *Life,* 149. For a detailed discussion of the working relationship between Haussmann and the emperor, see the chapter, "Le Paris d'Haussmann: à la recherche d'une rélance économique," in Louis Girard, *Napoleon III* (Paris: Fayard, 1986).

35. Chapman and Chapman, *Life,* 207.

36. Ibid., 226.

37. Ibid., 239 (emphasis in original).

38. Jordan, *Transforming Paris,* 293.

39. Ibid., 295.

40. Ibid., 216.

41. Chapman and Chapman, *Life,* 229.

42. For further examples of questionable financial practices by Haussmann, see ibid., 27–28.

43. Jordan, *Transforming Paris,* 57.

44. Ibid., 84.

45. Ibid., 88.

46. Ibid., 142.

47. Chapman and Chapman, *Life,* 52.

48. Jacques Godechot, *Les Constitutions de la France depuis 1789* (Paris: Flammarion, 1979), 298.

49. The points developed in the remainder of this chapter are discussed more fully in Rohr, *Founding Republics,* chapters 2, 4, and 5.

50. *Documents pour servir à l'histoire,* 2: 717.

51. François Luchaire, *Le Conseil Constitutionnel* (Paris: Economica, 1980), 31.

52. Didier Maus, "La Constitution jugée par son pratique: Réflexions pour un bilan," in Olivier Duhamel et Jean-Luc Parodi, *La Constitution de la cinquième République* (Paris: Presses de la Fondation Nationale des Sciences Politiques, 1988), 319.

53. This language appears in the preamble to the Constitution of the Fourth Republic, which was incorporated into the preamble to the Constitution of the Fifth Republic. It was the primary text the Constitutional Council relied upon in its decision of 16 July 1971. For more details, see Rohr, *Founding Republics,* 141–143.

54. For a full discussion and careful analysis of the decision of 16 July 1971, see Alec Stone, *The Birth of Judicial Politics in France* (New York: Oxford University Press, 1992), 66–69, and James Beardsley, "Constitutional Review in France," *Supreme Court Review* (1975): 189–259.

55. Louis Favoreu, "L'Application des décisions du Conseil Constitutionnel par le Conseil d'Etat et le Tribunal des Conflits," *Revue française de droit administratif* 3 (March–April 1987): 263–280.

2. THE UNITED KINGDOM

1. Leslie Wolf-Phillips, *Constitutions of Modern States* (New York: Praeger, 1968), ix.

2. Philip Norton, *The Constitution in Flux* (Oxford: Basil Blackwell, 1982), 4–5.

3. Philip Norton, *The British Polity,* 3d ed. (New York: Longman, 1994), 59. Richard Chapman mentions "legislation, including subordinate codes and rules," as constitutional sources in "Reasons of State and the Public Interest," in *Ethics in the Public Service: Public Administration in the 1990s,* ed. Richard A. Chapman (Edinburgh: Edinburgh University Press, 1993), 161.

4. Norton, *The Constitution,* 5.

5. Henry Parris, *Constitutional Bureaucracy* (New York: Augustus M. Kelley, 1969), 49.

6. Peter Hennessey, *Whitehall* (New York: Free Press, 1989), 252.

7. Norton, *The British Polity,* 60.

8. Ibid.

9. Richard A. Chapman, "Setting Standards in a New Organization: The Case of the British Civil Service Commission," in *Ethics in Public Service for the New Millennium,* ed. Richard A. Chapman (Aldershot, U.K.: Ashgate, 2000), 94.

10. Hennessey, *Whitehall,* 242.

11. Ibid., 243.

12. Richard Norton-Taylor, *The Ponting Affair* (London: Cecil Woolf, 1985), 96.

13. Clive Ponting, *The Right to Know: The Inside Story of the Belgrano Affair* (London: Sphere Books, 1985), 138.

14. Ibid., 150.

15. The Official Secrets Act is one of the old chestnuts of British public administration. The literature on it is overwhelming and for the most part critical. The act was substantially revised in 1989. For a discussion of the legal changes, see Rosamund Thomas, *Espionage and Secrecy: The Official Secrets Act 1911–1989 of the United Kingdom* (London: Routledge, 1991). For discussions of the act shortly before its revision, see Michael Hunt, "Parliament and Official Secrecy," in *Open Government,* ed. Richard A. Chapman and Michael Hunt (London: Routledge, 1987); David Hooper, *Official Secrets: The Use and Abuse of the Act* (London: Hodder and Stoughton, 1987); Rosamund Thomas, "The British Official Secrets Act, 1911–1939," in Chapman and Hunt, eds., *Open Government.*

16. Norton-Taylor, *Ponting Affair,* 102–103.

17. Gavin Drewry, "The Ponting Case: Leaking in the Public Interest," *Public Law* (summer 1985): 208.

18. Ibid.

19. Colin Turpin, "Ministerial Responsibility," in *The Changing Constitution*, ed. Jeffrey Jowell and Dawn Oliver, 3d ed. (Oxford: Clarendon Press, 1994), 111.

20. Robert Armstrong, "The Duties and Responsibilities of Civil Servants in Relation to Ministers," 74 H.C. Deb. 6S Col. 130–132 (26 February 1985).

21. Richard A. Chapman, *Ethics in the British Civil Service* (London: Routledge, 1988), 230.

22. Parris. *Constitutional Bureaucracy*, 103–105.

23. Ibid., 104.

24. Ibid., 105, citing A. L. Lowell, *The Government of England* (New York: n.p., 1926), 193.

25. David Marion, "The British Civil Service: A Political Excavation and Review," *Administration and Society* 24 (1993): 478.

26. Henry Taylor, *The Statesman*, ed. David L. Schaefer and Roberta R. Schaefer (New York: Associated Faculty Press, 1988), 117. The editors follow the 1878 version of Taylor's text.

27. Richard A. Chapman, "Reasons of State and the Public Interest: A British Variation of the Problem of Dirty Hands," in Chapman. ed., *Ethics in Public Service*, 108, citing Graham Wallas, *Human Nature in Politics* (London: Constable, 1908).

28. Chapman, *Ethics in the British Civil Service*, 288, citing Richard Crossman. *The Diaries of a Cabinet Minister*, vol. 1, *Minister of Housing 1964–66* (London: Hamish Hamilton and Jonathan Cape, 1975), 31.

29. Chapman, "Reasons of State," 105, citing Edward Bridges, *Portrait of a Profession: The Civil Service Tradition* (Cambridge: Cambridge University Press, 1950).

30. Chapman, *Ethics in the British Civil Service*, 290.

31. Richard A. Chapman, "Ethics in Public Service," in Chapman, ed.. *Ethics in Public Service*, 162.

32. Hennessey, *Whitehall*, 148.

33. Ibid.

34. Ibid., 155.

35. Colin Campbell and Graham K. Wilson, *The End of Whitehall: A Comparative Perspective* (Oxford: Blackwell, 1995), 18.

36. Norton-Taylor, *Ponting Affair*, 115.

37. *Economist*, 11 November 1997, 71.

38. Richard A. Chapman, "Minister–Civil Servant Relationships," in Chapman and Hunt, eds., *Open Government*, 54.

39. Ibid.

40. Colin Turpin, "Ministerial Responsibility: Myth or Reality," in *The Changing Constitution*, ed. Jeffrey Jowell and Dawn Oliver, 2d ed. (Oxford: Oxford University Press, 1989), 69, and Parris, *Constitutional Bureaucracy*, 298.

41. Diana Woodhouse, *Ministers and Parliament: Accountability in Theory and Practice* (Oxford: Clarendon Press, 1994), 87–106.

42. Ibid., 285.

43. Gavin Drewry, *The New Select Committees: A Study of the 1979 Reforms* (Oxford: Clarendon Press, 1985), 394, citing "Standing Orders of the House of Commons, 1979–1983," March 1983 (HC 307 1982–83).

44. Gavin Drewry, "Select Committees and Back Bench Power," in Jowell and Oliver, eds., *The Changing Constitution,* 146.

45. Ibid., 147.

46. Ibid., citing CSD gen. 80/38, para. 29.

47. Ibid., 137.

48. Gavin Drewry, "Revolution in Whitehall: The Next Steps and Beyond," in Jowell and Oliver, eds., *The Changing Constitution,* 3d ed., 155.

49. Ibid., 170–171.

50. Woodhouse, *Ministers,* 228.

51. Ibid., 253.

52. Richard A. Cosgrove, *The Rule of Law: Albert Venn Dicey, Victorian Jurist* (Chapel Hill: University of North Carolina Press, 1980), 113; see also Trowbridge H. Ford, *Albert Venn Dicey: The Man and His Times* (Chichester, U.K.: B. Rose Publishers, 1985).

53. Paul R. Verkuil, "Crosscurrents in Anglo-American Administrative Law," *William and Mary Law Review* 27 (summer 1986): 686.

54. Albert Venn Dicey, *The Law of the Constitution,* 10th ed. (Oxford: Oxford University Press, 1959, 1985), 40.

55. Ibid., 330.

56. E. C .S. Wade's introduction to Dicey's *Law,* 10th ed., xxiii.

57. Dicey, *Law,* 389.

58. Ibid.

59. [1914] 1 K.B. 160; [1915] A.C. 120.

60. Wade, introduction, cxlix.

61. Notably, *Board of Education v. Rice* [1911] A.C. 179.

62. Dicey, *Law,* 496; Dicey's 1915 article is reprinted in the 10th edition. Entitled "The Development of Administrative Law in England," it originally appeared in *Law Review Quarterly* 31 (1915).

63. Ibid., 496.

64. Ibid., 499.

65. Ibid.

66. Sir William Wade and Christopher Forsyth, *Administrative Law,* 7th ed. (Oxford: Clarendon Press, 1994), 504.

67. Dicey, *Law,* 350.

68. Ibid.

69. Ibid., 350, 381–382, and Wade, introduction, cxlv, cxlix.

70. Dicey, *Law,* 370.

71. Ibid., 369–381.

72. Wade and Forsyth, *Administrative Law,* 41.

73. Ibid.

74. Ibid., 42.

75. [1969] 2 AC 147.

76. Wade and Forsyth, *Administrative Law,* 302.

77. Ibid.

78. Ibid., 735.

79. Ibid., 503.

80. Bernard Schwartz, "Wade's Seventh Edition and Recent English Administrative Law," *Administrative Law Review* 48 (winter 1996): 179.

81. Wade and Forsyth, *Administrative Law,* 515.

82. [1964] AC 40.

83. Wade and Forsyth, *Administrative Law,* 511.

84. Ibid.

85. Ibid., 512. For further discussion of the *Ridge* and *Arlidge* decisions, see E. C. S. Wade, introduction, cxxxiii; Dicey, *Law,* 497–498; Wade and Forsyth, *Administrative Law,* 466 and 504.

86. Dicey, *Law,* 498.

87. Wade and Forsyth, *Administrative Law,* 468 and 512; the quotation is from *Cooper v. Wandsworth Board of Works* [1863] 14 CB (NS) 180.

88. *Economist,* 14 October 1995, 28.

89. Schwartz, "Wade's Seventh Edition," 177.

90. Ibid., 178, citing *R. v. Secretary of State for Transportation ex parte Factortame, Ltd.* no 2; [1991] 1 AC 603.

91. *Equal Opportunity Commission et al. v. Secretary of State for Employment* [1994] 1 All ER.910.

92. For further discussion of the European Union and British sovereignty, see Wade and Forsyth, *Administrative Law,* 30–31, 15–16, and 246–247; Alexander Andrew Mackay Irvine, "Constitutional Change in the United Kingdom: British Solutions to Universal Problems," *Supreme Court Journal* 2 (1998): 26–39; William Wade, "Sovereignty—Revolution or Evolution," *Law Quarterly Review* 112 (October 1996): 568–575; Paul P. Craig, "Sovereignty of the United Kingdom After Factortame," 11 Y.B.E.L.: 221.

3. CANADA

1. Margaret Atwood, *Survival: A Thematic Guide to Canadian Literature* (Boston: Beacon Press, 1972), 171, cited by Seymour Martin Lipset, *Continental Divide* (New York: Routledge, 1990).

2. An address delivered at the Woodrow Wilson Center, Washington, D.C., 29 April 1999.

3. BNA Act, section 91.

4. (Toronto: University of Toronto Press, 1995.)

5. Smith cites Maitland's characterization of the word *Crown* as "a convenient cover for ignorance" (27). His source is Frederic William Maitland, *Selected Essays,* ed. H. D. Hazelbine, G. Lapsley, and P. H. Winfield (Freeport, N.Y.: Books for Libraries Press, 1936), 155.

6. Ibid., 34.

7. Ibid., 35.

8. Ibid.

9. Ibid.

10. "PM Eyes Ways to Improve Federation," *Toronto Star,* 22 November 1995, reprinted in NEWSCAN, 24 November 1995.

11. These following citations provide examples of the connection between adminis-

trative and constitutional questions after the referendum of October 1995: "Today and Tomorrow: An Agenda for Action," Report of the Confederation 2000 Conferences, Ottawa, 1996; Steven A. Kennett, "The *Environmental Framework Agreement,* Reforming Federalism in Post-Referendum Canada," *Resources* 52 (fall 1995); "Environmental Management Framework Agreement," Canadian Council of Ministers of the Environment, Winnipeg, October 1995; Robert Matas, "Environment Pact Transfers Powers to Provinces," *Globe and Mail,* 20 January 1996; "PM Eyes Ways to Improve Federation," *Toronto Star* (reprinted in NEWSCAN, 24 November 1995, 22 November 1995; Mary Janigan and E. Kaye Fulton, "The Master Plan: A Draft for a New Canada Goes Before the Cabinet," *Maclean's,* 5 February 1996; "New Wisdom in Quebec," *Globe and Mail* (reprinted in NEWSCAN, 22 March 1996), 20 March 1996; E. Kaye Fulton and Mary Janigan, "Previewing the Budget," *Maclean's,* 29 February 1996; David Roberts, "Distinct Society Status Would Not Necessarily Mean Extra Power for Quebec, Dion Says," *Globe and Mail* (reprinted in NEWSCAN, 12 April 1996), 11 April 1996; Barry Came, "Finding Common Ground in Quebec," *Maclean's,* 1 April 1996; Alain Dubac, "Une Caricature du Québec Contemporain," *La Presse,* 16 avril 1996; Mario Fontaine, "Johnson, Rue dans les Brancards," *La Presse,* 16 avril 1996; Michel Vastel, "Le Canada . . . a minuit moins une," *L'Actualité 21,* 1er mai 1996, 14–16; Neville Nakivell, "Referendum Threats Raise Warning," *Financial Post* (reprinted in NEWSCAN, 3 May 1996), 2 May 1996; Edison Stewart, "Unity Panel Calls for Urgent Reform of Federation" (reprinted in NEWSCAN, 10 May 1996), 5 May 1996; Barry Came, "A Credible Effort," *Maclean's,* 20 May 1996; "Building a Stronger Canada": *Confederation 2000* Business Council on National Issues, 3–4 May 1996, passim; "Provinces Can Control Job Training, Ottawa Says," NEWSCAN, 31 May 1996, 2; Barry Came, "A New Tune in Quebec City," *Maclean's,* 17 June 1996, 14–16; Brenda Branswell, "A Hot Time in the Old Town," *Maclean's,* 24 June 1996, 12–14; "National Unity of National Securities" *Globe and Mail* (reprinted in NEWSCAN), 25 June 1996; Peter C. Newman, "A Revolutionary Twist on Indian Statehood," *Maclean's,* 1 July 1996, 33; Anthony Wilson-Smith, "Mission Accomplished," *Maclean's,* 1 July 1996, 17–19; "Co-operation the Focus of First Ministers' Meeting," *Canada Quarterly* 4, 3 (July 1996): 1–2; Howard Schneider, "Floods Let Canada Wave Flag of Federalism," *Washington Post,* 27 July 1996, 23A; Brenda Branswell, "Floodwaters on a Rampage," *Maclean's,* 5 August 1996, 22–25; Mary Nemeth, "On the Offensive," *Maclean's,* 2 September 1996, 11–13; Jim Bronskill, "CSIS Used Public Servants as Informants," *Ottawa Citizen,* 6 September 1996, 1; Jean-Pierre Proulx, "Les Ecoles confessionnelles ne sont pas toutes imposées par la constitution canadienne," *Le Devoir,* 10 October 1996, 7A; Brian Johnson, "Undiplomatic Service," *Maclean's,* 21 October 1996, 58–60; Brenda Branswell, "Quebec's Distinct Dilemma," *Maclean's,* 26 October 1996, 18–19; Debra Brown, *CBC News,* reporting on meeting of Human Resources minister Pierre Pettigrew with his provincial counterparts, 26 November 1996; Anthony Wilson-Smith, "Backstage Ottawa," *Maclean's,* 9 December 1996, 25.

12. See especially Premier Bouchard's remarks of 6 December 1995 at Laval in what *L'Actualité* called *"un véritable discours du trône"* (Michel Vestel, "Bouchard l'énigme," *L'Actualité* 21 [février 1996]: 17–25, at 20). See also "A l'écoute du Québec," *L'Actualité* 21 (1er mars 1996): 13; Jean Paré, "Le Grand théâtre de Quebec," *L'Actualité* 21 (1er mai 1996): 8; Jean Chartier, "Plan O: l'opération secrète de Parizeau," *L'Actualité* 21 (1er juin 1996): 11–12; Michel Vestel, "Le Bilan de Fernand Dumont," *L'Actualité* 21 (15 septem-

bre 1996): 86–96; "Lucien Bouchard and the Weekend Psychodrama," *Globe and Mail* (reprinted in NEWSCAN, 29 November 1996), 28 November 1996.

13. Other possible starting points for Canadian constitutional history are the Proclamation Act (1791), the Quebec Act (1774), or the Act of Union (1840).

14. The Constitution Act of 1982 retroactively renamed the BNA Act as the Constitution Act of 1867. Nevertheless, the earlier act is usually referred to by its original name.

15. *Parliamentary Debates on the Subject of the Confederation of the British North American Provinces,* 8th Provincial Parliament of Canada (Quebec: Hunter, Rose, 1865), 338(1c) (hereafter *Debates*). In referencing the *Debates,* I will give the page or pages, and where appropriate, I will also insert parenthetically the number 1 or 2 and the letters a, b, or c to indicate the column from which the citation was taken and its position with the column. Thus (2c) means the text cited can be found in the lowest third of the second column; (1a) means the top third of the first column; (1b) the middle third of the first column, and so on.

16. Ibid., 415(2b).

17. Ibid., 466(1a).

18. Ibid., 549(2b).

19. Ibid., 550(2b).

20. Ibid., 960(1a).

21. Ibid., 6(1b).

22. For further discussion of these topics, see John A. Rohr, "Current Canadian Constitutionalism and the 1865 Debates," *American Review of Canadian Studies* 28 (winter 1998): 413–444.

23. For the general statements, see *Debates,* 30(1c) and 131(2c); on public works, see 366(1a) and 920(1b); on education, see 95(1) and 411(1b–2b). The discussion of canals was pervasive throughout the debates. To sample some of the main arguments, see 79(1c); 639(1b–2c); 680(2c).

24. Although Newfoundland and Prince Edward Island did not join the Dominion of Canada in 1867, the Quebec Resolutions of 1864 included them because they had participated in the conference that drew up these resolutions. There was no way of knowing at that time what decision these two colonies would take regarding confederation.

25. *Debates,* 69(2); 93(2b); 377(1c)–379; 158(2c)–159; 178(1a); 258(2c)–259; 280(2b); 758(1b); 861(2a); 945(2b)–947(2b).

26. Ibid., 229(2c).

27. Ibid., 979(2a).

28. Ibid., 832(2c).

29. Ibid., 920(2b).

30. Ibid., 17(2b).

31. Ibid., 18(1c).

32. Donald Creighton, *The Road to Confederation: The Emergence of Canada, 1863–1867* (Toronto: Macmillan, 1964), 250.

33. Ibid., 250–251.

34. *Debates,* 336(1c) and 430(2c)–431(1a).

35. Ibid., 109(1c); 201(2a); 377–379; 386(2b); 415(2c)–416; 467–469; 512(1b–c); 553; 677(2); 681(2); 693(2)–694(1); 702(1b); 703(1a); 751–757; 762(1c); 791; 812–814; 901(1a).

36. Administrative questions were by no means neglected by the Americans of 1787

or the Frenchmen of 1958; quite the contrary, such questions were important in the founding debates in both countries. However, the French and the Americans tended to stress the formal powers of the administrative institutions rather than the financial management of specific regulated industries. For a fascinating account of the relationship between government and railroads in the early years of the Confederation, see Pierre Burton, *The Last Spike* (Toronto: McClelland and Stewart, 1977).

37. Norman Ward, *Dawson's The Government of Canada,* 6th ed. (Toronto: University of Toronto Press, 1990), 278.

38. Ibid.

39. For a balanced and penetrating study of Lord Durham's political thinking, see Janet Ajzenstat, *The Political Thought of Lord Durham* (Kingston: McGill-Queen's University Press, 1988).

40. *Debates,* 77(1a).

41. Ibid., 790(1b).

42. French Canadians have tended to dismiss Durham as a narrow-minded schemer with nothing but contempt for the French way of life in British North America. For a recent effort to rehabilitate Durham, see Ajzenstat. For examples of French Canadian resentment of Lord Durham, see *Debates,* 789; 844(1b); 850(2b)–852(2b); for a defense of Lord Durham, see 908(1c)–910(1a).

43. *Debates,* 52(1b).

44. Ibid., 251(2a).

45. Ibid., 356(2a).

46. Ibid., 901(2c).

47. For other statements linking railroads to confederation, see 896(1a), 227(1a), 132(2a), and 297(1b).

48. Robert C. Vipond, *Liberty and Community: Canadian Federalism and the Failure of the Constitution* (Albany: SUNY Press, 1991), 15.

49. Richard Gwyn, *Nationalism Without Walls: The Unbearable Lightness of Being Canadian* (Toronto: McClelland and Stewart, 1995).

50. Ward, *Dawson's Government of Canada,* 308, citing Macdonald's speech at the Confederation debates on 3 February 1865.

51. Amendment 10.

52. BNA, section 91.

53. Peter H. Russell, *Constitutional Odyssey: Can Canadians Become a Sovereign People?* 2d ed. (Toronto: University of Toronto Press, 1993), 38.

54. Ibid.

55. Vipond, *Liberty,* 24.

56. In the Privy Council (1881), 7 App. Cas. 96; I Olmstead 94. The decision is reported in Peter H. Russell et al., *Federalism and the Charter: Leading Constitutional Decisions,* new ed. (Ottawa: Carleton University Press, 1993), 37–42.

57. Russell et al., *Federalism,* 39.

58. Ibid.

59. Ibid., 41.

60. Ibid., 38. The year 1995 is mentioned because *U.S. v. Lopez* 115 S. Ct. 1624 was decided at that time. It marked a sharp departure from over half a century of judicial decisions favoring a broad interpretation of the commerce clause.

61. Vipond, *Liberty,* 47. My discussion of the office of lieutenant-governor relies almost exclusively on Vipond's treatment of this topic; for a fuller account of the development of this office during the early years of Confederation, see chapter 3.

62. There is no entry under "lieutenant-governor" in the most recent edition of Ward's *Dawson's Government of Canada* and but one covering less than a page in a seven-hundred-page text on public administration in Canada: see Kenneth Kernaghan and David Siegel, *Public Administration in Canada,* 3d ed. (Toronto: Nelson Canada, 1995), 185.

63. Vipond, *Liberty,* 48, citing a speech by John A. Macdonald during the parliamentary debates on Confederation in 1865.

64. BNA Act, sections 10 and 58.

65. Vipond, *Liberty,* 65.

66. Ibid., 64, citing papers of David Mills, Brief to the Ontario Court of Appeals in the Matter of Queen's Counsel, 1896, 136.

67. Russell et al., *Federalism,* 50, introducing *Liquidators of the Maritime Bank v. Receiver General of New Brunswick,* in the Privy Council (1892) A.C. 437; Olmsted 263. Along the way to their eventual triumph in *Maritime Bank,* the provincial autonomists had suffered some serious judicial setbacks; see especially *Lenoir v. Ritchie* 3 S.C.R. 575 (1879).

68. Russell et al., *Federalism,* 50.

69. The Constitution Act of 1982, sections 41–46.

70. Robert J. Jackson and Doreen Jackson, *Politics in Canada,* 4th ed. (Scarborough, On.: Prentice-Hall, Allyn and Bacon, Canada, 1998), 186.

71. *Maclean's,* 5 February 1996, 18.

72. Ibid., 19.

73. Ordinarily, I would not rely on a popular magazine article based on leaks from unnamed sources. In this case, however, subsequent policy statements and actions by the Chrétien government follow the script of the Massé report closely enough to allay my misgivings in relying on what it was alleged to have contained. Further, on 5 August 1997 Intergovernmental Affairs Minister Stéphane Dion assured me during an interview in his office in Ottawa of the general accuracy of the *Maclean's* article. Unfortunately, however, he also told me the document in question remained confidential and that I would not be allowed to read it myself.

74. Speech from the Throne to Open the Second Session of the Thirty-fifth Parliament of Canada, 27 February 1996, 7.

75. Ibid.

76. Ibid.

77. Ibid.

78. Ibid., 8.

79. Stéphane Dion, "Intergovernmental Relations Within Federations: Contextual Differences and Universal Principles," an address delivered at the Forum of Federations, International Conference on Federalism in Mont Tremblant, Quebec, 6 October 1999. This address goes into considerable detail on administrative decision making, emphasizing the domination of Canadian governments by the executive at both the federal and provincial levels and the important contributions of civil servants. See also Dion's remarks in "Are We Moving Beyond Our Constitutional Obsession?" an address delivered at the University of Toronto, 28 January 1999.

80. A "reference" in Canadian law is somewhat akin to what American lawyers would call an advisory opinion. In the United States, federal courts do not give such opinions, but some state courts do.

81. Reference re: Secession of Quebec, [1998] 2 R.C.S., 218.

82. Ibid., at 293, para. 150.

83. Ibid., at 294, para. 151. On the question of international law, the court found that a right to unilateral secession exists only when a people is governed as part of a colonial empire or is under alien subjugation and exploitation. These conditions do not apply to Quebec.

84. Ibid.

85. Ibid., at 267, para. 91. The French text reads: "Les écueils resident dans les détails."

86. Ibid., at 294, para. 151.

4. SEPARATION OF POWERS

1. Wilson, *Bureaucracy,* 28.

2. *Federalist,* no. 72; Article 2, sec. 2, U.S. Constitution.

3. Theodore Roosevelt, *An Autobiography* (New York: Putnam, 1913), 388–389.

4. The discussion of executive power follows closely the gist of my article, "Public Administration, Executive Power, and Constitutional Confusion," *Public Administration Review* 49 (March–April 1989): 108–114.

5. *Morgan v. U.S.,* 298 U.S. 468 (1936); *Morgan v. U.S.,* 304 U.S. 1 (1938); *U.S. v. Morgan,* 307 U.S. 183 (1939); *U.S. v. Morgan,* 313 U.S. 409 (1941).

6. 298 U.S. 468, at 471.

7. Ibid., at 473 and 476.

8. Ibid., at 481.

9. Ibid.

10. Ibid., at 482.

11. 304 U.S. 1, at 18.

12. Ibid., at 19.

13. Ibid., at 22.

14. Louis L. Jaffe and Nathaniel L. Nathanson, *Administrative Law: Cases and Materials,* 4th ed. (Boston: Little, Brown, 1976), 68.

15. 313 U.S. 409, at 422.

16. David H. Rosenbloom, *Building a Legislative-Centered Public Administration: Congress and the Administrative State* (Tuscaloosa: University of Alabama Press, 2000).

17. Ibid., 2.

18. Ibid., 24.

19. Ibid., 3.

20. Ibid., 57.

21. David Osborne and Ted Gaebler, *Reinventing Government: How the Entrepreneurial Spirit Is Transforming the Public Sector* (New York: Penguin Books, 1993).

22. Chris Wye, ed., "Forum: Implementing the Results Act," *Public Manager* 26, 3 (fall 1997): 1–38.

23. Harry P. Hatry and Harold B. Finger, eds., *Effective Implementation of the Government Performance and Results Act* (Washington, D.C.: NAPA, 1998).

24. Ibid., 30.

25. Magistrate judges are sometimes called Article 1 officers because their offices are created by Congress. This expression is somewhat confusing, because every federal court, other than the Supreme Court, is created by Congress. One magistrate judge suggested to me that he should be looked upon as an Article 2 officer. He points to the power given to Congress in Article 2 to vest the appointing power of inferior officers in "the Courts of Law." Since magistrate judges are appointed by federal district judges, their appointments are made pursuant to this congressional grant of power. For a statement describing magistrate judges as Article 1 officers, see Brendan Linehan Shannon, "The Federal Magistrates Act: A New Article I Analysis for a New Breed of Judicial Officer," *William and Mary Law Review* 33 (fall 1991): 287.

26. Magistrate judges also handle much of the pretrial work for cases heard by Article 3 judges. Magistrate judges may rule on nondispositive motions, e.g., a motion for discovery, but not on dispositive motions, e.g., motions for injunctive relief or to quash an indictment. See Carroll Seron, *The Roles of Magistrates in Federal District Courts* (Washington, D.C.: Federal Judicial Center, 1983), 7.

27. Carroll Seron, *The Roles of Magistrates: Nine Case Studies* (Washington, D.C.: Federal Judicial Center, 1985), ix.

28. Philip M. Pro and Thomas C. Hnatowski, "Measured Progress: The Evolution and Administration of the Federal Magistrate Judges System," *American University Law Review* 44 (June 1995): 1510.

29. Peter G. McCabe, "The Federal Magistrate Act of 1979," *Harvard Journal on Legislation* 16 (1979): 366.

30. Pro and Hnatowski, "Measured Progress," 1506.

31. McCabe, "Federal Magistrate Act," 343.

32. Ibid., 379.

33. Pro and Hnatowski, "Measured Progress," 1526.

34. Seron, *The Roles of Magistrates: Nine Case Studies,* xii.

35. Seron, *The Roles of Magistrates in Federal District Courts,* 3–4, 18, 55.

36. Pro and Hnatowski, "Measured Progress," 1505.

37. The discussion of delegation follows closely my analysis in John A. Rohr, *The President and the Public Administration* (Washington, D.C.: American Historical Association, 1989), 55–66.

38. *Lichter v. U.S.,* 334 U.S. 742 (1948), at 778.

39. *Wagman v. Southard,* 10 Wheat. 1 (1825), at 41.

40. *Field v. Clark,* 143 U.S. 649 (1892).

41. *The Brig Aurora,* 7 Cranch 382 (1813).

42. *U.S. v. Shreveport Grain and Elevator Co.,* 287 U.S. 77 (1932), at 85.

43. Lester S. Jayson, ed., *The Constitution of the United States of America: Analysis and Interpretation* (Washington, D.C.: U.S. Government Printing Office, 1973), 67.

44. Ibid., 63. I follow Justice Stevens's position that Congress delegates *legislative* authority to administrative agencies. He made this point to distinguish his position from that of Justice Scalia in his concurring opinion in *Whitman v. American Trucking Association* (2001). Justice Scalia wrote the opinion of the Court in that case (see n. 55).

45. John Locke, *Two Treatises of Government,* ed. Thomas I. Cook (1947; reprint, New York: Hafner, 1959), 193 (Second Treatise, paragraph 141).

46. *Schechter Poultry Corp. v. U.S.,* 295 U.S. 495 (1935); *Panama Refining Company v. Ryan,* 293 U.S. 388 (1935). The Supreme Court used the nondelegation doctrine in *Carter v. Carter Coal Co.,* 298 U.S. 238 (1936), but this argument was subordinate to arguments based on the commerce clause and the Tenth Amendment.

47. Ibid., at 537–538.

48. Ibid., at 553, 539.

49. Ibid., at 538.

50. Ibid., at 539.

51. John A. Rohr, *To Run a Constitution: The Legitimacy of the Administrative State* (Lawrence: University Press of Kansas, 1986), 47–48.

52. Edward S. Corwin, *The President: Office and Powers 1787–1957* (New York: New York University Press, 1957), 127, 241.

53. *Fahee v. Mallonee,* 332 U.S. 245 (1947).

54. Corwin, *President,* 127.

55. *Whitman v. American Trucking Association,* 121 S. Ct. 903 (2001).

56. 462 U.S. 919 (1983).

57. Stanley C. Brubaker, "Slouching Toward Constitutional Duty: The Legislative Veto and the Delegation of Authority," *Constitutional Commentary* 1 (winter 1984): 81.

58. 462 U.S., at 968.

59. *Clinton v. City of New York,* 118 S. Ct. 2091, at 2102.

60. Louis Fisher, "Judicial Misjudgments About the Lawmaking Process: The Legislative Veto Case," *Public Administration Review* 45 (November 1985): 706–707.

61. Ibid., 707.

62. Ibid.

63. Ibid., citing *City of Alexandria v. U.S.,* 737 F2d 1022 (1984), at 1026.

64. The discussion of serving two masters is developed more fully in Rohr, *The President and the Public Administration,* 31–54.

65. Robert V. Remini, *Andrew Jackson and the Course of American Democracy, 1833–1845* (New York: Harper and Row, 1984), 119. This book is the third in a three-volume series; my account follows Remini closely.

66. Ibid., 65.

67. Ibid., 77.

68. 12 Pet. 522 (1838).

69. Ibid., at 609.

70. Ibid., at 610.

71. "EPA's Asbestos Regulations: Report on a Case Study on OMB Interference in Agency Rulemaking," Subcommittee on Oversight and Investigations of the Committee on Energy and Commerce, U.S. House of Representatives, 99th Congress, 1st sess. (Washington, D.C.: U.S. Government Printing Office, 1985), 118.

72. Ibid., 109.

73. *Federalist,* no. 51.

74. For examples of judicial insistence on accountability from administrators even in the face of statutory language seeming to preclude a judicial role, see Kenneth C. Davis, *Administrative Law: Cases, Text, Problems* (St. Paul: West, 1977), 176.

75. 685 F2d 547 (1982).

76. 5 USC 557(d)(1)(D).

77. 685 F2d 547, at 557 (1982).

78. 5 USC 557(d)(1)(D).

79. 685 F2d 547, at 557.

80. Ibid., at 566.

81. Ibid., at 570 (emphasis in original).

82. Ibid., at 571.

83. Ibid., at 568.

84. 5 USC 557(d)(1)(A).

85. 685 F2d 547, at 594.

86. Ibid., at 594–595.

87. Ibid., at 597.

88. Ibid., at 598.

89. Ibid., at 598–600.

90. Ibid., at 622 (emphasis in original).

91. Ibid., at 623, citing 18 USC 1506 (emphasis in original).

92. 984 F2d 1534, 9th Cir. 1993.

93. Ibid., at 1545.

94. Ibid.

95. Plaintiff's motion for discovery was denied; the court found remand a more appropriate remedy.

96. 657 F2d 298, D.C. Cir. 1981.

97. Ibid., at 406.

98. Ibid., at 408.

99. Ibid.

100. 354 F2d 952, 5th Cir. 1966.

101. For a full discussion of the Pillsbury saga, see Michael Asimow, Arthur Earl Bonfield, and Ronald M. Levin, *State and Federal Administrative Law,* 2d ed. (St. Paul: West Group, 1998), 142–149.

102. 354 F2d 952, at 961.

103. Ibid., at 963.

104. Ibid.

105. Asimow et al., *State and Federal Administrative Law,* 146.

106. 354 F2d 952, at 964 (emphasis in original).

107. 989 F2d 1332, 3d Cir. 1993.

108. Asimow et al., *State and Federal Administrative Law,* 154.

109. Ibid., 155.

110. 989 F2d 1332, at 1345.

111. Ibid.

5. CIVIL SERVANTS' RIGHTS AND POWERS

1. For concise treatments of the constitutional positions of civil servants, see Phillip J. Cooper, *Public Law and Public Administration,* 3d ed. (Itasca, Ill.: Peacock.

2000), chapter 12, and David H. Rosenbloom and Rosemary O'Leary, *Public Administration and Law,* 2d ed. (New York: Marcel Dekker, 1997), chapter 6. The best source for the constitutional history of the public service is David H. Rosenbloom, *Federal Service and the Constitution* (Ithaca, N.Y.: Cornell University Press, 1971).

2. John A. Rohr, *The President and the Public Administration* (Washington, D.C.: American Historical Association, 1989), 19.

3. Rosenbloom, *Federal Service,* 16, citing *McAuliffe v. New Bedford,* 155 Mass. 216, at 220 (1892).

4. Ibid.

5. *Bailey v. Richardson,* 182 F. 2D 46 (1950); 341 U.S. 918 (1951).

6. Cooper, *Public Law,* 195.

7. 391 U.S. 563 (1968).

8. Ibid., at 564.

9. Ibid., at 574.

10. Ibid., at 568.

11. Ibid., at 571.

12. 103 S. Ct. 1684 (1983).

13. Ibid., at 1688.

14. Ibid.

15. Ibid., at 1690.

16. Ibid.

17. Ibid., at 1694.

18. In his dissent, Justice William Brennan notes that there was newspaper coverage of Myers's dismissal, but the coverage came after the event. Therefore, her firing was a matter of public concern, but her complaints were not. Apparently, Justice White believed the subsequent media interest in Myers's dismissal did not suffice to transform her grievances into matters of public concern.

19. 107 S. Ct. 2891 (1987).

20. Ibid., at 2895.

21. Ibid., at 2901.

22. Ibid., at 2904.

23. Ibid. (Scalia's emphases).

24. 96 S. Ct. 2673 (1976).

25. Plurality opinions are written when a majority of the justices cannot agree on the legal basis for a decision. For one party to prevail in a lawsuit, it is necessary that a majority of the justices agree that that party should prevail, but it is not necessary that they should all reach this conclusion for the same reason. For example, in the litigation of A versus B, five of the nine justices may agree that A should win; but three of these five may believe he should do so for reason X whereas the other two may think A should win for reason Y. One of the three justices who favored reason X would then write a plurality opinion. When five or more justices agree both on the outcome and the reason for the outcome, the opinion is called the opinion of the Court and sets a precedent for future cases.

26. 96 S. Ct., at 2684–2685.

27. Ibid., at 2687.

28. Ibid., at 2690.

29. Ibid., at 2681.

30. Ibid., at 2693–2694.

31. Ibid., at 2697.

32. 445 U.S. 507 (1980).

33. Ibid., at 518.

34. Ibid.

35. *Myers v. U.S.,* 272 U.S. 52 (1926).

36. 445 U.S. 507, at 527.

37. Ibid., at 521.

38. 110 S. Ct. 2729 (1990).

39. Ibid., at 273.

40. Rosenbloom and O'Leary, *Public Administration,* 201.

41. For a fuller treatment of Justice Scalia's ideas on "original intent," see his book, *A Matter of Interpretation* (Princeton: Princeton University Press, 1997). This book includes critiques of Scalia's position by Gordon S. Wood, Laurence H. Tribe, Mary Ann Glendon, and Ronald Dworkin.

42. 110 S. Ct. 2729, at 2748–2749 (Scalia's emphasis).

43. Ibid., at 2748.

44. Ibid., at 2749.

45. Ibid., at 2748–2749 (Scalia's emphasis).

46. Richard John, *Spreading the News* (Cambridge: Harvard University Press, 1995). My discussion of the post office relies heavily on *Spreading the News,* especially chapters 2, 5, and 7.

47. Ibid., 56.

48. Ibid., 30, 7–8.

49. Ibid., 60.

50. Ibid., 24.

51. Ibid., 170.

52. Ibid., 170–171.

53. Ibid., 171.

54. Ibid., 193 (emphasis in original).

55. Ibid., 177, 205.

56. Ibid., 264.

57. Ibid., 266 (emphasis in original).

58. Ibid., 269, 271.

59. Ibid., 279.

60. Ibid., 260.

61. 109 S. Ct. 998 (1989).

62. Ibid., at 1001.

63. Ibid., at 1001–1002.

64. Ibid., at 1003. Readers with an interest in political philosophy will find in the chief justice's statement that the Constitution protects us from the state and not from one another an implicit rejection of Thomas Hobbes's notion of the social contract. For Hobbes, the purpose of the contract is to authorize the state—or the Leviathan, as Hobbes would say—to protect us from one another.

65. Ibid., at 1004–1006.

66. Ibid., at 1006.

67. Ibid., at 1007.

68. Ibid., at 1011 (emphasis in original).

69. Ibid., at 1012.

70. 106 S. Ct. 1135 (1986).

71. Burbine also challenged the conviction on the grounds that the police behavior in his case violated the integrity of the attorney-client relationship.

72. 106 S. Ct. 1135, at 1141.

73. Ibid., at 1139 and 1142.

74. Ibid., at 1147.

75. For a further discussion of "structuring and confining" discretion, see Kenneth C. Davis, *Discretionary Justice: A Preliminary Inquiry* (Baton Rouge: LSU Press, 1969).

76. 110 S. Ct. 2465 (1990).

77. Michael Asimow, Arthur Earl Bonfield, and Ronald M. Levin, *State and Federal Administrative Law,* 2d ed. (St. Paul: West Group, 1998), 210.

78. 110 S. Ct. 2465, at 2471.

79. Ibid., at 2476.

80. *Rock Island, Arkansas, and Louisiana R Co. v. U.S.,* 254 U.S. 141, at 143 (1927).

81. *Foote's Dixie Dandy, Inc. v. Henry,* 607 S.W. 2d 323 (Ark., 1980), reported in Asimow et al., *State and Federal Administrative Law,* 211–212.

82. *McKnight v. Richardson,* 117 S. Ct. 2100 (1997), at 2105.

83. *Delaware v. Prouse,* 440 U.S. 648 (1976), at 650.

84. Ibid., at 651.

85. Ibid., at 659.

86. Ibid., at 650.

87. 357 U.S. 116 (1958).

88. Ibid., at 127–128.

89. 115 S. Ct. 2097 (1995).

90. Walter Dellinger, "Memorandum to General Counsels," Office of Legal Counsel, U.S. Department of Justice, Washington, D.C., 28 June 1995.

91. Ibid., 1.

92. As this book was about to be submitted for publication, the *Washington Post* reported that the Supreme Court had agreed to hear an appeal by Adarand Constructors from a decision by the U.S. Court of Appeals for the Tenth Circuit holding that the affirmative action program that the company had originally contested satisfied the demands of strict scrutiny (27 March 2001, A10).

93. Rosemary O'Leary, *Environmental Change: Federal Courts and the EPA* (Philadelphia: Temple University Press, 1993), 125.

94. Rosenbloom and O'Leary, *Public Administration and Law,* 232.

95. Gary L. Greenberg, "Revolt at Justice," in *Ethics and Politics: Cases and Comments,* ed. Amy Gutman and Denis Thompson, 3d ed. (Chicago: Nelson-Hall, 1997), 143.

96. Ibid., 151.

97. Marion Smiley, "Legalizing Laetrile," in ibid., 316.

98. Ibid.

6. FEDERALISM

1. Alexis de Tocqueville, *Democracy in America,* trans. and ed. Henry Reeve, Francis Bowen, and Phillips Bradley, 2 vols. (1945; reprint, New York: Random House, 1990), 1:404.

2. Herbert J. Storing and Murray Dry, eds., *The Anti-Federalist: Writings by the Opponents of the Constitution* (Chicago: University of Chicago Press, 1985), 103. This book is a one-volume abridgment of Herbert J. Storing's *The Complete Anti-Federalist,* 7 vols. (Chicago: University of Chicago Press, 1981). Historian Paul Leicester Ford believes that Robert Yates is Brutus, but Storing finds little evidence to support this conjecture.

3. Storing and Dry, eds., *The Anti-Federalist,* 133; *Federalist,* no. 23 (emphasis in original).

4. Storing and Dry, eds., *The Anti-Federalist,* 136.

5. Ibid., 134 (emphasis added).

6. Ibid., 135.

7. Ibid.

8. Ibid., 136.

9. Ibid., 137.

10. Ibid., 136–137.

11. Ibid., 141–142.

12. Ibid., 142.

13. Thomas A. Gullo and Janet M. Kelly, "Federal Unfunded Mandate Reform: A First-Year Retrospective," *Public Administration Review* 58 (September/October 1998): 381.

14. 117 S. Ct. 2365 (1997).

15. Ibid., at 2370 for Justice Scalia and at 2386 for Justice Stevens.

16. Ibid., at 2370.

17. Ibid., at 2387.

18. Ibid., at 2378.

19. Ibid., at 2379.

20. Ibid., at 2388, n. 2, citing *McCulloch v. Maryland,* 4 Wheat. 316 (1819).

21. Ibid., at 2370.

22. Ibid.

23. Ibid., at 2371 (emphasis in original).

24. Ibid., at 2389.

25. Ibid., at 2391.

26. Ibid., at 2392.

27. Ibid., at 2392.

28. Ibid.

29. Ibid., at 2376 and 2393.

30. Ibid., at 2376.

31. Ibid.

32. *New York v. U.S.,* 505 U.S. 144 (1992); *U.S. v. Lopez,* 115 S. Ct. 1624 (1995); *Seminole Tribe v. Florida,* 116 S. Ct. 1114 (1996); *Idaho v. Coeur d'Alene Tribe of Idaho,* 117 S. Ct. 2028 (1997); *Kimel v. Florida Board of Regents,* 120 S. Ct. 631 (2000); and *University of Alabama v. Garrett,* 121 S. Ct. 955 (2001). For commentaries on the rele-

vance for public administration of the changes in the constitutional law of federalism, see David H. Rosenbloom and Bernard H. Ross, "Toward a New Jurisprudence of Constitutional Federalism: The Supreme Court in the 1990s and Public Administration," *American Review of Public Administration* 28 (June 1998): 107–125.

33. C. Herman Pritchett, *The American Constitution* (New York: McGraw-Hill, 1959); Kermit L. Hall, ed., *The Oxford Companion to the Supreme Court of the United States* (New York: Oxford University Press, 1992); Alfred H. Kelly, Winfred A. Harbison, and Herman Belz, *The American Constitution: Its Origin and Development,* 2 vols., 7th ed. (New York: Norton, 1991).

34. *Black's Law Dictionary,* 4th ed. (Minneapolis: West, 1968), 1568.

35. Justice Scalia cites two recent Supreme Court decisions to support his reliance on "dual sovereignty": *Gregory v. Ashcroft,* 501 U.S. 452, at 457 (1991), and *Tafflin v. Levitt* 493 U.S. 455, at 458 (1990). For further discussion of the diminished aspect of state sovereignty, see Mark R. Killenbeck, "Pursuing the Great Experiment: Reserved Powers in a Post-Ratification Compound Republic," *Supreme Court Review 1999* (Chicago: University of Chicago Press, 2000), 81–140.

36. *Printz v. U.S.,* at 2394.

37. Ibid., at 2376.

38. Ibid., at 2378.

39. See ibid., n. 12, where Justice Scalia gives a brief and not very convincing solution to this problem.

40. Ibid., at 2396.

41. *Korematsu v. U.S.,* 323 U.S. 214 (1944).

42. *Printz v. U.S.,* at 2379.

43. *New York v. U.S.,* 505 U.S. 144 (1992).

44. *Printz v. U.S.,* at 2398 and 2380.

45. Ibid., at 2381.

46. Ibid., citing language used by Judge Sneed in *Brown v. EPA,* 521 F.2d, at 839, and Judge Fernandez, dissenting in the present litigation before the Ninth Circuit, 66 F.3d, at 1035.

47. Ibid., at 2398 (emphasis added).

48. Ibid., at 2404.

49. Ibid. (emphasis in original).

50. Ibid., at 2403.

51. Ibid.

52. Ibid., at 2402, n. 1.

53. Ibid., at 2375, n. 9.

54. Ibid., at 2403, n. 2.

55. *Adarand Constructors, Inc. v. Peña,* 115 S. Ct. 2097 (1995), at 2113.

56. Ibid., at 2102.

57. Ibid.

58. *Brown v. Board of Education of Topeka, Kansas,* 347 U.S. 483 (1954) and 349 U.S. 294 (1955).

59. *Bolling v. Sharpe,* 347 U.S. 497 (1954).

60. *Adarand,* at 2110.

61. Ibid., at 2124–2125.

62. Ibid., at 2124 (emphasis in original).

63. Ibid., at 2114.

CONCLUSION

1. Joseph P. Mitchell, "The Central Bankers: Administrative Legitimacy and the Federal Reserve System" (Ph.D. diss., VPI and SU, 1999), 276, 289, 298.

2. For scholarly analyses of the broader implications of constitutional norms and values, see Mark Tushnet, *Taking the Constitution Away from the Courts* (Princeton: Princeton University Press, 1999), and Wayne D. Moore, *Constitutional Rights and Powers of the People* (Princeton: Princeton University Press, 1996).

3. John A. Rohr, *Public Service, Ethics, and Constitutional Practice* (Lawrence: University Press of Kansas, 1998), 165–167.

4. Philip Bobbitt, *Constitutional Fate: A Theory of the Constitution* (New York: Oxford University Press, 1984); Louis Fisher, *Constitutional Dialogues: Interpretation as Political Process* (Princeton: Princeton University Press, 1988); Sanford Levinson, *Constitutional Faith* (Princeton: Princeton University Press, 1988); Graham Walker, *Moral Foundations of Constitutional Thought: Current Problems, Augustinian Perspectives* (Princeton: Princeton University Press, 1990).

5. *Austrian Federal Constitutional Law (Selection)* (Vienna: Federal Chancellery–Constitutional Advisory Service, 1995), article 10.

6. Ibid., article 11.

7. Ibid., article 12.

8. Ibid., article 14.

9. "Thaksin to the Rescue?" *Economist*, 23 December 2000, 46.

10. *Constitution of the Kingdom of Thailand*, B.E. 2540 (1997), chapter 10, part 2, section 297.

11. Ibid., section 301 (3).

12. The Thailand parliamentary election received considerable attention in the *International Herald Tribune*. See articles by Seth Mydans, 27 December 2000, and 6–7 January 2001; Thitinan Pongsudhirak, 10 January 2001; Thomas Crampton and David Ignatius, 11 January 2001; and Rajiv Chandrasekaran, 13–14 January 2001.

13. The English translations of the post–1968 nomenclature are somewhat inconsistent. I follow the version offered by Albert P. Blaustein and Gisbert H. Flanz, eds., "The Czech Republic," in *Constitutions of the Countries of the World* (Dobbs Ferry, N.Y: Oceana, 1993), 110.

14. Radim Marada, "The 1998 Czech Elections," *East European Constitutional Review* 7, 4 (fall 1998): 51.

15. Vojtech Cepl, "Ritual Sacrifices," *East European Constitutional Review*, 1, 1 (spring 1992): 24.

16. Ibid., 25.

17. "Czech Republic," *East European Constitutional Review* 2, 1 (winter 1993): 4.

18. Jacques DeLisle, "Lex Americana: United States Legal Assistance, American Legal Models, and Legal Change in the Post–Communist World and Beyond," *University of Pennsylvania Journal of International Economic Law* 20, 2 (summer 1999): 179.

Index

202 CIVIL SERVANTS AND THEIR CONSTITUTIONS